The Magic of Life

Freedom from the Mind

Kamla Beaulieu

BALBOA.PRESS

A DIVISION OF HAY HOUSE

Balboa Press books may be ordered through booksellers or by contacting:

Balboa Press
A Division of Hay House
1663 Liberty Drive
Bloomington, IN 47403
www.balboapress.com
844-682-1282

Print information available on the last page.

ISBN: 978-1-9822-6832-9 (sc)
ISBN: 978-1-9822-6833-6 (e)

Balboa Press rev. date: 05/24/2021

To Life

Contents

Introduction

My book is written as a giant letter to Jed McKenna—a homegrown American enlightened master. In *The Enlightenment Trilogy*, he encourages the reader to address their journey of self-discovery to him to facilitate the creative process. Voila! The key worked.

Given its loose structure, this book poured forth almost effortlessly. A couple of hours before I penned the first chapter, I had no clue that for more than a year I would be sitting at my desk recording my spiritual journey, which, up until then, had stubbornly resisted its expression.

My once hyperactive left brain language center, largely deactivated by solitude and meditative silence, needed to be brought back online. This task was accomplished by not merely reading but by *grokking The New Yorker* magazine. In my self-imposed isolation, I used the magazine as my muse, my creative writing instructor, a prodigious source of trendy vocabulary and trending modes of creative expression. It also inspired me to keep on writing through strangulating self-doubt.

Once, dejected, upon randomly flipping through the magazines, I was uplifted by the words of Adam Gopnik—that when life is the author one need not worry about the quality of prose and other prissy details. At another time, it dissolved my writing block with the wise Japanese words, *wabi sabi*, or, reverence for the imperfect. Further down in the book, an entire chapter titled "A Miraculous Success" was inspired by an article in *The New Yorker*.

I had no structure for the book and wrote whatever presented itself while I was seated in front of my iPad. More than 60 percent into the manuscript, I realized there was way too much Jed here, too much Osho, too much sex, and the all-pervading fragrance of *pakalolo* (Hawaiian for cannabis). Too many guru scandals. Too many ashram intrigues! It seemed to lack the wholesome fragrance of a spiritual journey!

Should I be embarrassed? Delete all and go my merry safe way? Nope! Cried my inner voice. Continue distilling the core message of your inner journey from human to being and beyond. I can only hope that I have fulfilled my purpose. No matter what, my unwavering focus is on being part of the human equation—that which is beyond all distinctions of race, religion, gender, color, caste, and even perfect and imperfect. I have found it to be of paramount importance to experience being part of myself rather than merely talking and thinking about it. Only the experience of being has the ultimate transformative power we all are seeking.

Chapter 1

My First Step

The First Step, However One comes to it, marks the end of one thing and the start of another. Until the First Step is taken, awakening from the dream state isn't possible. After the First Step is taken, staying in the dream state isn't possible.

—Jed McKenna, *Spiritually Incorrect Enlightenment*

"My Cave on Kailash" spontaneously rolls off my irreverent tongue as the name for my new casa on a hilltop in Mexico. I'm smoking a joint and pacing on my delightfully spacious terraza. The tranquil beauty of the holy Lake Chapala, guarded by the mountains at the back and full open skies above, never ceases to charm and uplift my visitors and me. I'm calling Lake Chapala holy because the Huichol Indians of Mexico regard the lake as one of their sacred places of pilgrimage. Once a year, Huichols offer prayers to Dios Hikuri (peyote god of ceremonial cactus) at the lakeside.

A new friend, Carlos, inspired by the shining and sparkling vista and glamour created indoors by its huge glass doors and glass walls, along with mirrors and more mirrors, called it the Hollywood Hills.

His name smacked of glitzy fiestas and friends, flowing goddess garb with ethnic accessories, book clubs, movie clubs, fundraisers, and volunteering at an orphanage. I had died to all that when I left Maui, Hawaii, with its aloha-blue beachy lifestyle. The express purpose of my gut-wrenching move was to die to the flesh and be reborn of the spirit.

The Hindu god, Shiva, well represents the spiritual journey of death and regeneration, along with uncertainty of the unknown. He resides on Mount Kailash in the Himalayas. On my journey into the unknown, it will be a boon to have the highest of all Hindu gods as my new neighbor.

My first step—concrete, decisive and surgical: leave the known Maui, Hawaii, not metaphorically but literally, for the unknown in Ajijic, Mexico. All the planetary ducks had at last lined up neatly, and the exit door was fully open. Yet a kick or two was still needed from existence to make my move. I had reached retirement age and sold my physical therapy practice. Economically, I was fully independent and fortunately single, with no sick parents, husband, children, or grandchildren to worry about. If I didn't make my bid for full freedom then, all would be lost. I had the necessary ingredient for my journey, an abundant secret stash of existential angst, which was molesting me mercilessly and poisoning my relationships with people. Psychological restlessness and confusion, on relentless increase since the reading of *The Enlightenment Trilogy*, was driving me bat-shit crazy.

I'm grateful to Jed, not only for providing me with inspiration, quiet confidence and clarity for my journey of self-discovery, but also for helping me with my new real estate needs. I frequently look at the sparkling Lake Chapala and think of Jed writing his book, *Spiritual Warfare*, looking at the very same vista. I know one day, I too, will finish my spiritual journey and record it here. Until then, I shall remain in self-exile. It's death or enlightenment.

Now that I have completed my inner journey, I feel compelled to record and address it to Jed. Why? He planted the seed of a book in me. He inspired and encouraged me to adopt the discipline of writing to nail down the cunning ego—a slippery and smooth shapeshifter. If I did that, he promised that instead of reading his books, I would be writing my own. My ego was enthralled! Writing as the super cleaning agent of the psyche is undeniable. Most importantly, writing by helping to connect the helter-skelter dots of my life, has magically revealed the invisible hand of existence, which hitherto I had only vaguely sensed. With teary eyes I acknowledge its perfect skill in guiding me through my dark and desolate inner labyrinth.

Another huge reason for calling out Jed, who is perhaps squeaky clean, is his interest in substance addiction. He has genuine praise for ancient Indian sages who imbibed soma, famed Indo/Aryan psychedelic of yore. Divinely intoxicated, they composed immortal songs of love and gratitude to existence, as recorded in Vedas. I'm by no means promoting drugs of any sort as a path to enlightenment. Drugs alone cannot explain my enlightenment or the enlightenment of ancient Vedic Sages. If that were the case, our drug peddlers, especially Senor El Chapo, the ultimate drug lord of Mexico, would be the granddaddy Buddha of all the buddhas in the lotus paradise. I liken my relationship to drugs to Mozart's relationship with the piano. What's a piano without a Mozart? It's the musician who brings life and music to the instrument.

From the spiritual literature I have read, I'm convinced existence loves new, fresh, one of a kind awakening and enlightenment stories. In my playbook, life goes to great lengths to create novel stories of awakenings and adventures to delight itself and us. I want to present to Jed, my readers, and existence my unique journey of sex, drugs, rock 'n' roll, plus marathons of meditation and writing. The result has been an ongoing melting into the sublime simplicity and boundless silence of Truth.

I begin.

Chapter 2

Making of an Addict

The journey of a thousand miles begins with one step.

—Lao Tzu

ALL BY MYSELF, I CAME to Quebec City, Canada, from India in the mid-60s on a work permit as a physical therapist. It wasn't my burning desire to immigrate to Canada, where I had neither family nor friends. Heck, I knew absolutely nothing about Canada, its history, or its culture. Europe and America were the destinations for most ambitious young Indians. My only ambition after graduation was to get married to a rich Indian guy, a doctor—better still, a surgeon. This, I was certain, would elevate my status in my mother's eyes. My mom had intense anxiety about my future as a good Hindu girl who is desirable and marriageable. In my mother's era, marriage and babies was the sole goal and ambition of every young girl and her parents. My mom worked diligently to mold me according to the specifications required by Hindu society at the time. Managing the complicated Indian kitchen, serving and obeying the in-laws and the husband, and handling babies, were some of the skills and attitudes she tried hard to drill into me, all to no avail. Reading books, especially in English, was my only interest in life.

"No man wants to marry a library or a woman smarter than him" was my mom's frequent warning to me during my teen years. I was on a very short leash as far as my virginity was concerned. She made sure my legs were always covered and crossed. To her credit, she supported me fully in my studies and was secretly proud of my brain power. After I graduated from physical therapy, she let me go to Delhi to work because my best friend had moved there.

One fine evening in Delhi, I was talking story with a bunch of girls, mostly about my handsome new boyfriend, an engineer soon to leave for Germany for further studies. At the same time, I was also leafing through The *Canadian Physical Therapy* journal. My eyes landed on a physical therapy vacancy at a hospital in Quebec. They were willing to help with travel and moving expenses. My friends and I had never even heard of Quebec. Still, we went crazy with excitement. Someone produced a blue aerogram (wonder if they still exist) with a tiny grease spot on it. Someone handed me the pen. Someone mouthed out the first few lines of the letter. Thus was completed my first job application for the global platform, in the midst of giggles and chuckles, teasing, and joshing. A friend grabbed the aerogram, sealed it, and took on the responsibility of mailing it, just in case I changed my mind. Things were truly so simple then!

My girlfriends and I quickly forgot about my job application letter, as it had been composed as a prank—upon whom, we didn't care. Within a couple of weeks, I was shocked and stunned to find a very official looking package from the hospital in Quebec. I was advised to go to the Canadian embassy for my ticket to Canada and for help navigating the complicated Indian bureaucracy to obtain my passport. My friends, including my boyfriend, assured me that I was being pranked and to be careful. I went to the embassy with a girlfriend and found out that it was a reality show! I was shown a one-way ticket on Swiss Air with my name on it and the departure date of less than a month. For the passport, they took my photos, helped me fill out the form, and advised me to get ready for my departure. I was a hyper excited emotional mess who simply had to move forward. The job contract was for a year. I started to see it as a great vacation, at the end of which I'd return home and marry my boyfriend, who would also be returning from Germany with awesome degrees and distinctions. What a grand and glorious future!

My drinking and smoking addictions started the day after my arrival in Quebec. My first day of work in a brand-new country, in a city torn by the French separatist movement, was truly dark and dismal. The physical therapy clinic was in the basement of the hospital and had been closed for years. I had been hired by an English hospital, but a few days before my arrival, according to the newly passed law, the hospital had to accept a certain number of French patients. As luck would have it, my first patient in the dark, musty clinic was a young French man in a wheelchair, holding on to his crutches. I had to teach him how to walk with crutches, negotiate stairs, and get in and out of the car so he could be discharged, all in French! The first time I ever heard French being spoken was on the PA system of Swiss Air, headed for Canada. When the Frenchman realized I couldn't speak French, he started to attack me with his crutches, swearing and cursing in French. I ran away and took shelter in a little convenience store next to my department, managed by a blind man. He calmed me down and handed me an Oh Henry chocolate bar. He walked me back to the clinic to help me with the patient, but the young Frenchman had left.

Totally exhausted, my heart heavy with despair and regret at the end of my first workday, I crawled back to my room in the nurses' residence. The loneliness of my life—not much English and zero French, no family or friends—hit me like a ton of bricks. What had I done! Why didn't someone stop me! It's because no one loves me, my secret theme song in those days. As I was about to bawl, there was a knock on the door. On opening it, I was greeted by two young and charming French nurses, fluent in English, holding a bottle of red wine, three glasses, and cigarettes. The door to the carnal sin city of the West had flung open for this Indian immigrant fresh off the plane, just like that!

While sipping on the red wine, my first ever, and puffing on a mentholated Cameo cigarette, also my first ever, I told my new friends that a few days before leaving India, I had gone to a very fancy farewell party for my boyfriend in New Delhi. There, I had met a couple of handsome and rich Indian boys who were heading for medical school at McGill University, in Montreal. We had promised to visit and call each other.

My new girlfriends both looked at me mischievously and said, "What are you waiting for!" The next weekend, the three of us were in Montreal partying and having sexual awakenings with the boys. And there were lots of them, brown and white, all of us young, open, eager, and excited! Goodbye, innocence, and hello wild pleasures.

From then on, cigarettes and drink became my loyal buddies, while human buddies came and went. I also did a makeover, exchanging my thick glasses for contact lenses, lots of eye shadows and mascara, fancy lingerie and mini dresses, and soon a car of my own. At the time, there were only a few Indian families and a few single Indian men in Quebec. They soon dropped me from their social circle, as my new Western liberal look was an assault on their orthodox Hindu values. I was happy to immerse myself in the much freer white culture, with its freedom of thought, expression, dress, food, religion, and marriage. I dated mostly white bad boys, great in bed but not great marriage material. The good and virtuous Hindu girl my mom had so painfully and laboriously crafted disappeared into vapor upon the lightest of contact with the liberal West. Surprisingly, there was no guilt and shame at betraying my roots and morphing into a certifiably bad girl, from the point of view of my mother and the Indian culture.

Two years later, I got a job in Toronto and fell in love with a Jewish-Canadian boy, who, after several years of coupling, was still hesitant to marry me. Emotionally exhausted by our on again/off again relationship, I decided to leave my job, sell everything, and buy an open around the world air ticket.

When I returned to Canada after more than a year of world travel, my Canadian boyfriend had recently got married. This was a good thing, even though I was crushed at the time.

I had a great job as a physical therapist, a few good friends, and a reasonable social life. But inside, I was fatally bored. I felt very guilty since I had everything except an intimate relationship. I decided to take some liberal arts courses at the University of Toronto in the evening. I enjoyed it so much that I gave up my fine paying job and various other perks and enrolled full time. I downsized my life to two jumbo size trash bags and moved into a rooming house within walking distance from the university.

In the early seventies, the university atmosphere in Toronto was still electrifying and saturated with drugs, free sex, and radical, edgy ideas. Hare Krishna folks were blissfully dancing and chanting in the university gardens, and Roshi Phillip Kapleau, of the book *Three Pillars Of Zen*, was to conduct a weekend retreat. TM folks were promoting their brand of meditation, and students were lining up for Ingmar Bergman film festival and discussion club. Almost everyone had read Ram Das' *Be Here and Now* and were eagerly awaiting his visit.

In the rooming house, on warm evenings, we used to sit outside on the steps and pass around a bowl of hashish or a joint and chat about our sex life, books, and movies. My first toke was as blissful as my first kiss. It seemed as if I had taken my first conscious deep breath ever, tasting existence for the very first time. I felt so alive and vibrant. I was instantly hooked. The next chemical suitor to show up was the granddaddy of the times, LSD, lysergic acid diethylamide. I was enamored with it from the get-go. We clung on to each other like long lost lovers. It was my gateway drug to existence itself!

I had gone to university full time with the intention of changing my profession. No more people in pain and suffering, no more physical therapy. I was going to be a professor of philosophy or psychology, maybe English literature. But the acid in LSD thoroughly dissolved all my academic dreams and ambitions, leaving me wondrously unrecognizable even to myself. I used to be a bookworm, glued to the chair. No more. My sedentary mental career of reading and writing died almost instantly. And I was reborn as a perennially pacing person whose body is still in gentle motion to this day — stretching, twisting, and rolling, etc.

I had to choose between academia and my growing devotion to LSD, and the latter won. No shame. Absolutely zero regrets. This was mostly due to the absence of my family in Canada, for which I shall remain eternally grateful — to them and to life. On the one hand, my life was lonely and challenging without their loving meddling, nagging, limits, and firm guidance. On the other hand, I had unlimited freedom to explore and experiment, to build or to wreck my life. Maybe I would die of drug overdose or insanity. My life was mine to do with as I wished. What a dare!

Chapter 3

Heavenly Visitations

> Think of a grasshopper caught in a spider's web, injected
> with a non-lethal poison and then cocooned in a layer
> upon layer of silk thread, kept alive for freshness but
> tightly bound to prevent thrashing or escape. It's
> still alive but bears no resemblance to its authentic
> grasshopper self.
>
> —Jed McKenna, *Spiritual Warfare*

I IMMEDIATELY IDENTIFIED WITH THE GRASSHOPPER as my pre-drug state: rigid, contracted, constipated, terrified, paralyzed, anxious, enraged, outraged (just chock full of rage but repressed), strained, twisted, frothing with frustration and perpetual violent screams inside. But on the outside, I wore a useful and practical, firmly fixed, serene and inscrutable Asian mask. Acid took care of my chronic inherited physical rigidity, especially the constipation part, in the first two to three trips, with lasting results. My digestion improved vastly, my metabolism woke up, and my body felt very alive. Before, my body had felt totally flat and lifeless, only I hadn't realized it. Now there was a marked contrast between dragging through life and dancing with it.

The five windows of sense perception, dusty and creaky with years of conditioning, were cleansed and revived. Pre-acid my taste buds felt numb and dead. In my teens I was plump because, in my family, food and love were entwined. In college I went on a strict diet, and to some, I looked anorexic. Now my interest in food and the sheer enjoyment of it had died. A gift from the gods, I thought at the time, as I could maintain my ideal weight with minimum effort.

On acid, my mouth became alive and excited. Fresh fruits and vegetables turned into poetry and prayer in my mouth. The process of eating turned into wordless meditation. Initially, I smoked cigarettes on my trips, but pretty soon, they tasted gross. Any kind of meat or canned food wasn't acceptable to my body during an acid trip. On a street dose of one mcg of LSD, I would be tripping for at least six to eight hours, sometimes more. My lifestyle became *sattvic* (pure) just like that for at least twelve hours.

The most utilitarian window of perception that opened for me was touch, which became tinglingly alive and enjoyable. As the door to academia was closing the self-closed door to physical therapy was opening up again. This new, full of life, dynamic person, one thrilled by physical movement for the sheer joy of it, who enjoyed touching, was going to work to bring home a regular paycheck. Even so, my exploration with LSD and marijuana would continue unabated. This new physical therapist was energetic, present, confident, open, empathetic, organized, kind, and cooperative. She was not only likable but now was enjoying working with people in pain, suffering, and trauma, inspiring them to move through pain. I tuned in and got totally turned on, but I didn't drop out.

For more than two years, I went to work regularly and tripped two to three times a week. Everything was swell. Meanwhile, I married a French Canadian in the food and beverage business. We were fed up with the long, frigid Canadian East Coast winters and moved to relatively warmer Vancouver, on the West Coast. We lived in a one-bedroom apartment in busy downtown Vancouver for a couple of years, me tripping regularly. Then we moved into a three-bedroom house in the suburbs of Vancouver. Across from our new home was a beautiful cemetery, huge and lush, with lovely trees, flat obituary stones, and totally tranquil! It was always a treat to look out of our windows. We also had a good size front yard and backyard, with landscape maintained by the owner.

Late one afternoon, while I was on acid and pacing around the huge house, I looked out a window and saw the two most revered gods of

Hinduism, Krishna and Shiva, about 100 yards away, sitting under a tree in my front yard. They were sharing a pipe. A jaw dropper! By the time my jaw and face found their proper resting places, the entire scene had vanished, leaving behind the usual tree and the usual yard. Later, I remembered admiring a greeting card with an American Indian chief in his gorgeous feather hat and Shiva. They were sharing a pipe.

What baffled me about this vision was that with my myopic eyes, I had seen them so clearly, even across the considerable distance, and without using my glasses.

The images of Shiva and Krishna had a dreamlike quality, and they faded like a dream too. Was I dreaming, or was I awake on acid with my myopic eyes wide open? How was that even possible? In dreams I see images inside my head without the need of physical eyes or my glasses. But this image was clearly at a distance, which my eyes technically should not have been able to see. I was still light years away from even formulating the question: Who is the seer observing images and the content in my mind?

Another waking dream in the same house on acid, was of Bhagwan Shree Rajneesh/Osho. It was twilight and the sky was aglow with shades of orange. He was standing at my front door in his simple white robe, luminous and lit up. His image was life size, and it didn't move or speak. Stunned and shocked, I too, was motionless and speechless! At this time, I hadn't been to Pune, India, but I had read his first book and seen his photo. By now, I had taken many trips, but these waking dreams of divine beings and sages were uncommon in my life.

I revisited my past trips the next day when I was not tripping, looking for the waking dreams. Only one clear memory surfaced. I had been studying American Transcendentalists at University of Toronto. I was tripping in my room, mesmerized by the beauty of the lit-up end of my cigarette, bright and glowing fiery orange, morphing and changing into different shapes. Then, out from this little glowing tip stepped five adult males: mystics and literary giants—Whitman, Thoreau, Emerson, Melville, and Hawthorne. They all fit into my tiny room, which was hardly big enough for one little chair. Call it dream logistics! They did speak to me and to each other, but by the end of the trip, I couldn't recall a single word. It all happened so fast, as in a dream. Only I was hyper awake. At that time, I wondered why them? Why not other writers who had impressed me and were part of my curriculum, like Malcom X of *Soul on Ice* by Eldridge Cleaver, or *Passage to India* by E. M. Forster, and a few others?

Much later, I'd find an explanation of these waking dreams in the book *Autobiography of a Yogi*, by Paramahansa Yogannanda. He mentions Kriya yoga techniques, in which yogis, in a state of pure consciousness, free from concepts and thoughts, use light to create 3D images of themselves, their gurus, and their gods, that move and talk. These techniques are laborious and have a basic requirement—a mind unidentified with thoughts. My own images on acid were spontaneous, basic, and 2D, with no speech and no motion. The chief yogi in the autobiography manifests his image to a disciple at a distance using light and purified consciousness and delivers an appropriate message. Very impressive but of no value to me on my path to enlightenment, I would realize only much later.

Chapter 4

A Daytime Nightmare

Ingesting a powerful dose of psychedelic drug is like
strapping oneself to a rocket without a guidance system.

—Sam Harris, *Waking Up*

B Y NOW, I HAD DONE more than 200 acid trips with few issues. If a
trip went south, I rolled with it, thus minimizing the consequences.
Once during my trip, I felt melancholy and desolate for no obvious
reason. The feeling morphed into sadness and continued to increase
in intensity. Eventually, the dark clouds burst, and I was bawling
inconsolably, as if someone near and dear to me had dropped dead, this
very moment, right in front of me.

I was sobbing and sniffling, and my inner voice said, "Take a deep
breath, hold it, lightly contract and dilate your chest sideways, and then
cry more and deeper." I did that, and the relief and unusual expansion of
the chest felt like some ancient bindings had come loose. I felt so light,
I could have levitated off my balcony.

From then on, despair and sadness had lost some of their powerful
grip on my psyche. I had mastered sadness, if that's possible. I had tools
to play with it and use it to my advantage. If a patient came to the clinic
looking sad and miserable, ready to bawl, I let them cry with abandon.
I'd hand them a large towel while giving them instructions appropriate
to their restrained and contracted energy patterns. They didn't feel as
much relief and benefit as I because of the deep seated Western societal
belief that it's weak and shameful to cry. Especially for men and that,

too, in front of a woman. Women too were full of profuse apologies and shame for crying, no matter how much I supported and praised crying as therapeutic. Most health care workers tend to be excruciatingly uncomfortable with their own and their patients' tears.

Repressed anger was uncorked for the first time when I was tripping with my husband Jacque's (name has been changed for privacy) free spirited and chronically optimistic friends from the restaurant where he worked. The time was perhaps around the late seventies. We were passing joints, snorting lines of coke, drinking wine, and making plans to take an acid trip together at a friend's spacious home, where there were many lovely crystals, several wind chimes, and great psychedelic music.

Jacque volunteered to be the chef at the party and wanted to make stuffed goose in some complicated Parisian style while stoned. His wonderful friends applauded his wonderful decision, except for me. I reminded everyone that we were going to trip on acid, which would immediately strip us of our habitual ways of thinking and being. I didn't think he'd be in shape to pull off such a complicated caper under the all-consuming influence of acid. And I certainly wouldn't want to partake of a rich feast at the end of my trip. They assured me and each other that the sumptuous feast would be a perfect expression of gratitude and appreciation for existence and its limitless bounties. I was absolutely against mixing up Thanksgiving with acid trips, and anyway, this was in the summer. I got the impression that everyone thought I was being a party pooper.

On the day of the trip, I arrived with my little bag of fruits and nuts. We all dropped acid, and the trip was unfolding beautifully. A couple of hours later, I wasn't feeling so good and ran for my bag of goodies. It was empty. People were hungry and were eating anything in sight. Jacque had done no prep work and was lying on a bed, blissed out in an alternate universe. For another couple of hours, he would be unable to stand up in the kitchen to roast the bird which would take several hours to cook. Despite their hunger, everyone else was able to maintain a facade of friendship and kindness, but not me. To my horror, I came unhinged. With no inhibitions, I shamelessly attacked and terrorized my husband and our friends. I had warned them, hadn't I, against their grand cooking fantasies! They had dismissed me as a party-pooper bitch. Now someone had finished my bag of goodies without even my permission. I went on and on saying things that should have been left unsaid. They were stunned to see me morph from a gentle, quiet person into a fire breathing freak. That was the first time my repressed rage had burst forth so fully, so publicly! Right in front of my husband and our friends with no regard for consequences. Jacque eventually roasted the bird, which we had for brunch. There was much boisterous and hysterical laughter over my wicked rageful behavior and lots and lots of hugs for me. That day, I was christened Kali Ma, Hindu goddess of wrathful destruction, who is bedecked in a garland of human skulls, with her bright red tongue hanging out. My newly freed anger, unlike my newly freed sadness, would become a problem for me throughout my spiritual journey.

Early on in my tripping career, I realized that going outward on acid, to big rock concerts with sensational stagecraft and pyrotechnics, was a fun Dionysius revel. But overall, it was a poor return on investment of my precious life energy, time, and sanity. I most enjoyed tripping in the solitude of my home, going inward and coming up with valuable insights and feeling supremely peaceful and energized the next day. Spending eight to ten hours on acid, three times a week, all by myself, week after week for a couple of years, thoroughly familiarized and made me comfortable with being alone. This would be of critical help during the final leg of my enlightenment journey in Mexico.

Meanwhile, I was still living in this house across from this lovely and serene cemetery in Vancouver, Canada. It was my evening for the magical acid trip. When I returned from work, there were a lot of cars parked in the cemetery and a lot of people around a grave, and the sun was about to set. Obviously, a fresh death of someone well connected.

The start of my journey was as usual—some physical discomfort marking the leap of consciousness from space to hyperspace, as I liked to think of it in those days. Cool visuals followed and then spontaneous dancing to music. My body felt floaty and feathery, an extremely desirable state. My eyes were closed, and I was soaking and swimming in bliss.

Then, suddenly, everything went dark—very, very dark. I heard an unfamiliar male voice, loud and rude, inside my head, viciously screaming, "Don't ever come back." Then the booming sound of a huge door being shut unceremoniously, rather obnoxiously, in my face. I didn't know what to think of it. I was in fatal shock, trembling uncontrollably with terror! I had been a dedicated devotee. My entire life revolved around my supreme chemical deity. It had supplanted and made all my previous spiritual practices of meditation, yoga, seminars, books, and discourse seem like slow and sleepy bullock cart rides.

The rescue techniques and remedies that had helped in the past were of no avail. My trip was quickly and irretrievably plunging south. I felt icy cold fingers, more than ten, inside my stomach, squeezing and pinching it. Then I felt them inside my skull, causing the same sensations of tightening and squeezing my brain. I felt suffocated and choked by countless invisible entities. My body was leaking life energy. My feet and hands became icy cold, like that of a corpse. My body was trembling with terror from inside, rolling and writhing on the floor. No matter what I did, death and insanity were tightening their stranglehold. A waking nightmare from which I was unable to awaken myself.

Eventually, a solution made itself known. Only the presence of a live human being could make this hell recede and awaken me from my waking nightmare. With trembling fingers, I donned my glasses, opened my phone book, and called a friend who, luckily, was at home. In a shaky and panicky voice, I pleaded with my friend to come over ASAP. When my girlfriend arrived, I clung to her physically like a forlorn child. Within a few minutes, my body temperature stabilized, the icy fingers disappeared, and the invisible entities vanished. Now I was feeling very stupid and ashamed for having troubled my friend over nothing. I had asked her to come immediately to save me from the phantasmagoria of my mind. She scolded me and urged me to stop taking acid and was not going to rescue me again in the future.

My first really bad acid trip, my first call for assistance from the outside world. I was very shaken and confused. What had gone wrong? It wasn't the contaminated quality of acid, because I used to purchase it in bulk. I'd had many successful trips from the same batch. After some analysis, I decided it may have been the fresh burial that evening which had caused this terrifying storm in my psyche. Was the set and setting so critical? I had many wonderful trips in my one-bedroom downtown apartment to the sounds of police and ambulance sirens. Also, I had several supernatural trips in nature.

WTF!

Chapter 5

Betrayed!

Resist not evil.

—Jesus Christ

I WAS IN DEEP DISTRESS. My god, my chemical lover, had abandoned me. Where to turn for help? No one to talk to. If I shared my pain with my husband or a few friends who were aware of my passion for tripping, they'd only be too happy that I had been freed from my madness. I could still hear the loud bang of a heavy door closing, but who the fuck was behind the door? No amount of meditation, or meditation on marijuana, revealed the face of the freak behind the door. Maybe it was an automatic chemical door that nature had kindly provided. It closed when a certain critical amount of LSD built up in the system. A most valid hypothesis!

More than a month had passed since my last scary ride, which no longer seemed scary. Not even a molehill had been found; I was making a mountain out of nothing and habitually harassing myself.

I had to take one more trip, maybe my last, to solve this chemical mystery. On a sunny Saturday morning, the cemetery across looked serene and beautiful. No fresh burial, not even the day before. In the late evening, I dropped my usual dose of acid. Everything was cool. I was even proud of my unflinching courage. And then the horror! From deep within me, I heard this same menacing male voice, totally unfamiliar, not resembling in the least any male authoritarian voices I had ever known.

In the most frigid and stern tone, he impatiently yelled at me, "We told you not to come back. You were warned very clearly."

There was no face, not even the outline of a person. The cold, icy fingers were all over me. Horror of horrors, they were inside me, violently groping, poking, and penetrating all my organs and tissues and twisting my joints from inside. I was rolling on the floor in anguish, writhing and resisting the sensations. Big mistake! I had learned again and again on acid that resisting negativity not only increased it exponentially but took it to a different order of magnitude. I was in face-to-face combat again with death and insanity. Yet, I couldn't remember the lessons from my past trips, of acceptance and embrace of negativity. Acceptance of these disembodied icy cold fingers would have instantly turned my trip golden.

Instead, I was a panicky, trembling mess, resisting, and begging to be left alone. Once again, my body and mind were on the brink of an existential catastrophe. My body might snap, resulting in death, which was totally acceptable. But insanity! What a horrendous fate! Only the presence of a live human could pull me out of my self-created chemical hell. I had to beg my husband to come home. He was working in the restaurant, which was out-of-control busy on Saturday night. Jacque, who seldom showed upset, was overflowing with irritation. I was clinging to him like a terrified child. Being glued to his body warmed, calmed, and energized me. He took control of my remaining acid stash and retrieved a promise from me that my tripping days, at least in that house, were over.

A couple of other mind-blowing things had happened to me before in this serene cemetery prior to my two trips to hell. During those times, I was not on acid or cannabis. Once it was on a summer evening when I was returning home from work. For the first time, I felt a strong pull to visit the cemetery. The sun was still high up in the sky. It was very tranquil, not a human in sight. I found a bench in a shady spot and was enjoying the beauty and color of this quiet landscape, feeling grateful for such supremely silent, non-interfering neighbors. Then, there was a pleasant tickle sensation in my ear, and I heard a woman's voice asking me to read her something from the Bible.

But I have no Bible, don't even own one, I silently said to the voice in my head.

Well then, get one, dearie, was her reply.

Yes. I nodded and said that could be done.

In retrospect, it all seemed very weird! Talking to a strange dead woman in my head! But it didn't seem at all weird at the time. After a brief, peaceful stay, I got up to go home, which was across the street. I noticed a handsome, lush tree and then a "Psst! Come here, you gorgeous one." I didn't walk but floated to the tree. I put my arms around it. I lifted one leg up and curled it around its trunk. Then I threw my head back, which served to bring my pelvis extra forward and almost locked it to the tree trunk, all in one graceful motion! I had not enjoyed such extreme pelvic proximity even with my male lovers. I immediately shrieked and ran home, terrified. I looked around to make sure no live human had witnessed my erotic encounter with a tree in the cemetery.

After smoking a joint at home, the whole episode seemed rather thrilling! So fucking erotic! The dance-like movements of wrapping my body around a gorgeous tree instead of a man were reminiscent of paintings and posters from erotic temples and caves in India. Stoned, I couldn't figure out my panicky behavior with such a handsome and hot tree. Was life showing me its deeply buried erotic aspects? But un-stoned and straight, the whole thing seemed certifiably insane.

I went back to the cemetery after a hiatus of a few days to fulfill my promise to the dead woman of reading the Bible to her. I had picked up the holy book from the drawer of an empty room at the hospital where I worked. As I settled down on the bench to read, I looked up and saw my husband standing in front of me. We were both shocked and stunned, as if we had seen a ghost version of each other. He had come home early and was looking for me. Then he saw a dark-haired head from the window and guessed, though not wishing to be right, that it could be me. Now he was distraught and doubly so to see the Bible in my lap. Nervously, hesitantly, I told him that a few days earlier, I had come to the cemetery, and a woman's voice had asked for the Bible to be read to her. Where had I gotten the Bible? From an empty room at the hospital, I replied. You stole it? Yes, you could say that, but I'm going to return it tomorrow. We walked home laughing at my crazy notions. Jacque assured me that all the dead ones in the cemetery had been thoroughly Bibled out and no one was waiting for me to save them. I did not introduce him to my hot and sexy tree or mention my erotic hug. Much too much for my grounded guy.

These episodes happened only to me, never to my husband or neighbors. My analysis: acid and marijuana were rapidly dissolving my ego, or the separate self, and I wasn't spiritually mature enough to cope with splendors of spirit—at least not yet!

Chapter 6

Me Still an Asshole!

There are more things in heaven and earth, Horatio,
than are dreamt of in your philosophy.

—Shakespeare, Hamlet

IN 2010, JED MCKENNA'S *NOTEBOOK* was published. The final section
of the notebook, titled, "The Golden Door" excited and mentally
stimulated me the most, having been an acidhead several decades
earlier. I wanted to respond but wasn't ready then. Now that I have
completed my spiritual pilgrimage, here are my thoughts, before I bid
adios to my beloved amigo, LSD. My psychic profile of an acid queen
causes shudders of shame and guilt for the chaste and virtuous Hindu
woman I should have been. How and when will the new woman emerge
from the toxic chemical ashes? If truth be told, her real spiritual journey
hasn't even begun!

In Jed's *Notebook*, Frank, a retired professor from California, a fan
and a friend of his, is pining for the lost golden key (i.e., LSD), which
has been declared illegal by the US government. It's not clear to me
whether Frank has taken any trips, but Jed certainly hasn't. Frank
believed that LSD promises "instant Buddhahood" and true freedom
for all humanity.

My version of the Buddhahood, or true freedom, is freedom from
ego, freedom from identification with all thoughts and concepts. It
means death to the ceaseless chatterer in the head! It means fathomless
silence. With an incalculable number of acid trips under my belt, did I

become free from my mind? Not even close! In fact, my head was filling up with new, fluffy and airy kind of celestial shit. But shit nevertheless!

Maybe I'm a low-grade moron, but what about the counterculture heroes Allan Ginsberg and Harvard professors Timothy Leary and Richard Alpert (a.k.a, Baba Ram Das)? Not to forget Jed's favorite, Ken Kesey, author of the award-winning book and movie, *One Flew over the Cuckoo's Nest*. They most certainly must have had glimpses of the unavoidable Buddha mind because we are all unconsciously soaking and swimming in it.

I did too. Vast glimpses of the ever-silent infinite that were unacknowledged because I was so addicted and identified with the content of my mind. I, along with other trippers, were looking for cool visions, delicate and delightful sensations, deep and spontaneous thoughts, intimate and juicy relations, divine images and exotic forms. We all got a lot of those. Tons for me. But Buddha mind, so plain and unsexy, so ridiculously obvious, went unnoticed.

Jed writes, "If chemical mysticism means you can drag any bum off the street after breakfast and have him experience a full-blown state of god-consciousness before lunch, then the rules have changed." By rules, he means, "All religions and philosophies and spiritual teachings have become obsolete." Not so fast, astronauts! Never mind the street bum, even the elevated and elite humanity didn't experience "full-blown" god-consciousness on their first trip or subsequent trips.

What does happen on acid invariably is that the ordinary becomes extraordinary. Does that qualify as god-consciousness? Maybe! The part of the mind that makes distinctions between ordinary and extraordinary has been chemically put aside or rendered inactive. My one such memory: at a traffic light, seeing the reflection of red light in the puddle of rainwater. Most ordinary and mundane! Yet I was overwhelmed by the sheer beauty and grandeur of the scene. What I saw was scintillating red rubies of the most fabulous, most dramatic red color I had ever seen, being reflected in the water. I was so lost in my blissful reverie of the mundane that when the light changed, the cars behind me had to honk. The entire phenomenal world becomes pulsatingly and throbbingly alive on acid.

Near death experiencers often describe heaven as similar to this world but bathed in radiantly shining and luminous supernatural light. They too have been temporarily released from the limitations of their mind. If that's what Frank and Jed mean by god-consciousness, you'll get oodles of it on acid. But, again, so what! Me? I'm still an asshole!

As far as I'm concerned, not even the most avid and famous worshippers of LSD reported lasting god-consciousness. If equated with the Buddha-mind, it amounts to pure emptiness or consciousness devoid of content. Not even Albert Hofmann, PhD, the noble and distinguished-looking scientist who serendipitously discovered LSD in Sandoz laboratory in Switzerland, had such great good luck. In his book *LSD: My Problem Child*, he reports having several cool trips in nature where the same-old, same-old morphed into a supernatural magic land which evoked deep feelings of joyous wonder and awe in him. I call them *soul feelings*. They come and then they go. Lots of those on LSD, but still nowhere near Buddhahood, which is uncreated, unchanging, and unmoving.

Timothy Leary, the most famous American acid head, in his book, *Change Your Brain*, shares a similar sentiment to Frank. An uneducated street bum on psychedelics could have visions of infinity like the English mystic and poet Blake. But the bum doesn't have literary skills to express his vision. Blake without drugs had glimpses of the infinite in its ever-changing forms. He saw angels and god, and then they disappeared. Here are his most famous visionary pearls. He saw "a world in a grain of sand. And Heaven in a wildflower." Very impressive indeed! I too saw a lot of these celestial visions, some of which I'll mention later. Blake had the mystical visions plus the literary skills, and yet, his ego gave him wicked runs around the psychological bushes, which made his colleagues doubt his sanity. However, having your sanity doubted is not uncommon for mystics.

I know Jed, unlike Frank and other acid heads, consider these visions to be *makio* (Jed's word from the trilogy), or illusions, fleeting and insubstantial on the enlightenment journey. Much later, I too, would see them as illusions, although sooo … delectable!

Timothy Leary may have provided me with a probable answer to why the acid door closed on me. First, I wish to spotlight his super elevated perspective of the human brain as "the key, the source, as god."

(Hello? Approximately 3 pounds of gray goo, although the most evolved and sophisticated goo in the universe, is god? The finite brain is god?) Is Leary even close to Buddha mind? Nowadays, the brain is given its due but is also seen as an inefficient machine filled with assumptions and biases. Leary explains in his book that the cerebral cortex is responsible for divine visions and the mystical illumination of the spiritual seekers. According to Leary, "There are more visions in the cortex of each of us than in all the museums and libraries of the world." My theory is that frequent acid trips perhaps exhausted all the visions programmed in my cerebral cortex. Another clue to this theory is my memory of a lot of spontaneous repeats of visions of *yantras*, or sacred geometrical designs, and other nonlinear states of consciousness.

For me, the most precious, most valuable gift of LSD wasn't celestial visions or Buddha mind, but succulent and juicy tastes of existence, of life itself. On acid, oneness with existence, though crazy making, is a deep, visceral experience, not an abstraction. Over reliance on my dualistic mind cut me off from the flow of life and energy, imprisoning me in my psychological straitjacket. Later, I would discover that liberated personal consciousness is the secret sauce of existence. Meanwhile, watch this acid and pothead sweat blood to find Buddhahood, which, actually, can never be lost.

Chapter 7

The Guru Appears

To live is the rarest thing in the world. Most people merely exist.

—Oscar Wilde.

A TEMPORARY PHYSICAL THERAPIST, A WHITE woman from South Africa, had joined our department in the general hospital where I was working. It was friendship at first sight. She had been living in Pune, India, as a follower of guru Bhagwan Shree Rajneesh (a.k.a Osho, henceforth addressed as Osho.) During the coffee break, when we two were alone, with a mischievous look, she pulled out her *mala* (beaded necklace with Osho's photo in the locket) from under her uniform top to show me his face.

From then on, she would regale me with jokes and stories of Osho and the ashram. I invited her and her drug dealing boyfriend for dinner with me and my husband one night. They both arrived dressed in smart looking Western style orange clothes, with their *malas* on the outside, displaying Osho's face. She explained Osho's *neo sannyas* to us over appetizers, wines, cannabis, and cigarettes, which they consumed in generous quantities, with deep enjoyment. *Neo sannyas*, they happily informed us, encourages a celebratory rather than ascetic lifestyle. Drugs, alcohol, and smoking although not permitted in the ashram's premises, were not condemned by the guru. Here she pulled out from her orange tote Osho's book *From Sex to Superconsciouness* as a gift to us. They told us that because of his open attitude to sexuality, he had been unjustly given the moniker of "Sex Guru," which was only a small part of his teaching. According to Osho, they told us, religion is an art that shows us how to enjoy life. We wholeheartedly agreed that all the religions of the past had been death oriented, a killjoy of condemnation and eternal damnation for enjoying life, especially sex.

Jacque and I instantly fell in love with this new religion from India, one of meditation, laughter, celebration, and creativity. My new friend's boyfriend promised me high grade hashish from Afghanistan, the purest LSD, or whatever else I wanted for free if we showed up at the ashram. Above all, I secretly wished to steam up our increasingly frozen marriage. What was not to like about our brilliantly adventurous and exotic future!

We both gave up our jobs, sold our belongings, and bought six month return tickets to Mumbai via the Philippines, Singapore, and Bali. We arrived in Mumbai a couple of weeks later, broke and exhausted, with infected wounds from a rented motorbike accident in Bali.

My family was distraught to hear about our plans to visit the Osho ashram. They told us he was a mad and crazy fraud, greedy for money. Time would prove them partly right. They had recently read a story about a German woman getting beaten up in some therapy group at the ashram. They also warned us that the culture and flavor of Pune, with which I was familiar, had changed for the worse. The white folks were everywhere in their orange clothes. The shameless white women, scantily dressed, hugged and kissed openly in the streets. All the good Pune restaurants were packed with these unkempt, wild, boisterous foreigners from all over the world. No Indian in their right mind would even call Osho a spiritual guru, while he called himself Bhagwan, which means god. What rubbish! He charged for his daily discourses, which no Indian guru had ever done in Hindu spiritual tradition. They tried to seduce us with several internationally known but traditional gurus, but we showed no interest. We weren't particularly interested in worship or meditation or longing to meet god or even enlightenment. We were looking for kindred souls for holiday sun, fun, and adventure.

The ashram in Pune immediately impressed us as an oasis of peace and beauty, natural serenity, and harmony. The locals were in a serious minority, mostly in administrative positions. Sparkling cleanliness, tranquility, and a feeling of order inside the huge, beautiful doors of the ashram stood out in clear contrast against the chaos, noise, and poverty outside. The ashram cafeteria, run by a Swiss devotee, was in an outdoor garden, with tables and huge sunbrellas. Their coffee and pastries deserved at least four international stars according to my gourmet French-Canadian husband. He was excited by the innovative menu, which was a fusion of European and Indian cuisine, created using only local ingredients.

The next morning, we showed up before 8:00 a.m. for the master's discourse in Buddha Hall, which holds a couple of thousand followers. We were told the day before to use non-scented toiletries and clothes washed in scent free detergent, as the master was very sensitive to chemical odors. Before entering Buddha Hall, we had to pass through an arc of human sniffers. They could deny entry to the discourse on the grounds of even the weakest whiff of chemical odor. We were happy to pass our first smell test.

Buddha Hall was without walls, with a covered roof and cement floor. It was surrounded by an abundance of shrubs and flowers and ancient tall trees. Inside the hall, it was orderly, peaceful, and very orange. At exactly 8:00 a.m., master arrived in his chauffeured white Benz. He was of medium height, wearing a simple white robe. He was bald on top, with long, curly black hair framing his sweet and serene brown face and he had a thinning, long black beard. He floated up the steps to his chair on the stage. He *namasted* his couple of thousand followers, making eye contact with those dear to him sitting close by. To me, he looked the embodiment of stillness and serenity. All his moves, especially his hand gestures, were fluid and flowing, like poetry in motion. Since the hall had no walls, the feeling of spaciousness seemed vaster, heightened by his timeless presence.

His current discourse was on Vigyan Bhairav Tantra techniques of enlightenment, given by the oldest Hindu god, Lord Shiva, to his wife Parvati, eons ago. Osho introduced Shiva as the first Hippie, first psychedelic freak, and first yogi, who presided over death and destruction. No amount of destruction is enough for Shiva because only the false can be destroyed, never Truth. He went on to describe Shiva's wedding to Princess Parvati, daughter of the king of Himalayas. The

Princess, dazzled by Shiva's transcendental radiance, overwhelmed by his legendary unfathomable silence, begged him to marry her. With much difficulty, she convinced her parents that she had found herself a husband worthy of her in every way.

Royals came from all over India to attend the illustrious wedding. The kingdom folks were very excited and had decorated their homes. One look at Shiva's wedding procession of weirdos and freaks—the groom looking the wildest and freakiest of them all—the citizens ran home in horror and locked their doors. Shiva was covered in ashes and matted hair, accessorized with snakes of various sizes, playing ghoulish music on his little drum and dancing with perfect abandon. At the palace, after one glance at Shiva, Parvati's mother, leading the bridal welcome procession, fainted and dropped like a ton of bricks. Fear and panic had replaced the palatial celebrations. Parvati fell at Shiva's feet and begged him to behave properly just this one time. Shiva then transformed himself. The royals' jaws dropped on seeing his radiant form. The presiding priest presented the bride's ancient royal lineage. Now it was time to present the groom's lineage. Shiva, sitting on the groom's throne, remained still and silent. Restlessness was in the air as the auspicious time for the wedding was passing. Nothing! Absolute silence from Shiva and his procession. Eventually famous Hindu sage Narda started to scold the priests and the royals for being blind, dumb, and stupid. Looking condescendingly at their gilded and glittering forms, he reminded them they had been blinded by worship of meaningless names and forms. Shiva, he told them, is unborn, uncreated, deathless, causeless, pure existence—the inexhaustible source of all names and forms. The humiliated royals fell at Shiva's feet begging for forgiveness.

I was ecstatic! I had never heard this story before. My LSD trips had been sanctified without my asking.

Chapter 8

Osho Resort

You know what a bitch is? Someone who simply believes what she thinks.

—Byron Katie

T HERE WAS NOTHING TRADITIONAL ABOUT Osho and his ashram, populated by mainly European and American followers. We felt as if we had found our club, a tribe of global misfits and weirdos. In order to really belong, to go deeper, we felt the need to be initiated. We reminded each other of the motto of the B.C. Lotto: "You can't win if you're not in." Also, we assured each other we would drop the whole thing if we felt unhappy, deceived, or exploited. With new orange robes, *mala*, and new names, we started our new lives as committed seekers of Truth.

My husband's new name was Swami Prem Bodhi, which he loved more than Jacque. His name had to do something with loving the Buddha-mind, the essence of us all. My name was kept the same, but he added the prefix *deva*, which made it Deva Kamla, meaning divine lotus flower. Osho told me sweetly while gazing gently in my eyes that the lotus flower is the symbol of "in" the world but not "of" the world. He added in a soft voice that the lotus grows in the mud but remains untouched and uncontaminated by its surroundings. In my new incarnation, I was to remember not to get mixed up with the mud of the mind. Very pretty! We had no clue at the time what Truth or Buddha mind meant or what we were doing. For me, though, unbeknown to me at the time, the search for Truth would consume my entire life.

Ashram offered a whole variety of therapies based on the Western human potential movement; body awareness therapies from standard massage to Rolfing, and a variety of meditations, including Vipassana. We had money, and we had time. We threw ourselves in the giant washing machine of groups, individual therapies, and meditations. We were each assigned to different groups and meditations. Most groups were done in the nude to promote the dropping of all pretensions and postures and to represent total nudity and naturalness of truth. We had no problem with nudity because we had spent time at nude beaches in Vancouver.

In one group, in an afternoon session, I arrived nicely stoned, although I had removed the traces of it by rinsing my mouth and washing my hands. There were about twelve to fourteen people, all white except me and all naked. The group had no structure, no agenda except to be in the here and now and to speak and act from there rather than the past and future of our finite minds. After a few minutes of silence, I stood up and started to sing a devotional song in Hindi. I don't know where the urge came from (most probably from the joint I had smoked), as I don't have a singing voice and have little public confidence. A swami (male follower) stood up and hugged me from behind as I was singing. Soon, another *sannyasin* stood up and put his arms around us. I felt a hand on my vagina. Pretty soon, we were engaged in an orgy, piled on top and around each other.

Then the group leader blew her whistle and asked us all to shower without touching, hugging, or exchanging a word with each other. When we returned, she read us a page from Osho's book on tantra and meditative sex. She said ours had started innocently and spontaneously but soon devolved into mind fuck. She said she could see that some people participated in the party driven by peer pressure and boredom.

Ashram was the most unique playground and laboratory for experimentation and exploration of human spiritual potential. We were constantly being urged to let go of our psychological hang ups and societal inhibitions and explore our liberated natural selves. Never, ever, had such a concept or such an oasis of freedom existed at such a grand international scale in the spiritual history of mankind. Most Osho meditations have a cathartic component, based on his observation that modern man is carrying tons of emotional and sexual repressions which are preventing him from being meditative and peaceful. In some group settings and segments of meditations, we had license to scream, shout, yell, and howl. We were free to hurl out International cusses and obscenities, of which the German word for shit, *scheisse*, was the most popular.

In one group, I was enraged at the leader because he laughed in my face and said I was playing at being angry but hadn't even scratched the surface. This wasn't a movie but real life, my life, and I wasn't showing up for it. I couldn't believe my ears. I screamed that I wanted to kick and strangle him. With a bored expression, he yawned in my face and defiantly asked, "Why don't you! Who is stopping you? You're terrified of life. Your anger is a pretense, a convenient cover up for your terror. Therefore, your anger is hollow and cold, like your life. A life of pretense is not worth living."

A near unbearable ouch! I was shocked! Me pretending! Me pretending anger! I had thought of myself as being not only brutally but dangerously honest and authentic on LSD. Maybe I was more honest with myself than the world because of fear of consequences that we were constantly urged to toss out. On LSD, so much anger had surfaced, most of the time not at anyone or any event. Anger was noticed, and it passed through me like a steaming whirlpool. I was aware that maybe my husband and some of our friends secretly thought of me as a bitch, and here this man was telling me that I was not bitchy enough for his group. My ego was hurt and confused.

Several days later, I had an appointment for an individual session of rebirthing. It consists of uninterrupted breathing through the mouth until some deeply buried emotion or memory surfaces, which is processed with the therapist. The therapy chamber was in the basement of one of the ashram buildings. I was asked to wait, as my therapist hadn't arrived. The waiting area was dark and damp, with no magazines. There were a bunch of *sannyasins* (the initiated ones), men and women, laughing and horsing around in the adjacent rooms. When they would pass me in the waiting room, they would never acknowledge me or even look at me. I would have to stand up every ten minutes and interrupt their crazy horsing around and ask for the status of my appointment. It was clear they were irked by me. This is well before the cell phone era. After about half an hour of waiting and marinating in my rage and resentment, I stopped one of the *ma* (female initiate) prancing in glee through the waiting area. She gave me the nuisance look and said impatiently, "I guess your therapist is not coming today," and disappeared. No apology, no sympathy, no nothing. Not even a humanitarian hug!

I left the therapy chambers so filled with rage that I could barely see the road. This is the new humanity, harbinger of a new world, founded on love and compassion, where everyone is a meditator and therefore peaceful. What rubbish! I had done my meditations and my groups. And yet, my soul was a fire that was escalating out of control. I started to silently yell obscenities at Osho and his orange tribe. I was stomping my feet and railing at the heaven with my fists. I yanked the *mala* off my neck so forcibly that all of the 108 beads went rolling off in the dirt. I jumped on the locket framing Osho's photo, cussing uncontrollably, using my newly learnt international cuss words. Then I kicked the beads and the locket into the open sewer.

Fucked up and fuming, in the hotel room, I immediately reached for a joint. I was feeling calmer, but my ego was firmly fixed in the position that it was all their fault. They ... they were the ones who told me I was fake, that my anger was fake (many years later, I'd peacefully acknowledge they were right). They ... only told me that this orange tribe was my new family, very different from the old. The new family was authentic, unconditionally loving, and unconditionally allowing. Ha, ha, haaaa!

Maybe I'm really a bitch, violent and bloody, Ma Kali, as my acid tribe had dubbed me! All the drugs, therapies, and meditation had only made me worse and more inflammable than before. Maybe I have to accept her bitchiness with no hope of ever tenderizing her. What horror!

P.S.

A fresh outrage toward the end of my manuscript had me running to *The Work*, by Byron Katie, whom you're going to meet going forward. *The Work* helped me discover deeper layers of old emotional pain of yearning to be included in the fun and frothy horseplay of *sannyasins* around me in the waiting area. I longed to be included but didn't know how to ask, and they didn't make any moves. My twisted psyche, ashamed of her vulnerabilities, instead reflexively indulged in volcanic eruption.

Chapter 9

Meet the New World, Same as the Old World

"The truth." Dumbledore sighed. "It's a beautiful and terrible thing, and should therefore be treated with great caution."

—J. K. Rowling, *Harry Potter and the Sorcerer's Stone*

RAGE HAD BURNED ITSELF OUT. Nail biting anxiety, shame, and guilt had taken possession of my psyche. What was I going to do without my *mala*, or holy necklace? It was my passport to the inner sanctum of the ashram, to many therapies to which only the initiates were permitted. Above all, it was a symbol of my bond, albeit a weak one at the moment, to the master and the orange tribe. I was worried that when I got back to the ashram tomorrow, those who know me are sure to ask, "What happened? Where is your mala?" Shall I tell the shameful truth or create a fiction—a tearjerker in the tradition of Bollywood? Like a little girl, I was scared and ashamed to face my husband. My worst doubts about me—an out-of-control, impossible-to-handle bitch—had been confirmed.

Later, when I told Bodhi about the event with residual steam and anguish still bubbling up from within, he was stunned. He warned me that if I told the story truthfully, the ashram authorities were not going to like it one bit. His suggestion, although I had thought of it too—convenient, quick, and so efficient—was to lie. Something like, I went to Mumbai for a day to visit my family, preferably a very sick, terminally ill family member in the hospital. Maybe a death in the family. In any case, I was extremely distraught and went to the beach to settle myself down. Before going in the ocean, I took out my *mala* and put it in my beach bag, which was stolen. We both thought of adding my wallet with credit cards and driver's license to the stolen beach bag for extra gravitas and drama. How many times in the past had I killed my grandma and grandpa, whom I had never met, to save my ass? We both laughed at the dark side of our creativity—a necessity in a society believing in the power of the punishment.

At dinner, we talked to our *sannyasin* couple friends, both practicing psychotherapists in the United States. They were shocked and speechless. I told them I was thinking of dropping the whole thing and returning home to Canada sooner, which would cost us some money. Bodhi was visibly upset to hear my new plan. He complained that I had dropped a bomb on his head and expected sympathy and cooperation. Our friends were on his side. Our friends warned me there'd be blood and there'd be consequences. The *mala* that Osho had personally put around my neck at the time of initiation was the most sacred symbol of truth, of the new and free world. And I had desecrated it! It was tantamount to desecrating the flag of a country. I reminded them how Osho laughed at any country that reacted vengefully at the burning of their flag. "It's only a piece of cloth to which we have attached our human values and meaning," he had said. So I had destroyed a necklace of beads in my rage. I hadn't harmed him or anybody. All I had done was pulled the plug from the container of my rage at the behest of their therapist. Truly, I assured them, I wouldn't dare to be so red-hot rageful in the real world. I was stubbornly trying to convince myself and them of my good and virtuous woman status: always peaceful and poised! I solemnly declared that the new me was going to explore honesty and authenticity to its core. No approval or support was forthcoming from my orange tribe.

The next day, feeling sweet and serene after the master's discourse, I walked into the ashram's office. I got the head honcho, Osho's alter ego, a local Indian *ma* (a woman seeker), to interview me. When I told her my story, which I toned down several shades, her face changed from gentle and soft to hard and stern, of a mean nun mixed with a serious and stern schoolteacher. She gave a short lecture on how immensely lucky we, the *sannyasins*, and the world were to have a living god, a living Buddha amongst us. I vigorously nodded my head in agreement. I explained that I was reacting to my therapist, who had said my anger was phony and impotent. She wouldn't have it. With shock and disgust on her face, she called me insincere and fake. She haughtily declared that my punishment was not to show up anywhere near the ashram for two weeks. After that, I would be interviewed by a panel of *sannyasins*, and then the decision would be made to restore my disciple status or to expel me. She abruptly rose from her chair and walked away before I could plead for mercy.

I knew if I told my mom or she found out what I had done, even though she didn't care at all for my guru, she would be deeply distressed. She had taught me by her example and by instructions to be respectful to sacred symbols of all rituals and religions. But that's the old world, based on unquestioned beliefs and unquestioned respect and veneration of authority. My new world, smelling so fresh and vibrant, with its new orange wardrobe, accessories, and lingo, had turned out to be no different. Gut-twisting disillusionment!

I simmered and stewed and vigorously continued my marijuana meditations for two weeks in the solitude of my hotel room. Bodhi continued to participate passionately in all the ashram activities. I decided to take an acid trip, but it was just flavorless and boring. I totally believed in LSD and its magical transformative powers. After all, it had revived my physical body. Now I desperately needed psychological tweaking, but no luck. I laughed at my plight. I felt like a freak and realized I had always felt freakish but had hidden it successfully from others and myself because of fear of disapproval and isolation. I was being roasted alive for using the freedom license given to me by my new orange tribe. I was being punished for flying my freaky freedom flag. Maybe the fire was good and holy. Maybe it was burning my unreasonable expectations, my arrogance, and my rock-solid stubbornness.

The person who walked into the ashram office after two weeks of solitude was relatively humble and properly chastised. With deep disappointment, I had silently swallowed my personal vision of a new world. If anyone would have asked me about my expectations of the ashram, which no one did, not even my friends, I had a ready answer.

To me, it seemed to be in alignment with the teachings of the master. Help and guide rather than punish. In my newly born orange fantasy, the ashram head honcho would have hugged, kissed, and congratulated me on my authentic expression of anger. She would have asked how it felt to express my deeply repressed, uninhibited anger at our symbol of highest authority, our godlike master? She would have assured me that it's not unnatural for us humans to rage at god—the ultimate authority! She would have reminded me never to forget there's no sin except unconsciousness. At this point, it would have been appropriate for her to praise the master as an ocean of compassion who has given us the full freedom to be ourselves, our genuine and authentic selves, no matter where it leads us. I would have totally agreed, perhaps prostrated at her lotus feet. Finally, the head honcho would have recommended an ashram therapist to fully process my anger and learn how to express it in a manner so that my needs were met.

Dream on, girlfriend!

Instead, for the panel of four ashram heavies, I had to put out a piece of performance art of deep sorrow, shame, and guilt, along with tears and repeated promises to mend my ways. It worked. I was welcomed back in the fold.

Chapter 10

Dance On!

What counts in making a happy marriage is not so much how compatible you are but how you deal with incompatibility.

—Leo Tolstoy

OSHO ONCE TALKED OF A letter from a *sannyasin* who wanted to come to his ashram but was concerned it would ruin his marriage. Master's answer: yes, it would. There's so much choice here, he said. She would find a better man and he would find a better woman simply because of increased understanding and maturity of both the partners. Osho was anti-marriage, anti-family, and anti-celibacy. Jealousy and possessiveness in marriage, he said, is a killer of love and passion. He was all for love and sex and birth control, which he said was a gift of unparalleled value from science on par with fire and wheel. Celibacy, promoted by all the major religions of the world as the highest virtue, he said, was the cause of all sexual perversions. Later he would call AIDS a religious disease, born in monasteries. All the religions of the world condemned him, Hinduism and Christianity the loudest.

My marriage to Bodhi had barely survived multiple emotional dents and scars from the open-love environment at the ashram. It was on life support, and we were going to throw it consciously into a roaring bonfire by coming to Pune for a whole year. My family had gotten us a condo in a middle-class neighborhood, from an uncle who had temporarily moved to Hong Kong.

We quickly settled into our new rhythm at the ashram, this time with a brand-new set of *sannyasin* friends. We went to master's daily discourses, which were dazzlingly brilliant, profound yet entertaining, hilarious, liberating, and always spontaneous and fresh. He resurrected and animated his favorite global mystics, enlightened masters, sages, and philosophers. Our day would start with an abundance of spiritual nourishment and end at the ashram run disco or bar outside the ashram's precinct. The disco was in a big, open field under the stars, with a huge wooden dance floor. We would quietly smoke in a corner and discreetly pass around the joint or pipe. Most of us danced with a blindfold, which was encouraged. The reasoning being that with eyes closed, unmolested by the mind and its toxic comparisons, the dance becomes meditation and the disco a temple. Freed from the ego, the dancer and the dance become one, and only the dance remains. This state of oneness was highly prized as being existence itself, and also for its dizzying floatiness and ecstasy. The vast and open set and setting and popular disco music would elevate a few tokes of cannabis to the level of dropping ecstasy.

After a few months of fun and frolic, we decided to do some volunteer work at the ashram. I was working in the printing department. On this particular morning, I was a floater, an extra. In came a tall, beautiful blonde *sannyasin ma*, holding a backpack. She grabbed me by my arm and asked me to help her count the money. She unloaded her backpack on a huge table in the very back of the printing department. It was one day of earnings of the ashram, from therapies; boutique, bookstore, and coffee shop sales; and Osho discourses. My first instruction was to make separate piles of 50-, 100-, and 500- rupee bills.

She proceeded to tell me about her life in the ashram and in India. Whenever she needed money for her personal expenses, she went to Mumbai, where she had super-rich Indian and Bollywood clients. A couple of hours of sexual work, and she would have enough money to live luxuriously for several months in Pune. I was enchanted by her easy-breezy style. Then she hurriedly rubber banded the piles of cash, depositing them in careful stacks in her backpack. She had to be somewhere, and I could join her if I wished. The thought of separating from her alluring presence so soon was unbearable. On the way to her appointment, she told me about the opium dens of Mumbai, where they were and how she occasionally made a quick drug run to Europe. I was in awe of her!

She remembered she had to deliver a quick message to someone in the pussy garden. As we were going up the steps, I, in all my innocence, asked, "What's a pussy garden?"

She opened the door to a terrace, and about six or seven very European looking, fair blonde women *sannyasins* were nude sunbathing. She quickly asked me to look at the pussies, how different each one looked, how tender and vulnerable, while she delivered her message to her friend. I was shocked, shamed and embarrassed and unfortunately couldn't look directly at the variety of pussies available to my gaze. She grabbed my arm again, and we were on the move. I was awed by her total lack of guilt and shame and wanted a tiny bit of that for myself. Outside, I got caught by a fellow worker and sadly had to dash back to my assigned workplace. I was overwhelmed with gratitude and silently wondered where else on this planet, especially in super conservative India, could I get such an authentic education in earthly matters of sex, drugs, and money—all universally condemned! Osho had taken the ancient Tantric concept of existential inclusiveness and given it a living laboratory to prove its worth. Stunningly bold and daring experiment!

The next new experiment was waiting in the wings for me. At work, I had made friends with a Swiss *ma*, an artist who had been living in London with her artist boyfriend. She was in Pune by herself, so we were able to spend time together. She told me she was bisexual and shared her failed suicide attempt in her teenage years. With simmering resentment, she talked of how the crushing conformity of her upbringing and culture had squeezed the wild and the natural out of her.

One evening, I invited her to my condo for happy hour. My husband wasn't home and hadn't been home for a couple of nights. We were sitting on the balcony, toking and drinking beer. We were giggling and laughing over our nasty commentary about the hundreds of obnoxiously loud birds returning to their nests in this huge tree next to our balcony. As the evening grew darker and the birds settled down, my friend suggested meditation. We both assumed a half-lotus posture and closed our eyes. After a period of quietude, I found myself reaching for her body and stroking her knee. She was very welcoming. It was the first time I had ever made advances toward anyone, let alone a woman. Later, she asked how it had been for me, being my first. I certainly didn't feel guilt or shame, but, rather, a feeling of liberation from judgments and suffocating societal rules and norms—a blessed state for an Osho follower.

My friend was scheduled to depart within a couple of days, so I invited her again. As we were making it in the shower, my husband came home. We didn't hear him. Confused to the core on hearing the chatter and sighs and giggles, he opened the bathroom door. He profusely apologized and said he had come to change clothes and was leaving. When I met him next, I assured him that I hadn't suddenly discovered my true identity as a lesbian and that it had all happened very spontaneously. He shrugged his shoulders and said he understood. I felt worryingly uncertain of his nonchalant attitude. That however was the required and necessary attitude to thrive in Osho's wild Tantric gardens of thrills, wonders, and delights.

Chapter 11

Om Namah Shivaya

In India, *bhang*, a marijuana-based drink, is called
Shiva's Regal (a pun on Chivas Regal brand of malt
whisky).

W E HAD SPENT SEVERAL MONTHS in Pune, and my family was
pressuring us for a visit. We also wanted to visit the opium dens
of Mumbai. At the Pune train station, we met a French couple whom
we hadn't met at the ashram. They were leaving for France and boarding
their plane from Mumbai. They were sorry to leave the ashram and,
above all, India.

Within a couple of days it would be Maha Shivratri, the Grand
Night of Shiva, moonless and dark. Our new friends told us there
would be all-night worship and singing at the Shiva temples. Free
bhang would be served, made by crushing the leaves and the buds of
marijuana in mortar and pestle and mixing it with milk and spices. I
made a disgusted *ew* face, imagining drinking room temperature milk
with marijuana paste. They assured us it was very tasty and supernatural
in its potency. Some of their best psychoactive trips and meditations had
happened under the influence of *bhang*.

We were flying high just on their stories of groups at the ashram—
how once she had left her body at an evening gathering, when Osho
touched her third eye, and of their wild New Year's bash in Goa. We
seemed to come up with no stories of our own to match their altitude.

We had almost forgotten about Maha Shivaratri, but my mother,
who faithfully consulted her lunar calendar, informed us of meatless

meals because of Maha Shivaratri. Looking forward to an auspicious *bhang* trip, our souls did joyful flips, certain that all the stars were in alignment. In the evening, on the way to the temple, which was about a fifteen-minute walk from home, Bodhi asked whether my parents had ever done *bhang*. It was considered sacred, after all, and my mother was so holy moly!

No, I replied, because of their classist, racist, and sexist conditioning. *Bhang*, in their playbook, was something that poor low-class people did: those who didn't care about losing control, those who had no class and no shame and danced the night away with abandon in sheer madness. My mom, in her younger days, went to Shiva temple in the mornings. There she worshiped with hordes of conservative and orthodox Hindu women by pouring a cup of milk on Shiva Lingam, which to any human eye around the world looks like a representation of a phallus. For Hindus, it's much more than Shiva's divine penis. It's a spiritual icon, a symbol of cosmic mysteries and a representation of the great void that contains the entire cosmos.

By the time we reached the Mumbai temple, the sun had set, but there was still plenty of light. There were no people anywhere, which was rare for Mumbai, especially in a temple on a holy day. We were either too early or too late. There was a table outside with a good size steel container and a bunch of clean glasses. A priest showed up his forehead, adorned with horizontal lines in sandalwood paste and a bright red circle in the middle. He handed us two six-ounce glasses filled with very light green milk, which looked like a pistachio shake. We quietly gulped the contents, and I led Bodhi to the nearby shoreline of the Arabian Sea, which was piled with huge black rocks.

The effect of *bhang* was almost immediate, starting with a pleasant buzzing in our heads. We found a private, secluded spot and settled on a huge rock where we could sit or lie together. The rocks felt cozy, still warm from the sun. The gentle sea breeze caressing our faces and hair was a huge turn-on. We refrained from dropping our clothes, which had become thoughtlessly easy by now. We didn't feel safe because even though we had procured a private spot, we were perilously close to the main road. I told my husband that even though we were in the country of erotic Kama Sutra temples (Khujrao temples dedicated to Shiva) and had drunk existential elixir at Shiva temple, the physical body and sex were deeply denigrated in this weirdest of all countries.

At one time in recent history, the authorities had planned to cover the temple statues of lush-breasted and butted women, as well as all the big, virile penises sculpted on the temple walls. Fortunately, it didn't come to pass. The missionaries of the colonial era had called these erotic sculptures obscene, puerile, and vulgar. We imagined covering Shiva's big, divine penis, usually sculpted from smooth, slick black stone, in some awesome underwear, maybe gold or red silk. We both burst out laughing at this image and couldn't stop. Through peals of laughter, I told him that there's a circle at the base of the divine penis that represents the vagina. He laughed uproariously at this image of a poor little circle, barely noticeable, so unassuming and unpretentious! And the erect penis, so potently penetrating!

"So awesomely aggressive, like a missile," I chimed.

"Like a rocket ready to take off," he retorted.

"For the mystic void," said I, completing his epic thought. "Hey, and women have breasts for show-and-tell," I added. Even Shiva and Christ, gods with five-star power, need a womb to manifest their form. Interdependence ran the engine of the universe, we philosophized.

Even though we were sitting in the heart of the densely trafficked area of Mumbai, it was quiet and serene. The traffic noise, like a distant wave, mingled with the gentle sound of little ripples of the ocean, soaking us in the richness of the moment. Our eyes naturally closed in meditation. Holding his hand, I fell into deep silence. My finite chattering mind had at last been tranquilized. There was only an ocean of emptiness, of timeless Shiva consciousness. Not only my mind but also my body had disappeared. What was lying on the still-warm rock was a network of energy lines. Very weird! But not terrifying. It all felt deeply nourishing!

Bodhi stirred from his meditation and gently whispered in my ear that it was time to go. We had missed the dinner hour, and he could feel my mom's agitation a mile away. More unstoppable laughter, which I milked to the max by consciously joining the jiggling of my stomach, opening my mouth even wider, throwing my head back, and laughing louder until there was no more left. When we felt properly settled in our normal consciousness, we left our divine oasis with gratitude to deal with Mumbai madness out on the roads.

After a few days of family fiestas, we were ready for the opium den. And my anxiety at the thought was growing faster than my excitement. I knew it was related to being busted in an opium den and bringing shame and societal condemnation upon my family. I knew I wouldn't feel so much anxiety but rather total excitement, like Bodhi, if we were going to opium dens in Hong Kong or Holland, for example. I tried all the tricks I had learned on my spiritual journey to make my anxiety manageable such as, *neti, neti* (not this, not this). If it can be perceived, it's clearly not me. Breathe it out and disengage. Above all, don't feed it with your attention. Ha ha, fat chance.

My pretension of being cool for the sake of Bodhi was only increasing anxiety's chokehold on me. So, I decided to share my thoughts with him. The opium dens, I guessed, were in the neighborhood of one of the largest and seediest red-light districts in Mumbai, perhaps Asia. I didn't want to get the directions from the men in my family. If they knew, we would be forced to cancel our adventure and I would receive heaps of shameful verbal abuse. I was wanting to impress upon Bodhi that the Mumbai red-light district was going to be unimaginably raw, shocking, and squalid compared to its European counterparts. As a precaution, he had to empty his wallet of all sorts of cards, including his driver's license. We decided to drop our *malas* and watches, and even my wallet and purse. We took just enough cash for cabs, opium, and some food and drinks later. We wished we had our ordinary clothes, like jeans and T-shirts. I didn't want us to look like two monks (saffron or orange being designated monk color in Asia) roaming in the red-light district looking for opium dens. The Western style of our clothes, such as pants and shirts, even though they were orange, was our possible safety sticker.

We let the cab go in the proximity of the neighborhood and decided to find the dens on foot. We were greeted by a labyrinth of filthy, squalid, dark and narrow lanes. We found ourselves frequently bumping into very dark-skinned, mean, macho-looking, paan-chewing (betel nut) *goondas* (gangsters). We were nervous but pretended our Canadian cool. We asked for directions and were told we were standing in front of a den. It was a seedy-looking establishment with dusty doors and windows. A dark-complexioned man with greasy coal-black hair, shabby clothes, a bulging tummy, and huge, pointy, mean-looking rings on all ten fingers let us in.

The front room was small and dark, with several wooden tables and chairs. He showed us another room, with single wooden beds and no mattresses, just straw mats. Two men, looking rather catatonic, were lying on their sides with long pipes resting on the wooden tables beside them. The setting was dark and depressing, and my mindset was even gloomier. I refused to lie down even though we were told it was the most effective delivery position for the opium vapors. I was concerned for our safety and, above all, my family reputation, as we were about to do something highly illegal and shameful even by chaotically maddening Mumbai standards.

Two long pipes were brought with clay bowls attached containing a brown looking pellet of opium. I wanted us both to share one pipe. The good man assured us we needed to smoke at least several of these pea-size pellets to get a happy lift-off. He heated the opium with a special lamp, and when it was ready, we were asked to inhale. We both weren't feeling anything, but I absolutely insisted on leaving, as pure, unstoppable terror was coursing through my veins. When we came out of the den, my body was trembling, and my mind was inconsolably rattled. I would have been quickly soothed if I had asked my husband for a long, warm, all-encompassing ashram style hug, but there was rawness and violence in the air. It bespoke of intolerance for such a display of affection, even between a married couple, in the most immoral and hellish-smelling place on earth.

We found our way to the main road and took a cab to a beach near my home. In the cab, we both became enveloped by a sweet sense of well-being, turned euphoric by the time we reached our safe beach. The effect of the joy plant was peaking. The darkness at the beach provided us with a safe cover. Behind us, the traffic and city lights, heat, humidity, and press of humanity were doing their thing. We found comfortable rocks to sit on with a patch of cool wet sand for our feet. Out of deep silence, Bodhi had an attack of uncontrollable laughter. He had to stand up to catch his breath. His eyes were shining in the dark with mischief and madness. I told him his crazy abundant laughter reminded me of Carlos Castaneda's Don Juan, who frequently laughed uproariously at man's follies, especially Carlos'. I went on to say that although Osho promoted laughter by peppering his daily discourses lavishly with jokes and anecdotes, I had never seen him, or even a photo of him, laughing with abandon, his mouth fully open, shaking from head to toe. His signature, we both agreed, was meditative bliss. Bodhi said master was right to criticize old religions for being serious and life, negative. With Osho, it's always party time, with his frequent emphasis on rejoicing, dancing, and singing. He was also heavy on meditation, on liberation from ego — the extinguisher of joy, the destroyer of peace, the damned party pooper!

I mentioned my family — so uptight and stiff, totally devoted to suffocating Hindu values, completely clueless about ego and meditation. He promptly brought up his own family — stiff and buttoned up, strangled by their Catholic values. We assured each other it was not just our families but most people on the planet were suffering from various levels of existential angst and pretending otherwise. Yes, we had both been there once upon a time and we still got sucked into the black hole.

We broke into gales of laughter and regretted not smoking a couple more pellets of opium. He asked if I would have felt the same about my one-week residential silent retreat at the ashram. Did he mean to ask if I had wished for another week of silent retreat, back-to-back, like wishing for another opium pellet to smoke? I replied mischievously that he was blowing my holy cover. Another sitting meditation for one more week would have given me butt sores, and perhaps premature Buddhahood. During the final hours of the retreat, I told him, my mind was out of control with fantasies of sleeping in a comfortable bed, eating tandoori chicken and other goodies at an air-conditioned restaurant with him. And above all, the anticipation of smoking my first joint after a week of hiatus. Just before departing, the instructor urged us not to fritter away the inner peace we had laboriously gained. Peace, he had said, is so subtle and insubstantial compared to the interminable noise and cunning of the mind. We were reminded that to value this silence, which is our innermost essence, is true self-respect. I was imagining how much this peace and silence inside me was going to grow and blossom with the first few tokes of my joint, which was ready and waiting to be consumed. I was like a kid returning home from the boarding school.

With excitement, I had opened the door to the condo, sure to see Bodhi lovingly waiting for me. Nope, he wasn't there. My faithful joint was in the drawer where I had left it. I knew he wouldn't smoke the joint on his own, because it wasn't his thing. He usually toked half-heartedly in social settings to blend in and get along. Food, alcohol, and cocaine were the drugs of his choice. To me, smoking felt so euphoric, so groovy. At the same time, there was a painful lump in my throat and in my heart, a sign of a shitstorm brewing. I tried to comfort myself with the thought he'd be home soon and that something important must have come up. Goodbye, hard-earned peace and silence of the supreme! Hello, anxiety and anguish, my familiar friends!

I spent the night in deep despair, crying and sobbing and moaning to myself that he just wasn't into me anymore. The next day, I saw him at the discourse with a *ma*, the two of them cozying up to each other, not having seen me. I had neither expressed nor processed with him or even by myself my heart-rending emotional torment.

Bodhi's innocent question sucked up the last traces of opium in my brain, triggering the soul-choking memory. The joyful exuberance of opium high of a minute ago seemed like a distant dream. Had it even happened? He was flying heavenward, while I was flailing in a hellish swamp, struggling to suppress again my thought monsters. We had acquired a few tools at the ashram to help us transcend these inconvenient and ugly emotional beasts. These reminders were, "Choose to live in the glory of here and now," "The past is over and dead," and "Breathe and release the mind consumed with the past and future." He was sure to get agitated and scold me for living in the dead past. Wasn't he with me and fully present in this moment? He was so damn right!

Also, we were getting close to my home, where we all specialized in keeping our emotional pain and agony behind a peaceful mask. I spent the night tossing and turning in silent suicidal despair, while he seemed to be sleeping peacefully. Why was I feeling so raw and bloody after so many groups, meditations, drugs, body therapies, books, and discourses? Nothing was working. Even opium had failed. It had brought my anguish to the surface but at the wrong time and wrong place. Why didn't these monsters come out in the therapy groups and sessions, proper places for expression of their violent strength? Two ashram mantras—*be in the now* and *be authentic*—seemed to be at odds with each other, at least for me. It's true, my jealousy, anger, and pain had roots in the past, even though I felt them in the present. I wished I could have vaporized, like the opium pellets, my monsters of possessiveness and jealousy, so disliked by Bodhi and bitterly condemned at the ashram.

No such luck!

P.S.

The thread of not paying attention to my essence, which is peace and silence attained with one week of silent meditation, runs throughout my journey. My personal consciousness is still in total service to the ego.

Chapter 12

Celebrate, Come On!

Guru Nanak, accompanied by his disciple, was resting under the shade of a flowering tree. A disciple of a famous Sufi master of the town showed up holding a cup of milk, filled to the brim, which he presented to Guru Nanak. At that moment, a flower from the tree fell into the cup of milk. Guru Nanak gestured to the Sufi disciple to leave. Guru Nanak's disciple was very confused because no verbal messages were exchanged. Guru explained that the full cup of milk sent by the Sufi master meant there are too many god-men and enlightened masters in the town and one more was not needed. A flower from the tree fell in the cup of milk filled to the brim, but it didn't disturb the milk or cause it to spill, not even a drop. The Sufi master would interpret it to mean, "Rest assured. Guru Nanak, like the flower, shall cause absolutely no stir or disturbance in the town."

—An Osho story, translated by me from my misty
memory of his Hindi discourse delivered in the
eighties.

B ACK AT THE ASHRAM, ANXIETY and uncertainty were in the air. There was a lot of noise about Osho being ill. About Osho having stubborn back pain. The most terrifying for the devotees: Osho was

51

planning to go silent, but when, nobody knew. After all, he had spoken gazillion words, immortalized in six hundred books or so, as well as his audio recordings and videos, all aimed at bombing and destroying our emotional fortresses, thus revealing vast wordless and immaculate silence of the spirit.

The ashram was vitally alive and growing at an unsustainable rate. Lots of talk about acquiring land for a new ashram and how the Indian government was being an uncooperative nuisance. There was also gossip about the ashram owing billions of rupees in back taxes.

Now we had a new set of friends, and this time they were Americans and mostly professionals—a gay couple, one a general surgeon and the other hospital admin and a pot head. They introduced us to another couple, a middle-aged woman, also a hospital admin but at a different hospital, with her acid-tripping pot-head musician boyfriend. Their two-week trips were ending, and they were envious of our great good fortune—our open-ended pilgrimage, still replete with resources.

It was a pleasant afternoon, and we were hosting a farewell lunch for them in an Indian restaurant outside the ashram. We were all sitting around a long wooden table under the lavish, generous shade of a huge tree. Big bottles of chilled Kingfisher beer and baskets of pakoras (fried veggie fritters) with small dishes of various chutneys and sauces had already crowded our table. Someone at the table brought up Osho's favorite topic: how traditional religions were ugly and anti-life. Imitating the master's singsong Indian accent, he looked at us with a mimicry of Osho's soft, compassion-filled eyes and proceeded, "I say unto you, religion is an art that shows us how to live, how to enjoy life. Existence is a celebration, an orgasmic dance. I say unto you again and again, rejoice and be happy! Be happy! You need do nothing else, not even meditate."

Thunderous applause and roaring laughter from us. We all got boisterously joyous, an outcome of orange group power. Another friend, a woman with large breasts, shared a funny and mildly disturbing story she had heard on an Osho audio recording. A hot European *ma* at the Pune airport was being helped by a young Indian employee to locate her suitcase. His eyes had found a resting spot on her luscious and perky breasts. To break his unconscious trance, she pulled out her fake foam breasts from her bra and invited the man to touch them. Horrified, the man ran away. The woman had had a bilateral mastectomy.

We were all laughing hysterically, a few of us choking on our beers. During a brief lull from the laughter, she added that Osho says the breasts are just a bunch of glands but the entirety of humanity, including women, are obsessed with them. The breast is the initial contact of the infant to the outer world and also a source of nourishment, comfort, and love. We all laughed, imagining titties of various shapes and sizes haunting the dreams of that poor man and wondering whether he'd ever be able to screw normally. We all agreed that only a liberated *sannyasin* who had embraced her cancer could pull a trick like that.

We were filled with gratitude for Osho, the most unique of all gurus and masters. He was so wild and wonder filled, endlessly charismatic, dazzlingly brilliant, utterly eloquent, passionately promoting a singular, bloodless rebellion. His brand of rebellion promised the most precious and most unpopular form of freedom—freedom from the tyranny and cage of the ego, the false self. Indeed, very few on the planet since the dawn of civilization had successfully overthrown the egoic stranglehold and established a new life in Truth. We were amazed that such an oasis of freedom existed or was even allowed to exist on earth. We wondered who among us, although we wished it would be all of us, would succeed in the inner rebellion of demolishing the ego.

The ashram, even though it exploded daily with new arrivals, remained a miracle of efficient organization, aesthetics, beauty, and, above all, shining cleanliness and hygiene. We all cheered for our five-star toilets and showers. Everybody had their own India horror stories of ubiquitous offensive smells, pollution, and dirt. We all noisily toasted Osho, raising our chilled glasses of beer. He had manifested a practical, down to earth, witnessed and enjoyed-by-all, modern mega-miracle of an ashram in India, a country lost in ancient time warp.

Everybody agreed with everybody else that Osho was the guru of their heart. For me, there was some resistance to the paean of praise, devotion, and deification of Osho. My first and original guru, I said, was drugs. "I believe in them. They brought me here, and I somehow feel they'll lead me to the victory over false self."

Shock and dismay on everyone's face, including mine. A blasphemous statement even for this most allowing of groups. It should have been left unsaid. Too bad, so sad!

As we approached the auto-rickshaw stand for the short trip home, our musician swami friend broke out in the latest soul hit from United States— "Celebration" by Kool and the Gang. He sang in a full-throated voice, "Let us all celebrate and have a good time." We all joined in singing, clapping and dancing, and asked the rickshaw drivers to join. They indulged us by adding cool Bollywood moves to our innovative choreography. The first flash dance at the auto-rickshaw stand in Pune! Our singing swami added, "Come on!" "Celebrate good times." I added, sort of singing, "Celebrate also the bad times—come on."

We had a mini duet going, him belting good times and me adding also the bad times (although, never mind me celebrating bad times, which I believed in resisting with all my might). Amid the din and dance, Bodhi started to tell the group of a truly sad and traumatic story turned joyous, uplifting thousands of sannyasins.

The story goes that a German prince of Hanover, a *sannyasin*, a karate teacher at the ashram, had sustained a fatal cerebral hemorrhage while teaching karate. He was rushed to the hospital and was kept on life support. Osho said for three days, he worked on his soul getting it ready to leave his remaining attachments and sink into the pure spirit. Osho said that when he was certain this noble soul had successfully crossed over to the other shore, he ordered life support to be removed. The body was brought back to the ashram, where we were all meditating and chanting. We were all asked to accompany the body to the burning *ghat*s (open-air cremation grounds), singing and dancing. At the burning *ghat*, we were asked to find a secluded spot and meditate on the age-old questions, "Who dies? Who died here? Who or what's burning in the fires of the funeral pyre?" We were to imagine our own death, our prized mind and cherished body burning to ashes. We were to remind ourselves, again and again, that only the false is consumed by the fire, while truth—the immortal, indestructible essence of us all—remains untouched by the fire. At the burning *ghat*, there were several other pyres flaming, surrounded mostly by wailing and chanting men. We found a secluded spot at the very edge of thick smoke and the unforgettable acrid stench of burning flesh. A few vultures circled above and swooped to the ground, pecking at the leftovers. At the end of my long meditation, which felt as tedious as an endless school day, I opened my eyes. A whole lot of *sannyasins* were still dancing and singing around the dying flames of fire, looking like fiery flames themselves, in their orange robes.

Upon hearing this story, all of us were immersed in deep silence, wanting to speak but speechless while our singing swami continued,

> "It's a celebration
> Nevertheless
> Come on
> Let us all celebrate
> And have a good time."

We parted to the dying sounds of "have a good time" amidst a flurry of hugs and kisses and promises to see each other when back home.

Chapter 13

Last Mango in Pune

The trick is in what one emphasizes. We either make
ourselves miserable, or we make ourselves happy. The
amount of work is the same.

—Carlos Castaneda, *The Power of Silence*

THE MOST DREADED, MOST UNWELCOME morning had at last
arrived, the morning of the Great Silence. Master sat silently with
his eyes closed. We were all soaking in the rapture of his presence. The
sweet songs of the birds, usually at the edge of our consciousness, were
in the foreground. An exotic symphony of various tweets and notes,
including the obnoxious cawing of the ubiquitous Indian crows. The
cool morning breeze was flirting and caressing us through the wall-
less Buddha hall. The sublime, pulsating silence, vast and boundless,
dissolving all distinctions, enveloped us all in its oneness. Who thought
that silence would turn out to be an ocean of ecstasy?

These silent "discourses" with the master eventually gave way to
us meditating silently around his empty chair. The gossip was that he
had intractable low back pain. My physical therapy friend, whom I had
briefly befriended in Vancouver but seldom saw at the ashram, happened
to be standing in front of me. She told me in whispery tones that Dr.
James Cyriax, the most renowned orthopedic surgeon from the UK, was
being flown in a private jet to treat his low back pain.

Several weeks passed, but Osho hadn't shown up for the silent
morning meditations. The vibes at the ashram, of uncertainty and

anxiety, were getting dense and denser. One late afternoon, as I was entering the ashram for Kundalini meditation, I collided with Bodhi. On his face were shock, confusion, and questions. He blurted out inconsolably that Osho had left and his destination was unknown at the time. He had seen him leave in his white Rolls with his girlfriend, Vivek, and few other *sannyasins*. Later, the destination was revealed to be the East Coast of America. We were all advised to go back to our home countries until further notice.

We were all in shock. It felt like a sudden and abrupt death. It was indeed death, with scary, unknown changes written on the wall for all of us, including master himself. We marveled at the success of their undercover departure operation, as it required so much prep work, especially for Osho. Perhaps he didn't even have a passport. The puzzling mystery of how his American visa had been obtained would later be revealed by his secretary, Sheela, in her book.

Meanwhile, we decided to boogie on and visit the south of India and plan our return trip from there. Rather than visit famous temples and tourist spots, we did a lot of beaching. I had obtained a bag of dope from a temple of Hanuman (our famous monkey god). It was very mild but did the job. We were itching to do some nude sunbathing but luckily lacked the dare as vibes everywhere were suffocatingly conservative and orthodox. One day, we took a bus in the morning to a faraway beach. When we arrived in the afternoon, the beach was cooking. We could see the shimmering waves of heat vapors emanating from the sand. Our feet were burning through our rubber flip-flops. We rushed to the shoreline to cool our feet, but the water was warm. Not a soul in sight except us two looney tunes.

We found a relatively shady spot. The clothes were immediately dropped, and we rushed into the warm ocean, which was soothing for me but uncomfortable for Bodhi. We funed and frolicked for a while, jumped and twirled like dolphins, swam underwater and tickled each other's naughty bits.

After Bodhi's hot body had cooled down somewhat, he wanted to rest. I continued my frolics, floating and twirling, from very fast to very slow. Ocean had decided not to wave in my honor. I was exploding with ecstasy to have this immensely huge bathtub of an ocean all to myself, that too in nude. As I was floating, my body became very still and my mind quiet. Gentle currents of the ocean were thrilling and delighting, now the soles of my feet, now between my legs, gently rolling over my pussy, and now my breasts. Out-of-control bliss, which my body almost seemed unable to tolerate. I remembered to breathe slow and deep while I remained floating with my eyes closed. Was it possible, me, always ravenously hungry, insatiably greedy for high times, had collided with a ceiling in the Indian Ocean? Nope, not possible! My floating meditation was deepening all by itself. My body sense disappeared, along with my mind and sense of time. Only vast oneness with all as I gently and rhythmically swayed and bobbed in the water. The overall feeling was of being held, caressed, rocked, pampered, and kissed softly, again and again, by life itself. There was only a blissful ocean of energy, holding the sky, the ocean, the entire beach, all of humanity—nay, the entire universe, including me, within itself. I, as I knew myself, was not to be found, which evoked a mild sense of anxiety that I simply observed. I don't know how long I stayed in this no-mind ecstatic state.

The discomfort of pruned hands and feet brought me back to my body. When I stood up, I was vibrating and subtly trembling. The disorientation and destabilization was so great, I could hardly walk out of the water. I wobbled and wavered toward the only human, lying on the beach in maddening heat. One look at his flaming red penis, ruby red balls, and glistening crimson stomach, and I freakin' screamed and shrieked in sheer panic. He was peacefully snoring, with his face and upper body covered with the last-mango-in-Pune saffron T-shirt, under the shade of a palm tree. He woke up immediately, panicked and confused, groping in the sand for his glasses. I kept muttering and moaning, "Bodhi, how could you have fallen asleep in this friggin' hell fire! Look at your penis. It's about to self-combust, and your balls are ready to explode and are already swollen. Oh, my god! What are you going to do? What are we going to do? You have fucking third-degree burns."

He was totally flustered and distraught and in great physical and emotional pain and embarrassment. At that moment, I seemed to myself a younger incarnation of my mom, who had the unconscious habit of scolding and shaming if you made a mistake. Hello, I'm already feeling miserable and ashamed of myself. I don't need further help from you. It wasn't only my mom but her entire generation—my aunts and uncles too. Maybe old societies reflexively shamed and berated erring and fallen folks. I immediately apologized and became caring and compassionate.

We were walking on the wet shoreline toward the main road but missed our exit. We were mind-blowingly startled to see an ancient black stone temple. It was mostly on the dry sand, but part of it was still buried in the wet sand, being rhythmically washed by the ripples and foam of ocean water. I recognized the stone statue of Shiva, sitting yogi straight in a figure-four pose (right ankle resting on left thigh). His well-proportioned consort sat with both feet, planted solidly in stone. It looked as if the temple had surfaced from unfathomable depths of the ocean during our very presence at the beach. We wondered what period of history it belonged to—certainly one that had hard tools to carve from hard rock such details as Shiva's blissful face, with half-closed eyes, and the round breasts of his consort.

Boddhi, wrapped in my sarong minus the underwear, forgot about his steaming hot discomfort and became completely lost in the splendor and grandeur of the moment. I suddenly remembered that at Shiva temple in Mumbai, we had behaved like barbaric foreigners. In the excitement of trying *bhang* for the first time, I had forgotten to go inside the temple to bow my arrogant head at Shiva Lingam. Boddhi said he felt guilty later that night for not putting any money in the donation box at the temple, which I hadn't even seen. Here was the divine couple, giving one-on-one audience and blessings to us two most undeserving of humans. Bodhi was soaking up the divine grace, both of us overwhelmed with gratitude, the kind that mists your eyes and chokes your throat.

Back in the air-conditioned cab, we felt lucky we were staying at a five-star hotel, with fierce AC, in-house doctor, and a small pharmacy, for this leg of our journey.

Chapter 14

London ... New York ... Vancouver!

Life is either a daring adventure or nothing.

—Helen Keller.

THE SPIRIT OF ADVENTURE WAS still roaring within us. We bought our one-way tickets from Mumbai to Cairo, then on to London, New York, and San Francisco, before reaching Vancouver, which we thought of as home though we had no address there yet. In Cairo, we spent two nights at the Nile Hilton, with magnificent views of the Nile from our room. We did a lot of sightseeing and wined and dined at fabulous restaurants. In London, we visited my bisexual girlfriend.

In New York, while walking in Times Square, I had a massive temper tantrum of projections, blames, and accusations. Our marriage was unraveling faster than our personalities. Inside, we were both feeling very shaky, raw, and vulnerable but didn't know how to express these feelings without consciously hurting each other. For example, instead of honestly expressing my diminishing love for him, I blatantly blamed him for no longer being in love with me. I was holding on to a catalogue of complaints. I was judging him silently as an exploiter (another theme song of my psyche). As a result, I was drowning in a smelly swamp of meta feelings of guilt and shame over my judgements. Underneath all that was intense existential angst and a black despair that I had failed in my most expensive search for a better me.

Not only I had failed, but guru, god, meditations, drugs, therapies, travels, friends, and love itself had failed me. My mind was eating me alive for being a dismal failure, and it was all my fault. My inner emotional swamp was getting smellier! There was a man-eating gator growing in it, ready to attack and eat sweet Bodhi alive. And, of course, he was running away and resisting the man-eating gator.

In his defense, he angrily retorted, "Do you realize how I felt in Pune when you said drugs are your first guru? Did you even notice how shocked our friends were?"

He had delivered the disgustingly bitter answer as to why Pune had failed me. Shoving all the shit down, I replied in a dulcet tone that I had noticed the look of embarrassment on every face and that I too was embarrassed by my own statement. What he was saying and what I wasn't willing to hear was about my unacknowledged addiction, my devotion to drugs, and my experiential belief in their efficacy. These were fast becoming unacceptable to him.

In San Francisco, our *sannyasin* friends wanted us to move and be close to them. I went for a job interview in a state-run hospital and was told that I was in; however, my job application had to be approved by the hospital board, which met once a month. There would be a waiting period of three weeks or more, for which we didn't have the financial resources.

We got to Vancouver with enough change for bus fare to downtown, where we rented a hotel room on a credit card that was barely breathing. Vancouver was our home, and we could have stayed with friends, but we wanted to avoid cringe-inducing moments. We felt silently judged as being financially reckless and irresponsible for our frequent long trips, lasting anywhere from six months to more than a year. My family in the United States was upset with me for my lack of ambition. According to them, I was a loser, a failed immigrant owning neither property nor business. They mocked, teased, and harassed us for our pseudo monk robes and lifestyles.

In the morning, I made a few phone calls and went for a job interview. By afternoon, I had a job in a skilled-care nursing facility— mainly geriatric clientele. My job was to keep them as mobile and flexible as possible so they could perform their daily functions. Later in the afternoon, Bodhi and I were going through one year's worth of mail, bags full. An envelope from a financial institution was screaming with stamps such as Immediate! Urgent! Open! Inside was a check for six hundred dollars that I could cash at any bank with a photo ID. I called them to find out if I could pay the entire amount with interest next month. They were agreeable. We were not walking but floating on golden waves of joy in downtown Vancouver, having cashed the check with ease.

Then we bumped into a physical therapy friend of mine with a seeing eye dog named Zoe, who adored Bodhi because of his offerings of fresh and juicy bones. Standing on her hind legs, pawing and licking him, she was grumbling and groaning that he had been gone for too long. My friend owned a lovely home in an upscale neighborhood. Her one-bedroom basement had just been vacated, and we could move in that very day. She was okay with no security deposit and no rent until we got paid by our jobs. She had a well-kept gorgeous garden in the back, which was our entrance to the apartment. She was fine with me smoking weed in the garden. Our free and crazy lifestyle was blessed by life itself!

It was tough adjusting to an eight to four work schedule after more than a year of play and more play. However, it was easier to hunker down this time as our global playground in Pune had closed down for the time being. Within a few months, we were debt free and fantasizing about future adventures.

P.S.

In spite of individual and group therapies, I didn't know what to do with my negative emotions. In meditations, I could bypass them, but that wasn't enough. The old default strategy of repression/explosive expression continued to run my life.

Chapter 15

Another (Yet Another) Door Closes

People who think only good things should happen to them are unfit for life. If you don't know how to go through harsh situations joyfully, you'll avoid all possibilities.

—Sadhguru, *Wake Up to Wisdom*, "Mystic Quote"
09/07/2019

THERE WERE A FEW BEAUTIFUL group *sannyasin* houses in Vancouver, celebrating master's discourses, meditations, and dances, which we attended infrequently. Bodhi's circle of friends at his restaurant job was free-spirited, bohemian, and addicted to substances of all sorts. My tribe of the health care workers tended to be conservative, serious, and very straight—at least that's the mask we wore up front. He was in a group that was into spouse swapping. Our marriage, even though we loved each other deeply, had no heat left. The swapping enterprise, we figured, would either revive or at last kill our nearly dead marriage. The latter happened because of my uncontrollable jealousy and paranoia.

The master key the ashram had given us to resolve all emotions, positive and negative, was: don't touch or get entangled with them. The basic spiritual rule is that whatever can be observed or witnessed can't be our essence. "I am" is the subject, the observer of the passing emotions and thoughts. The no touching, just watching rule worked on lightweight negative thoughts and emotions, especially in Pune. My jealousy, arising from my belief in thoughts of lack, had an embarrassing beggarly quality to it. Nobody loves me, oh my god! The ghost of my loveless childhood of crumbs and starvation, of wounds and heartbreaks, had me by the throat. I was enchained to my history!

Most of the wives of Bodhi's friends were professionals—polished, dressed in trendy beige, white, and black, carrying designer handbags and smelling of expensive French perfumes. I felt so un-chic and classless in my bright orange garb and my brown beaded *mala* with Osho's photo in it. Bodhi tried to assure me that it was just my mind molesting me and that I was sucking up this shit like it was reality. Out with another couple, Boddhi would be all over the guy's seductively welcoming wife while her husband twirled and sniffed and commented upon the expensive wine we had brought. Pretty soon, the wife and Bodhi would smoothly slip away, leaving us two to fend for ourselves. No choice. We had to fuck just to kill time! He was a perfectly nice guy. When I inquired how he was dealing with his jealousy, he said he had none. He loved his wife so much that he wanted only her happiness. I wished I had such a magnanimous heart. At the time, mine was feeling like a desiccated lemon.

One night Bodhi didn't come home. In Pune, we had consciously given freedom and permission to each other to play; otherwise, it would have been impossible to stay. There, my mean and petty ego was tranquilized by the joyous milieu, meditations, drugs, and frequent reminders that identifying with thoughts is the main disease of humanity. But now in Vancouver, besides thoughts to navigate, what else did I have? The silence revealed by marijuana and meditation was awesomely nourishing but not enough to guide me through my self-created swamp. That Bodhi loved me, there was no doubt in my mind, but most of the time, I felt like his childhood pet dog, Toto. The bitter choice for me was uncertainty and openness of the unknown or known misery and loneliness. I chose the first, and we started our trial separation, followed by divorce.

I started going to Sunday morning discourses at *sannyasin* houses. There would be lots of excited talk from those who had attended annual Guru Purnima Day (day of the guru) in Antelope, Oregon, USA. They would say it was a miracle how fast the "big muddy ranch" was coming along. Rajneesh Mandir was so grand, much larger than Buddha Hall in Pune. Soon, we'd have a city all to ourselves, and so forth. *Sannyasins* were going on Saturdays in a hired school bus to work for a day at the ranch. Next day, the workers would look radiant and shiny recalling masters' "drive-by" *darshan* (seeing) in his impeccable white Rolls while they showered him and the car with rose petals.

The time was around the fall of 1984. I decided my shriveled soul could use a divine soak and some shine. I signed up for Saturday volunteer work. We left very early in the morning and reached the ranch after ten. It was cold and gray. My jaw dropped with awe and admiration at the sheer scale of the operation. Everything was super-sized and opulent, in the American style. I was given a shovel and shown where to dig with a bunch of other workers. I silently groaned at my fate. I had barely swung a hammer in my life, and now a shovel! I had handled a shovel maybe once or twice in rehab centers in the work-hardening department. My job was to demonstrate to the patients returning to work ergonomics and correct low back position for using the shovel. Within less than ten minutes of my feeble digging, my hands were complaining of friction burns, my upper body was starting to collapse, and the ache in my lower back was increasing. It made no difference how I held my back or how firmly I engaged my core muscles. My now awake inner bitch was getting ready to roast and grill me on her favorite seldom extinguished fires of inadequacy and worthlessness.

I had come for some shine, but my soul was drowning in startlingly dark and violent-shaped clouds. Should I go and ask for an indoor job that was doable for me. What if they threw their favorite concepts of surrender, acceptance, and obedience at me? What if I hurt my low back? Would there be sympathy and support for me? Pretty soon, the joyous news ("He is coming. He is coming") was all around. Everyone immediately threw down whatever they were doing and lined up on the road with folded hands. It reminded me bleakly of Lord Krishna's power to charm. Whenever Lord played his flute on the banks of river Yumna, his fan club dropped whatever they were doing and ran to meet and greet him.

We were given a handful of rose petals to shower on the beloved master as he drove by. I, too, stood there with my folded hands. He was driving very slow with gun-bearing guards on either side. Sheela, his personal secretary, and others, were walking slowly around his car, some joyously dancing and singing. As his impeccably white and shiny Rolls approached, his sublimely seductive smile and the despicable ooze of deep devotion of his followers triggered my temperature to unbearably explosive heights. I turned my back on dizzyingly blissed-out devotees, who were screaming and jumping with uncontrollable joy. I heartlessly crushed the rose petals in my fist and then stomped on them. Global rock stars and royals eat your heart out! The gods and gurus rule! Even now in the century of science!

Chapter 16

Bitch Strikes at the Empire

"You take yourself too seriously," he said slowly. "You are too damn important in your own mind. That must be changed! You are so goddamn important that you feel justified to be annoyed with everything. You're so damn important that you can afford to leave if things don't go your way. I suppose you think that shows you have character. That's nonsense! You're weak, and conceited!" - Dom Juan"

—Carlos Castaneda, *Journey to Ixtlan*

THE QUESTION THAT WAS SIZZLING and painfully swirling in my brain was, *What crimes have I committed that brought me to this, where I'm digging ditches while the divine royal is feted with rose petals, loving smiles and deep bows?* I saw Osho as a modern-day Pharaoh and myself as a lowly Jewish slave. The only big difference was I and thousands of others were here of our own free will. Through a curtain of free-falling tears, I found a restroom, with toilets and a sink, immaculately clean, away from the work, crowds, and the Rolls route. I set myself up in the last toilet and bawled my brains out.

What is wrong with me? I silently screamed at myself. There was something hugely wrong with me; of that, there was no doubt in my mind. These people had gathered from around the globe, thousands of them. They had renounced their countries, and far bigger and more brilliant careers than mine. Some had renounced thriving businesses, fame, and families. Obviously, they had found something immensely precious and unspeakably valuable that was totally eluding me. Despicable me! In less than ten minutes of labor, with barely a few pounds of dirt to show for it, I had brought a sudden, unstoppable shitstorm on myself. *No!* I screamed inside, it wasn't the shovel and the digging. It was the obscenely perverse deification of a man who said he knew god, he *was* god. He was addressed as *Bhagwan*, which, in popular Indian parlance, means god. The word also has other meanings, he said, such as the Blessed One, the Luxurious One, One in Whom the Divine Is No Longer Hidden. Imagine, god, the Luxurious One, showing up in a golf cart or Nissan Sentra, or most appropriate for the big muddy ranch, a pick-up!

Be glad, I said to myself, *his Rolls isn't made of gold in the gaudy style of India and decked with diamonds.*

I had heard that his hard working, deeply and selflessly loving devotees had expressed their wish to worship him with new Rolls for each day of the year. What horror! But then, he was in America, where affluenza and bluster never fail to capture the imagination of the media and the public.

I felt brutally betrayed and disappointed with Osho, myself, and the Westerner devotees. Them, yes, them white folks! Super civilized, highly educated, yet behaving no better than uneducated and superstitious Indians, prostrating themselves at the feet of any and every asshole who uses god-speak. True, Osho's existence-speak is of super high caliber and astonishingly clear, perhaps the best ever in any century. Osho had said over and over again that we were all potentially Buddhas but we hadn't realized our Buddhahood. That's the only difference between me with the shovel, digging away the dirt for the sake of my enlightenment, and him being already enlightened. But to show up in royal robes of shimmering silks and velvets, looking and behaving like the King of kings in his impeccable Rolls in democratic America! Okay, I was aware of Osho's penchant for theater in India. But this smacked of Hollywood extravaganza!

My whole being shrieked with pain at the toxicity of this equation. Shameless exploitation of humanity had a timeless stench to it. The poor Jewish slaves, for the sake of miserable survival, had to put up with the oppression of their overlords. But what was driving these white elites, the crème de la crème of Western civilization? Perhaps the golden carrot of enlightenment, which they had been led to believe grows miraculously in the presence of an enlightened master when offers of selfless service are made. I flushed the hope and aspiration of my enlightenment down the toilet.

I remembered Osho's injunction to us that if his behavior seemed irrational and illogical to us and the world, it was a conscious device. Its purpose being to deliver a shock to our brain to wake us up from our coma. Instead of trying to understand his behavior with our minds, we should drop our minds, which is the ultimate purpose of meditation. He also said he used these devices to get rid of deadweight, stupid, and know-it-all followers—perhaps like me. His device had worked on my brain to inflame it into suicidal self-loathing, but luckily, there were no means of destruction around.

The public toilet I was camping in was in a secluded area, used infrequently. If someone came in, I would go quiet until they left. Once or twice, I went out for a brief walk in my shades to cover my red and swollen eyes. Our bus was scheduled to leave after 5:00 p.m. I arrived early, crawled in at the very back, and stretched out on the back seat. Pretty soon, the bus, filled with *sannyasins*, left for Vancouver. The jubilant and exultant bunch were excitedly discussing the drive-by as heart-to-heart communion with the master, so worth the effort, so very fulfilling! The physical labor had quieted their churning minds, and they agreed work was indeed worship in the most sacred environment of the ashram.

At home, the first thing I did was throw my *mala* down the incinerator chute with a goodbye to the orange club. I had a couple of friends, so I had thought, and an on-and-off lover in the orange club. No one ever called to find out why and to where I had disappeared. My exit from the cult was a non-issue.

Chapter 17

My First Clean-Up

Anger, sadness, frustration—all signs you're at war with reality.

—Byron Katie

MY MOM IN INDIA HAD developed health issues that required a lot of care. I resigned from my job to help look after her. She had fallen, the worst challenge for the elderly, the day I arrived in Mumbai. She was in extreme pain but didn't want to go to the hospital. One look at her twisted, swollen leg, and I knew she had sustained a bad fracture. She looked very weak and frail, as if she could die any moment, which would have been a blessing for her. Meanwhile any movement of her body, even receiving a bedpan, was excruciatingly painful for her and us.

Eventually, she agreed to go to the hospital, and surgery was scheduled the next day. I was with her all the time, holding her frail and delicate hand, which she let me do. The tough woman who would have resisted such gestures of tender affection was swiftly losing her grip. She was semiconscious, but when she would open her eyes, I would ask her in very soft tones, "Where are you?" or "What is going on for you?" Her reply, in a weak and barely audible voice, was that she was roaming and floating. Then she would be gone, inaccessible again. When she would open her eyes after a while, I would ask her where she was floating, and was she alone. After an hour or so, the answer would come: though she was still lying in the bed in the hospital, in actuality, she was floating above her bed. Another hour or two would pass, and she would give me the names of people who were floating with her in the room. I wrote the names down, not being familiar with them. Later, on checking the names with my dad, I was told those names belonged to her family members who had departed a long time ago, before even the India-Pakistan partition. My current interpretation is that her soul/attention had freed itself from her ailing body and mind and was floating above her body with other souls known only to her.

Next day, after her surgery, she was unconscious and didn't look good at all. I was harassing the nurses when my brother-in-law showed up to take me home for lunch. I didn't want to leave her, but he convinced me that it was best for all that I take a little break. At home, we were all eating, when I suddenly stood up, grabbed my purse, and lunged for the door, screaming that I should be at the hospital. My family members ran behind me, urging me to wait. As I was getting in the cab, I heard more yelling from my family members to stop. The hospital had just called to tell us that she had passed away. In retrospect, I had noticed an outburst of energy in my stomach area that had pushed me up from the chair in one powerfully swift and spontaneous motion. I had interpreted it as an absolute emergency. Actually, she had died around that time, and I had for only a second or less intimately experienced her departing energy, her immortal essence.

After the elaborate Hindu funeral rites and services, I had a couple of weeks left to kill on my air ticket. I decided to visit Pune ashram for old time's sake. Osho was back after he had been deported from the United States and denied entry by twenty-one countries. He had rebranded himself from Rajneesh to Osho. The new avatar was infinitely more popular than the old. All the intrigues, scandals, and his brief imprisonment in the US had indisputably enhanced his new global brand and guru power with his followers.

Even though I had arrived before the discourse, I was seated in the fairly crowded terrace of the building close to Buddha Hall, which, I was told, was packed to the max. From where I was seated, I could see neither Buddha hall nor Osho. I could hear his discourse clearly on the loudspeakers. The discourse was a full-throated denouncement of the US government as well as the European Union. He urged the world to put the monster America in its place. He presented himself and "his people" as great holy innocents, victims of "the stupid and idiotic" people of Oregon and the idiot US president, Ronald Regan. I wanted to remind him of his own wisdom—that there's no sound of one hand clapping. I knew of his habitual disdain for the religious and political leaders of the world and his penchant for conflict and legal battles. I left the discourse when his spin became intolerable, filling me with certainty he wasn't going to own up to his responsibility as the failed leader of the US commune.

When I returned to Canada, I decided to work part time and as a temp, which gave me just enough money to cover my expenses and a lot of free time to myself. My ex-husband was in a relationship, which was good for us both. I was caught in a vicious circle of deadly boredom of my terribly tedious life. Just then, a parcel showed up at my doorstep—a can of marijuana cookies and approximately one pound of quality homegrown, sealed airtight. It was a gift from a friend in New Mexico who used to grow her own stuff. Her mother, ravaged by Alzheimer's, almost rigid with rigor mortis, unable to recognize her devoted daughter, was a patient at the nursing home where I had worked a few years earlier. It was a miracle the parcel had moved safely undetected through the US and the Canadian customs. An unexpected windfall of high times to generously celebrate the upcoming holiday season. I was nibbling on cookies and smoking ceaselessly. If I woke up in the middle of the night to pee, I would smoke a joint.

For Christmas, I had plans to visit my family in Virginia Beach. I had my last heavily laced marijuana cookie at the Seattle International airport. My next desire was for coffee and a cigarette. Overnight, smoking had been banned in all public places at the airport, except a few corner tables in a dimly lit bar. No serving of plain coffee, I was told, but yes for spiced ones, Mexican or Irish. I boarded the plane, all smiles, high as a kite. On board, the handful of smokers were displeased and agitated, it being the first day of ban. A very charming and diplomatic air hostess went democratic on us and asked for a show of hands from passengers to decide yes or no for smokers. As expected, the smokers suffered dismal defeat. My family in Virginia, also lately woke to the harmful effects of secondhand cigarette smoke rightfully insisted I smoke outside, if needs be, with my gloves to keep my fingers from freezing.

I needed a gift, preferably a book, for a girlfriend back home. We, her friends, would sympathetically advise her that her hot Latino boyfriend whom she adored was not that into her. While offering her tissues for her tears, we would look at each other with sad eyes and whisper, shaking our heads, "No wedding bells for her. We can't hear them!" A book on romantic addictions that described my lovelorn friend's love sickness to a tee fell into my hands. I couldn't put the book away, as it was reflecting in high definition more my addictive personality than my friend's: Low self-esteem, fear of being alone, fear of change and hard times, difficulty letting go emotionally and moving forward. I imagined letting go of dope, having worshipped it for about two decades in near secrecy from most of the world. In those days, marijuana was considered not only a vice but a crime. Nowadays, it is an essential health product.

The book had stirred up waves of shame, guilt, embarrassment, and terror that were choking me to death. Me, an addict! The label simply wouldn't stick. The mirror confirmed that I didn't look the part—gaunt, ugly, unkempt! You're a high-achieving, high-functioning professional, my deflated ego feebly argued. Sure, my family was dysfunctional, and I was working at healing my childhood wounds, but so was everybody else. Outside, I maintained the facade of holiday cheer, while inside, I was sinking in a quagmire of self-loathing and shame.

The day I was to leave for Canada, I woke up with full blown symptoms of flu. By the time I reached home at night I was an aching, dripping, coughing mess with a fever. Smoking the welcome joint I had left at home prior to my departure was clearly out of the picture. I collapsed on the bed, wishing I were dead. By now, it had been more than two weeks since I had smoked dope. I was determined to clean up my act and prove to myself I wasn't an addict.

In the morning, I called my gay friend, who was living a block away from me, to come over with some food and medication. I still had more than half a pound of superior quality homegrown organic shit. I handed the bag of cannabis over to my friend, who hated how marijuana made him feel, for safekeeping. He was very encouraging of my cleanup plan and suggested I visit a government drug rehab agency to get free counseling. My lungs were so full of crud that the very thought of smoking anything made my body cringe with nausea. Smoking cigarettes and drinking coffee all day long and wine in the evening—accepted social addictions in the West—were habits I began immediately after my initial arrival in Canada. Within a couple of years, I had added illegal substances.

After doing intense spiritual practices and enjoying the peaks of spiritual experiences, going to a drug rehab counselor was despairing devolution. My counselor was a compassionate, sensitive, and kind woman. I proudly declared to her that I had dropped all my addictions: nicotine, marijuana, alcohol, and coffee. With a worried look in her eyes, she told me it was typical of an obsessive addictive person to take on sure-to-fail extreme cleanup operation! I told her I was carrying zip lock baggies full of carrots and celery, which I was chewing consciously to soothe my insatiable mouth fixation. To qualify for free counseling, I had to attend a twelve-step program, and my therapist suggested Narcotics Anonymous. I hated those meetings; everybody smoked cigarettes and drank terrible coffee with Coffee Mate, except this newly purified saint!

At the clinic where I worked part-time, I was leafing through *American Physical Therapy* journal, which posted job vacancies from Honolulu to Houston. My mind immediately revved up the engines of her fantasy private plane and headed for warm Hawaiian paradise, complete with the long yearned for romance on the beach under a full moon. The next step of my life was slowly coming into focus—except for one huge dark cloud that was blocking my paradise fantasy. In order to work, I needed to pass the US physical therapy board exams, which were much like final exams. This meant I needed to be competent and fluent in all the medical material learnt over a four-year period for a basic bachelor's degree.

How was I going to do that? It had been eons since I graduated in India and eons longer since I had passed my Canadian board exam. I desperately needed a change. I wanted to move to the United States, but what to do with the monster size challenge of studying and cramming endlessly? And then the big exam, which I might or might not even pass. And then what? That was the unscalable wall that plunged me into deep depression and suicidal despair. I couldn't see a way out. I resisted making an appointment with my psychotherapist, when merely remembering her positive suggestions and affirmations were nauseating to me at the time.

I spent ten days in dark hell with my sober and clean monster of a mind, whose only and oft repeated advice was suicide and ways to accomplish it.

I was straightening a book on my shelf when a folded paper, which I had been perhaps saving for dark times like these, fell into my hand. The lines were from Goethe, dictated to him by life for mortals like me, struggling to be or not to be. Goethe writes,

> "Until one is committed, there is hesitancy, the chance to draw back, always ineffectiveness, concerning all acts of initiative (and creation). ... The moment one definitely commits oneself, then providence moves too."

I read the last line again and again. With each repetition, I felt the dark cloud dissipate and life returning to my deflated and harassed soul. Goethe writes, "All sorts of things occur to help one that would never otherwise have occurred." My whole being was in agreement and had personal examples of providence going out of its way to bring much needed assistance at the time. My mind was falling in alignment with her wish to move to America. It was getting ready for the big battle of disciplining and applying herself to the singular task of studying with single pointed focus. Goethe continues, "Whatever you can do, or dream you can, do it. Boldness has genius, power and magic in it. Begin it now." I repeated the last two lines loudly several times, first in a neutral tone and then with passion and conviction, as if I were auditioning for a part in a play. Although nothing had changed as yet in the outer world, my inner world was roaring with a fresh infusion of life energy and a new direction. I noticed I was standing straight and strong, ready to meet the new challenges from my future.

Chapter 18

Recovery/Relapse

Humans need to be a little crazy, spontaneous, unusual, free- flowing, and creative.

—Stuart Wilde, *Whispering Winds of Change*

NEXT DAY AT WORK I mentioned to my boss that I wanted to immigrate to the US, but my board exam was a real problem, and I didn't even know where to start. She informed me that the hospital library had all the latest physical therapy books and that she would ask the librarian to loan me the books I needed, since I was not regular staff and entitled to borrowing privileges. Hallelujah! Providence was indeed moving for me. Two days later, my boss called me at home and said that at a party, she had met a physical therapist who had fractured her leg in a skiing accident. She had plans to move to the United States and had gone to Seattle to attend a weekend seminar on how to prepare for the American board exam. She not only had a list of books to read but also exam questions and papers from the past several years which gave the exact guidance needed to pass the exam. The injured therapist had changed her mind about moving to America and was willing to give me all the material for free.

I cried with gratitude as Goethe's providence had gone out of its way to make my dream come true. When I looked at the test material, more precious than gold, I knew exactly how and what to study and that my success was guaranteed.

I was eager to make my move and called one of the headhunters listed in the *American Physical Therapy* journal. I was focused on Hawaii, while they were adroitly directing me toward New Mexico. Within a few days, they had set up a job interview in New Mexico, complete with airline tickets, hotel, and car-rental vouchers. I wasn't happy but decided to look at the interview as an all-paid adventure. I didn't like the dry and dead beat town of Farmington, and tried my best to blow up the interview, but to no avail. The director of the rehab center was so charmed by me that she agreed to all my requests and then some. I had six weeks or so to prepare for my exam and wrap up my several decades of life in Vancouver.

It was my last night in my apartment. The telephone was to be disconnected at midnight. Fifteen minutes to midnight, I received a call from a *sannyasin* couple from California, with whom I had lost touch for several years. They called my family in India to find my whereabouts. They were excited beyond belief that I was moving to Farmington, New Mexico, as they were also planning to move to New Mexico but hadn't decided where. They promised to visit me as soon as they could manage time off work. I was trembling with excitement at the memories of warm and wonderful times with them.

Moving to America from Canada was no culture shock for me, it was more of a welcome party. The rehab clinic, affiliated with a medium-size general hospital, was a mini world, with therapists from all over Europe, Asia, and a few from different parts of the United States. The European and Asian therapists would look up to me for professional guidance and emotional support. Most of us immigrant therapists were housed in a gated community of townhouses. We would visit each other, and a party would materialize spontaneously, out of nowhere.

The day my friends from California were to arrive was here. I picked them up at the airport in my brand new-smelling car, and they both immediately lit up their cigarettes. I fell into unspeakable shock and dismay. I had completely forgotten that they were my high-times friends. It hadn't occurred to me to inform them of my total sobriety. Then one of them pulled out his pipe and started to smoke highly fragrant Humboldt County dope. They assured me they weren't going to share their high times with me, not even the classy California wines they had brought as a gift. Meanwhile, I stuck to my resolve of "just say no." My friends loved Farmington so much, they purchased a ranch-style house in a tony neighborhood closer to Durango, Colorado, but still in Farmington. They both got jobs as teachers. My no to high times, step by step, morphed into a total yes.

One evening, while smoking and drinking with my friends, I expressed the deep gratitude I felt for marijuana and that it hadn't affected my brain adversely. I had scored an A in my board exam—incontrovertible proof of faultless memory, clear reasoning, and winning mental strategies. However, I was certain, if I hadn't gone on a cleanup binge, such a torturous idea of writing the board exam for the third time in my life would not even have dared to peep in my brain. Basking in the twilight glow of a red and orange sky, soaking in the unimaginably open views of La Plata, I enjoyed a rare winning smile, inside and outside. I felt no shame or regret at having fallen off the wagon. My first cleanup venture hadn't failed; rather, it had succeeded in delivering a new possibility and promise.

I often spent weekends with my ex-*sannyasin* friends, getting stoned, meditating, watching spiritual videos, listening to audio recordings of different spiritual teachers, and practicing being authentic. I also did lots of hiking and outdoor activities with my therapist friends. Not one weekend did I stay home to ponder the yonder. Who would have thought that a life rich in dollars, warm global friendships, career perks and privileges, and unimaginably high times awaited me in the boonies of America? By now, Osho had died. His ashram had turned into an immensely successful corporate machine.

And then came winter. My friends were going to California for Christmas, and they wanted me to stay at their house and look after their pets. I was supposed to drop them off and pick them up at Durango Airport—a drive of less than an hour. The day of their departure, a light snowfall started early in the morning, ramping up at fierce speed by mid-afternoon. My American therapist friends warned me it had been forecasted to turn into a savage storm by evening. I needed a four-wheeler with snow tires and chains to navigate, not a toy Nissan Sentra. I was very nervous and trembling with fear at the thought of driving home alone in the relentless white storm. My ex-sanyassin friends continued to assure me I was needlessly fussing, as was my wont; everything was going to be all right, as always.

As soon as I dropped them at the airport and turned around, the snowfall started coming down faster than my brand-new windshield wipers could cope. I was in the midst of a great endless white freeze, unable to distinguish between the road and the pavement's shoulder. Mine was the solitary car on the road. Even at low speed, the car was skidding and eventually fell sideways into a ditch. No vehicles passed by, no houses, no sounds of distant cars to orient me. Should I stay warm in the car with the heat on until some help comes or venture forth on my freezing feet and look for help? Anxiety and restlessness drove me to choose the latter course.

After walking for about fifteen minutes in a desolate white wonderland, I saw a light from afar that energized and injected me with hope. It was a tiny one pump gas station with a live attendant. I fell into his arms sobbing. The guy had a pick-up with chains and snow tires. Within a few minutes, he had my car straight on its four wheels, unhurt and unscratched. He warned me that side roads to La Plata were sure to be more treacherous than what I had just gone through. Should I go to my place in the city, clearly more accessible or to my house sit at the secluded ranch in the middle of snow covered fields where there were live pets needing to be fed. I arrived at the ranch past midnight, having spent more than six hours on the road. It was wickedly dark. Eerily still. Not even a coyote cried. Their porch light was off. I kept the car lights on and slowly groped to find a light switch. No lights! No heat! No water! At least the pets were happy to see me.

When I woke up in the morning, the sun was shining brightly, the snow had started to melt, the heat in the house was on, the pets were playful, and the car was unharmed. The only reminder of the previous night's frigid nightmare was stiff neck and shoulders and a steely resolve to move to Hawaii. The fun I experienced in Farmington had been unimaginable in Vancouver, where only the dreams of blue Hawaii had inspired me to the discipline of studying.

Chapter 19

Who Am I?

We don't want to eliminate the ego completely. Otherwise, we'd be wandering around the house each morning, drinking coffee for hours, saying, "Who the hell am I?" We need the ego to sustain a sense of identity.

—Stuart Wilde

Ah, Hawaii! I was awake and luxuriating, looking at colorful Hawaiian prints on the wall, tropical wicker furniture, drapes and quilts with Hawaiian motifs. My cardboard box with miscellaneous stuff, in which I had hidden a bag of homegrown cannabis from Taos, New Mexico, had safely arrived at my new clinic without a hitch.

The phone rang in my hotel room, and it was my new manager. One of the therapists had called in sick. Could I please replace her at such a painfully short notice, even though it was my day off? Yes, I replied, and there I was, in my new clinic, with my new family. The boss, who lived in the mainland US, was scheduled to arrive in Maui in the afternoon from the Big Island (Island of Hawaii) where he owned two more clinics. By late afternoon, there was an unusual amount of activity in the clinic. Men in Aloha shirts and women in designer clothes and accessories were arriving bearing gifts for the boss' birthday. I was in my office finishing my notes for the day when my office manager came in with tentative body language to invite me for the birthday celebrations at the coolest joint in Lahaina. Yes, to party with the coolest gang on my first day at the office! Drool!

We all piled into a stretch limo, packed with balloons, which I'd soon find out were filled with nitrous oxide, the famed laughing gas of the dentists. The pipes and joints of Maui-Wowi, which looked and smelled divine, along with champagne and lines of coke we were doing the rounds in the limo.

The gorgeous Latina receptionist at the clinic shared how they had hemmed and hawed whether to invite me to the wild, wild party in paradise on my first day of work. Now they felt relieved and thrilled with my coziness with high times. I told them that the most precious content of the cardboard box I had mailed to the clinic with no return address was a bag of organic dope from Taos, NM. Applause and interest in trying the new varietal. As I was preparing my bag of dope for travel, hiding it in plastics and clothes to muffle the fragrance, my friends in Farmington complained, "Oh! Ye of little faith." They were so right.

The ease with which I moved around the clinic on my first day, handling with not a glitch the entire day's load of patients who were totally unknown to me, had been noticed by the boss and the others. The dinner was divine at the seaside Italian restaurant, with a light ocean breeze pouring in from the fully open French doors and windows. After, we moved to the upstairs bar with live music. My new Latina friend and I danced and laughed the night away. Late the next morning, she picked me up for a picnic at the beach with her boyfriend and his friends. Off-the-chart high times, yearned for intimacy, and an Aloha sense of belonging! A feeling of pure paradise inside and out. At work, it was a dream team, hard-working, harmonious, helpful, and efficient.

There was lots happening on the island in human growth and spiritual areas. I had a patient—middle-aged, blonde, and attractive, always dressed in flowing silks and delicate cottons, called goddess wear on the island. She was managing one of the finest spiritual bookstores and boutiques, known for goddess wear and accessories. She was attending *satsangs* (gathering of Truth seekers) with an enlightened American woman whose Indian Guru had named her Gangaji. My patient and I loved each other's company, as I was still a dedicated seeker of truth. One day, she was my last patient, and she insisted I go with her to *satsang*. It was my first drive upcountry, and I was enchanted by full-on open views of blue Pacific as the car ascended the high altitudes. Gangaji's discourse on non-duality and living without the story was an instant click for me. Pretty soon, I signed up for a weekend retreat with her and husband, Eli Jackson Bear, in breathtakingly beautiful gardens and church upcountry. There, I bought a video of Ramana Maharishi's life.

After dinner, I settled down in the well-padded comfort of La-Z-Boy chair to watch the video, which was in black and white. It brought out in high relief the dry and drab poverty and his totally comfortless environment. Ramana, as he was called, was a teenager when he left his school and ran away from his home in search of truth. The day before, I had asked Gangaji the most frequently asked question by the seekers: "Why am I not enlightened yet?" I felt I had done intense spiritual practices and had sacrificed much for truth already. But the returns on my investments had been rather poor. She gave me her signature sunny smile and said my resolve was still feeble and weak. Asked me to contemplate Buddha's story as he sat under the Bodhi tree, with no intention of moving, no matter what befell him, until he was fully enlightened! Well, I tried that night, sitting half lotus in my La-Z-Boy chair, with my back straight but fully supported. I sat in sublime stillness for about two hours, until I absolutely had to get up to pee. I felt familiar peace, lots of it, but no enlightenment. Or was the peace itself the enlightenment? I was certain that Buddha must have been able to sit for interminably long periods. After all, he had raised himself above all physical needs since he is portrayed as horribly malnourished and dehydrated during his reach for the finish line.

Now, watching teen Ramana's single pointed resolve, his courageous (or was it reckless) gamble with his family, his future, his very existence, for Truth, filled me with shame and deep despair. LOL for me. No hope of ever meeting Buddha or Ramana at the sunlit peaks of consciousness. Suddenly, I didn't even want to meet them. His death-defying deprivation of all human comforts—nights in the airless, dark, and damp basements of temples, where his starving, naked, and defenseless body was an offering to hungry critters and crawlers—was a total turn off for me. During the day, he was harassed and tormented by children pelting him with pebbles. Eventually, he was rescued by a kind man and nursed back to whatever physical health could be restored to his severely neglected body. It seemed to me his body had burnt itself out in single pointed quest for truth. After his death, his poor and humble village was elevated to the status of holy pilgrimage place for the world. He is now universally regarded and revered as the eternal light of enlightenment by the seekers and devotees of Truth. His photo always graces Gangaji's *satsangs*.

Big friggin deal, I silently screamed into the midnight stillness. But when I looked at his photo and gazed in his eyes, I was met with peace and more peace, absolutely infinite peace and bottomless silence. In the photo, his face and his features looked ultra-refined to me. I had to admit that the refinement and grace he radiated were clearly otherworldly. I then compared in my mind an imagined popular rendition of a coarse-featured Neanderthal to Ramana's face and saw a clear and well-defined evolution of man's consciousness.

But what was I to make of his near naked body, in loincloth, displaying frailness and fragility, devoid of any muscle tone, sometimes in a slumped posture? I know without a shadow of a doubt that I'm not the body, and neither was Ramana. If I wanted to delight myself with virile, buff, and handsome male bodies, I was looking in the wrong place. The purpose of the video was to intensify the longing of the seeker for the formless truth, not to condemn and criticize the most revered sage of the world for not taking care of his body. Wasn't the body supposed to be the temple of the spirit? In his case, the top of the temple was radiating gold, while the bottom was in ruins.

When I brought my pain and dismay to Gangaji in *satang*, she dismissed me as if the question was a no-brainer: we are not our bodies. Is it not clear to everybody? A thunderous "yes" from the group, composed of well-nourished and well-groomed bodies. I too nodded, still painfully muttering to myself, "But this!"

I remained disturbed for a couple of weeks. On drugs, I felt my consciousness had awakened from centuries of Indian cultural conditioning—body was evil, dirty, sinful, sex a curse and a woman's body even a bigger curse and damnation! My body had become the temple of the divine and I treated it as such most of the time. Increasingly, it felt sensitive, sensuous, light, and playful. Above all alive, thrillingly alive, dancing with life. I was testing life through my senses, in my body, and it felt sublimely delicious. Pre-drugs, I was a walking, talking zombie! I decided to trust my experience and go my own merry way, experimenting with meditation and drugs.

P.S.

When I started my inner journey in earnest, its Ramana Maharishi's existential question, "Who am I?" that was critical in leading me home. The answer to his question is not mental but experiential. With profound gratitude, I humbly bow my old but flexible and fairly fit body at his lotus feet.

Chapter 20

Wake Up Call from Jed

The price of truth is everything, but no one knows what everything means until they're paying it.

—Jed McKenna, *Spiritual Enlightenment: The Damnedest Thing*

M Y DREAM TEAM AT WORK was dismantled after several years due to market pressures. My boss wanted to revamp and restyle his clinics and sell them to the highest bidder. Much to mine and everyone else's surprise, I was the one who was given the pink slip. I was drowning in shock and despair as I was driving home. The old feeling of worthlessness had reared its ugly and violent head and was feeding itself on me for having grown old and unwanted. A liberating thought from my latest teacher, Esther Hicks, who channels Abraham, blossomed forth in my brain, misting it with sublime fragrance. Most people, when misfortune strikes, go swiftly sliding down the what-if ramp of hopelessness and despair.

No one will hire me at my age.

It's all over for me.

Everyone wants younger therapists, as they are cheaper and more flexible.

And so on.

However, Abraham urges us forward with a possibility of another kind of what-if—going upward. My loss of identity and income could be the best thing that could have happened to me. Hard to believe, but I wasn't completely closed to the possibility. Maybe a better job, or a more rewarding one. Maybe I would meet my soulmate in my new future. Perhaps something unimaginably magnificent was waiting in the wings that needed me to be free from this job to reveal itself. By the time I got home, the vibes of positive "what if" had filled me with a helium high of Hawaiian heaven.

I got home as the sun was getting ready to set. At the time, I was living in a one-bedroom ocean-view apartment with a lovely, long covered lanai (balcony), with a hammock chair suspended from the ceiling. A patient had gifted me with a set of rainbow-colored glasses. My favorite was seeing the world in purple and red—happy, happy! I had money in the bank, a full bag of dope, and lots of time for sun and fun! *What, me worry?* was the final decision of my regal purple world seen through my purple glasses. I also decided to visit the unemployment office and take my sweet time to regroup.

The news of me getting laid off traveled faster in my professional community than I would have liked. The job offers were coming in from other Hawaiian Islands. I remained firm in my resolve to stay free and structureless for as long as possible. My official reason for refusing employment was I felt too emotionally traumatized, crushed, and diminished by the pink slip at my age, and I needed time to heal. The reality was I had a bag of Maui-Wowi and the spirit of play in magical Maui. Well, life doesn't get any better than that. The best I could do was drag out my vacation for four weeks. A rehab center in Honolulu had two clinics in Maui, and they wanted me to run the clinic in Lahaina. So much for terrifying myself with ageism! Whatever demands I was making, they were ready to fulfill and then some. The new management was conservative, serious, and squeaky clean.

After a couple of years, one fine morning, my boss from Maui and another big honcho from Honolulu informed me they were going to close my clinic due to financial reasons. They wanted me to manage their new flagship in Kihei, less than a ten-minute drive from my home. They were certain I was going to be thrilled to death at their proposal. Instead, what came out from my mouth shocked me more than them. I declared that I was going to take over the clinic. They did their best to dissuade me. They warned me that they were unable to make it work with their deep pockets. Within a few minutes, I had a clear HD picture of my downsized clinic of 450 square feet from the original 1,600 square feet. I negotiated a reasonable rent for a lease of six months.

My new clinic was born in less than three hours, all the federal and state paperwork completed. America the great! In the evening, unexpectedly, a friend brought me a stack of papers that she had designed with my new letterhead, which I was going to need the next day. The old company had generously left me the equipment I urgently needed, such as a treadmill, wall pulleys, and ultrasound, etc. I was amazed to see my overnight transformation from a business moron to a savvy entrepreneur.

My life was very sweet. My dope habit had dropped away all on its own a couple of months prior to starting my own practice. Some evenings, I simply forgot to smoke. What a blessing! I packed up my smoking paraphernalia and gifted it to a friend. I didn't attend the twelve-step group. A glass of wine with dinner was my only high-time treat.

I had booked a seminar on a cruise ship to Alaska with my favorite channel, Abraham. I had bought an elegant made-in-France skirt at a boutique in Maui. My only challenge was to find, in costume jewelry, a pair of long, delicate earrings in rubies and gold. And departure time was nearing.

And then, it was Sunday evening! A regular meeting of noble friends, where we practiced being authentic and telling the truth, was planned at my place. Noble friends were all seekers and had been through the rigors of the spirit in some form or the other. One friend was carrying a cardboard box containing books. He was browsing on the internet and had come across these books on enlightenment with lots of testimonials and a good discount if he bought in bulk. None of us had heard of the writer and enlightened master, Jed McKenna. I immediately bought the set of two books, *Spiritual Enlightenment: The Damnedest Thing* and *Spiritually Incorrect Enlightenment*. I was touched in my heart that I had effortlessly attracted reading material for my cruise trip. Ha, ha, ha! Little did the innocent me realize that the books were not a bubbly beach read. They were nuclear, and my ego was toast, and so was her make believe world of romantic dreams and fantasies for the cruise ship.

I had bought the books to be read on the trip. However, the minute the meeting ended and everybody had left, I picked up the first book. Had I been smoking *pakalolo* (Hawaiian name for cannabis), I would have reached for a joint and saved the book for the trip as planned. As it was, I couldn't put the book down. My ego structure was being intensely rattled; its solidity threatened. It was 2:00 a.m., I hadn't even had my dinner, and I had a full workday in front of me. The read certainly wasn't joyously uplifting or inspiring. On the contrary, it was mocking the peace, joy, and warm friendships that had at last blossomed in my life after much striving and struggle. My personal take-away message from the so-far-half-read book was as follows: I was still totally spiritually blind. I was living in a self-made world of *maya*, or illusion. My head was filled with crap, not with wisdom, as I had believed. My spiritual practices so far had been in service of fattening my ego rather than starving it. My spiritual ship was stuck in the mud but making fake impressive sounds of moving forward, which I and my friends were mistaking for the real deal. Who, me? I cried inconsolably. At my age of more than fifty years, I was supposed to chuck my past as a sick mistake! Start afresh with a new technique of *spiritual autolysis*, which would hopefully bring *abiding non-dual awareness*, the ultimate destination of all seekers. Nevertheless, my ego knew it was being totally disarranged, and it was not going to be the same again ever!

I carried the book with me to work, hoping for cancellations. I did have a few, which on any other day would have irked me, but not on that day. In less than twenty-four hours, Jed's potent prose of dire urgency to wake up from spiritual sleep had stripped my life of all meaning. I didn't want to go on my trip. The image of me dressed in my fancy French skirt, with all the cool accessories, partying and dancing with beautiful people aboard the cruise ship, was now causing me embarrassing nausea. I felt fatally flakey! I decided not to share my pain and confusion with my friends. Not even my noble friend, through whose agency Jed had dropped by unasked, uninvited, right in my living room, on my coffee table. I had never come across a book that had burned my world to ground zero in one hasty read, especially since my life was flowing like a sweet song! It was clear to me that the universe cares heartbreakingly for my spiritual growth but absolutely zilch for anything else in my life.

That's been its way and its pattern for my life. A loving relationship, more like-minded friends, a warm and compassionate personality, a sexier body, an ocean view condo, and a very successful business—no matter how much *Abraham* I practiced, these weren't in the cards for me. I realized how exhausted I was, of constantly desiring and asking for and not being able to even consistently manifest a parking spot. Ask and I'm sure not to receive! Don't ask, and a nasty alarm clock wrapped up skillfully in a book with a cool cover lands into my life.

Shall I not go on the trip! I had hired a therapist for a month. After the cruise, I was flying to Virginia to visit my family and then to California to do a continuing education workshop on vestibular system and balance. I felt emotionally unbalanced and shaky and convinced that sharing my emotional state with my friends was going to earn me a future niche as a dim-witted lunatic!

On the cruise, I read the second book, *Spiritually Incorrect Enlightenment*. My *Abraham* cabin mate, an Aloha-filled, attractive woman from Honolulu, read the *Spiritual Enlightenment* book. She shared with me that some time ago, she had spontaneously experienced an all-inclusive, overwhelming peace that "passeth understanding" for several months. During that time, she had been delightfully invincible to misery and struggle. And then... it left, just like that! Since then, her main desire had been to regain the paradise lost, but to no avail! Sitting in the back row at the *Abraham* meetings, I wondered about the connection between manifestation and enlightenment. The former has to do with the person, her dreams and desires fueled by lack and manifested by following *Abraham's* mind-designed strategies. The enlightenment was about the death of the person: her desires, dreams, hopes, and fears as being not her. What is left is the enlightened state. The enlightened sages, including Jed, have unfailingly assured us that we are all already enlightened, which is something not to be created or attained and accomplished with human effort and planning. The only requirement is to sever our attachment to the personal self, which is obscuring enlightenment like clouds covering the sun.

It was obvious I had graduated from *Abraham's* school of manifestation. She had taught me appreciation, gratitude, and transformation of negative to positive emotions, which had served me well in the dream world. Now, the universe was asking me to wake up from my prolonged sweet dream and, for fuck sake, stay awake. I was resisting fiercely, and a bitter battle of my will against Thy Will of Existence had begun.

My family bought my pretense of all-is-so-well in my life. But upon arrival in the hotel in Los Angeles, the emotional distress of going back to my life in Maui, which had suddenly become increasingly stale and meaningless, hit me like a lightning bolt. Uncontrollable heaving and sobbing! Edgy energy and waves of restlessness! Not once did I think of smoking dope to make it all go away like a bad dream. I decided to either sell my practice or give it away or hire somebody to run it for two years with such sweet terms that they couldn't refuse. Jed's assertion of two years in solitude, filled with contemplation and writing, was sure to significantly enfeeble or hopefully destroy my ego. It seemed so doable. At the workshop, I decided to advertise my two-year job opening in fabulous Maui with an ocean view apartment. Only $1000 a month to be paid to me and a net profit of anywhere around $5,000 and more a month, plus salary for the therapist. No takers. A number of therapists took my ad to put it on the classified boards in their hospitals and clinics. Nothing.

Back home in Maui, I was feeling even more destabilized and demoralized. I arranged a meeting with my noble friend, who, I was sure, must have read both the books by now. He arrived in his colorful Aloha shirt, looking very breezy and cheerful. He laughed at my misery and seriousness. Gently and insistently, he tried to convince me that Jed McKenna didn't exist and that books are fake records of a fake man's fake journey! He assured me that he had searched the net, but nobody had met the elusive Jed McKenna face to face. *That's because he doesn't exist.* Later, a noble friend pointed out Jed's huge ego, and the other called him a cold-hearted bastard! My friend felt very guilty and responsible for my sorry state. He urged me not to do anything rash and reckless with my future and the clinic, which had turned from a blessing into an albatross. He agreed that the book is written very powerfully, passionately, convincingly, and clearly! Still, it was only fiction trying to be real. Not for me! Both the books had made a deep imprint on my soul, and there was no going back.

I hated to close the clinic with the sign "Gone to find her True

Self." A good number of my patients were involved in legal cases, and it seemed very irresponsible to vanish into thin air overnight. Yes, I could die suddenly of natural causes or in an accident. Then what would happen to all those legal cases and files? Well, not dead yet, so back to work!

Chapter 21

What Has God to do with Ganja?

When you smoke the herb, it reveals you to yourself.

—Bob Marley

BY AND BY, AWAKENING AND enlightenment moved into the background and my life found its center in work, beach activities, noble friends group, and meditation. It had been more than a year since I had been sober and clean of cannabis. I had a pothead patient/friend who had been coming to me for several years for various physical conditions. This time, she had had surgery on her hand and wasn't doing well either physically or emotionally. Late one afternoon she came in for her appointment looking sad and teary-eyed. It was her birthday, and no family members or friends from the mainland or Maui had called. I offered to take her out for dinner wherever she wanted to go. She picked an ocean view bistro in a five-star hotel. Prior to dinner she wanted to smoke a joint in the lovely garden of the hotel. She knew of my recovery/relapse history with cannabis and found my struggle with it meaningless and empty. Why would anybody choose to fight against an herb, against medicine, against a sacred plant? Giving up ganja for god served nobody! She kept offering me the joint, and I kept politely refusing it. When I'm clean, I don't like to put myself into temptation filled situations, I had unconsciously done once again. The main reason for my persistent refusal was we were in Ka'anapali Beach, far, far away from my home in Kihei. It was getting dark, and my friend agreed that driving through the treacherous narrow and winding roads stoned at night wasn't a good idea. She pulled out a fresh joint and with eyes filled with love and gratitude, gently put it in my hand. I realized she was having a hard time accepting my gift of dinner, so I accepted her gift and put it away in a never used pocket of my wallet, where it would stay for several months.

One evening, while returning home from work, I was involved in a multiple car accident, and my car was more or less in the middle. My car was totaled, and I sustained a moderate whiplash. Being a therapist, I decided to treat my own neck and not go to a doctor for pain pills. One evening I was worn out and depressed from dealing with my car insurance company and other heavy work-related issues. My head and neck were throbbing with pain. The image of the joint resting in the dark pocket of my wallet popped up in my mind. A few tokes, and heaven! Everything in my little private garden, where I was smoking, was rippling with delight! I started to massage my scalp and neck. A ton of weight that I had been carrying on my bruised neck lightened up, and my head found its proper resting spot. My garden had a tall bamboo fence covered with a vine of bright yellow flowers that seemed to be waving and smiling at me. Feeling of oneness with existence felt intensely delightful. The sky was streaked with gold and orange from the setting sun. The contrast between my habitually uptight, separate state of mind and Maui-Wowi state of oneness was in ultra-high relief, especially since I hadn't smoked for more than a year. It felt festive, like a union of two lovers. Daddy Cool was back in my life!

I had been meditating regularly while clean, which gave me peace of mind as well as flexibility. My mind was much less mechanical and reactive. However, lightness, playfulness, wondrousness, and the poetry of life still eluded me without the presence of Daddy Cool. Life was good without, but with it, it was a fun-filled festival of wow, wow, wonder and exuberance! My body was, in reality, addicted to these powerful jolts of pure life, which were often expressed as spontaneous dance, coming from the fountain of existential eroticism. During my clean-out phase, a brief and weak version of these spontaneous physical moves is all I would get. Reading books, my oldest habit since I learned to read, would be back in the center.

Dancing with delight, I called my friend to get me more goodies ASAP. She laughingly accused me of being a masochist who loves to torment herself like old-world ascetics. Oh! how they whipped and slashed themselves to purify for a fucking god who they hadn't even seen or met. None of us to this day have been able to understand what he wants from us. To give up ganja is a dumb move unworthy of a smart and independent woman like me. She informed me in no uncertain terms that cannabis, sex, and masturbation were divine blessings and medicines for the new woman of the twenty-first century. The woman of the past, prissy and compulsively pleasing, sexually uptight and nonorgasmic, an obedient baby-making machine overwhelmed by mundane details of her life, is *finito*, toast, forever. By smoking, I was not only celebrating life but paving the way for the new woman, free from the sturdy fetters of dependence and slavery of all kinds. Lots of deep nods of agreement on my side.

The next day, I went to visit my friend in the art gallery where she worked as an associate. As it was Friday evening, their doors were wide open to the tourists, and there was a table with bottles of wine and a cheese platter. My friend poured us two glasses of wine and made a plate of cheese and crackers and led me to the viewing room. It was dark and soothing save for the light over the seascape painting, reflecting myriad colorful underwater creatures with all their finest details, playing and doing their thing. We sat on the ultra-padded leather sofas, and I pretended to be the wealthy potential art buyer.

My friend had a great natural aesthetic sense of presentation. She usually purchased my dope for me — awesome quality, pricey stuff! She rolled thirty impeccable joints and put them in a colorful metal chewing gum box. The joints and the metal boxes were always a fit. This time, she had tied a delicate gold rope and made a tiny, clever, and complicated bow. Controlling my teary eyes, I held both her hands and wondered aloud to her, "I'm always pleasantly stunned how you do such fine and refined work with your hands."

She had mean Dupuytren contractures in both hands. As a result, the fascia of her palms was tight and contracted, making it hard for her to fully open her hands. While driving home, I couldn't get the feel of her hard, ropey, and clawed hands out of my mind. They were symbols of her life's heartbreaking suffering. She was a post WWII East European immigrant with history of incest, multiple rapes, and a pedophile uncle whom she hated for sexually abusing the children in her family. So much chronic pain, as well as tons of unresolved rage had perhaps manifested as breast cancer and contracted hands. Smoking dope was her way of temporarily unloading herself of a massive burden of guilt, shame, and rage. For a brief period, she could fly!

Chapter 22

Another Existential Crisis

God is merciful, but the journey toward god is merciless.

—Meher Baba

Time: FALL OF 2007. I'm scheduled to leave on vacation to Vietnam with a friend from my medical world. A call from a noble friend that Jed McKenna's new book *Spiritual Warfare* is out.

The book arrived from Amazon a day before my departure. I was very happy but shouldn't have been. A couple of years earlier I had taken two of his books with me on my dream cruise to Alaska, and all hell broke loose. Monsters of shame, guilt, and despair had wrenched and ruined my good times, from the swimming pools to dance floors and hiking in supernatural Alaskan glaciers. It had taken me a couple of months to regain my balance and full function. Where did those mean memories disappear to, and why?

Here I was, sitting in the plane, sipping white wine, totally reveling in the first lines of his book: "How many spirituality books start with a chase scene? And how many where the enlightened guy writing the book is being chased by the cops?" Early in the chase, he comes across young men smoking dope who ditch their joint thinking they are the target of the chase. *Don't be fooled by the lightness and humor*, I warned myself. *Serious substance and significance, Jed's signature, is sure to be afoot.* Later, in the hotel room, my friend fell asleep while reading her book. I switched off the lights and moved into the bathroom with my book, where I collapsed into tears on the floor.

So what ails her? Why do Jed's books twist and torment her soul?

At more than sixty years of age, she is increasingly and acutely aware of her race against time. But somehow, she manages to muffle her sense of urgency. She feels ashamed of having chosen economic security, safety, and the relevant perks and privileges. These have overshadowed her gnawing hunger and thirst for spiritual enlightenment. Has she sold her soul? Absolutely!

Her head was throbbing with confusing concepts and unquestioned beliefs. Since reading Jed's last two books a couple of times, a few layers of her false egoic self had been destroyed. She knew her essential self to be no-thingness, sky-like, boundless openness. And yet ... she felt locked in a house of mirrors and mirages. A spasm of envy, for her friend and all the people sleeping peacefully, unaware of their illusions and ignorant of their essential self, was molesting her heart. She was starting to nod off while being cooked in this complicated quagmire, still holding on to the book.

I returned to bed in the wee hours of the morning. I had barely closed my red and swollen eyes when my companion and I bolted upright to the savagely loud sounds of Alvin and the Chipmunks. They were screaming and screeching, "You better not cry. You better not sigh. Santa Claus is coming to town."

We looked at each other in sheer stupefaction. He is coming to Ho Chi Minh City in November! At a little past 7:00 a.m.! Is this a sign of a failed communist revolution? We quickly got dressed to more screechy Christmas songs by the Chipmunks. We later found out that the music was coming from a terrace of a mid-size building a block away.

Time for sugar and caffeine fix. Time to soak in the early morning hustle on the streets of a mega city coming back to its high-octane status. By early afternoon Ho Chi Minh was in full, vibrant flow. Traffic in the city was intense and chaotic, and the air smelled of poisonous exhaust fumes. Crossing the roads was an even worse nightmare for me than in chaotic Mumbai. I found it hard to keep my wits about me. Swarms of scooters, motorbikes and motorcycles overloaded with passengers, stacks of baskets of chickens and pigs, coming at me from all directions like a 3D video game. I clung with my sweaty hand to my dear friend, who was able to walk slowly and confidently through the gaps in the traffic.

A flashback: I'm clinging to my younger sister, who is leading us slowly and steadily through near homicidal Mumbai traffic. Humiliating pangs of ancient inadequacy were harassing me, which had never surfaced on the roads in the West, where traffic rules and laws are obeyed.

The next day's visit was to the War Remnants Museum, heartbreaking for my already crushed psyche. The photos of Vietnamese farmers on fire from napalm, running in desperate panic, was more than I could handle. My own psychic pain felt obscenely bourgeois. At the souvenir shop, seeing the deformed and stunted second generation victims of Agent Orange making trinkets, was truly sobering.

In Hanoi, we visited a Buddhist temple with lovely gardens and colorful statues of ethereal and angelic Chinese-looking Buddha and Quan Yin. The temple had a huge hall with lovely carved pillars. There were rows and rows of long, shiny yellow lacquered boxes that looked to us like coffins. I thought the monks were practicing some form of death meditation, an integral part of Buddhism. I wanted to open one and lie down to experience the utter darkness and total silence of death. Pretty soon, a whole bunch of Vietnamese boys, dressed in yellow monk robes and heads shaved, walked into the hall. Upon inquiring, our guide was told that the boxes contained their personal belongings. Our guide told us that a couple of these mini monks were offended to hear I had thought the boxes were coffins for practicing death meditation. Collectively, they gave us demeaning "barbaric tourists" looks. In the souvenir shop, scented with incense, I bought a Vietnamese bamboo flute meditation music cassette, elegantly wrapped as a gift for a friend back home. On playing the cassette he called to say thanks for the thought, but the tape was a blank dud!

On the last day of our trip, we were having our dinner in an elegant restaurant with panoramic views of the city and the Saigon river. I shared with my friend how surprised I had been to find fourth century Hindu temples near Hoi An. They were built by the Champa dynasty, which ruled Vietnam for several centuries. The museums had well preserved sculptures of Shiva, his Lingam, and his son, Ganesha. There was a temple to ancient god Vishnu.

WTF are you Hindu guys doing in Viet Nam?

I told my friend there was no mention at all of the Champa dynasty in my history books. My friend reminded me of Hindu temples of Angkor Wat. Wow! India has been exporting its exotic brand of gods and divine ideology since almost the dawn of history. Hare Krishna and gurus are just its latest iteration!

We wrapped up our amazing dinner by sharing memories of other delicious meals that we had eaten, of crispy spring rolls, sizzling Vietnamese crepes, bowls of steaming soups, richly spiced and overflowing with organic green herbs and delectable sauces. I reminded my friend of the joke by our tour guide: "Anybody for grilled field mouse swirled with five-spice powder?" As I gleefully said, "Not me," I broke into an unstoppable cough. I confessed to my friend that I hadn't been feeling well and my throat was sore. She offered me her antibiotics and suggested warm salt-water gargles.

As we were catching a red-eye flight home, we had some time to rest. I had finished the *Spiritual Warfare* book and my ego had been mercilessly crushed and deflated. I was grateful to Jed for that. I was even more grateful to his book for strengthening and fortifying my resolve to seek truth. In Jed's words, "It was Truth or Die" for me from now on. Jed said that truth is contagious, and he was hoping to infect more people. I was certain that was a metaphor. The pages of the book weren't dipped in an enlightenment virus that had attacked my soul from inside. But, even so, my body was hacking, dripping, and coughing on the outside.

I arrived home a wobbly near-dead woman. After a couple of days of rest, I called the two therapists who were managing my clinic for a meeting. I offered them extremely generous terms if they would run the clinic for two years. They happily agreed, and I started to fantasize about devoting 100 percent of my resources to my search for Truth. After two days, one of the therapists called and said she would be leaving for the mainland, as her husband had landed a job of his dreams. Good for them, but not so good for me.

Chapter 23

The Last Door Opens

The choice to make this inner journey was not mine.
When the ship of life moved, it took me with it and I
had no say or control in that matter.

—Patrick Drysdale, *The Journey to No-Self*

I DIDN'T COME UNHINGED THIS TIME. I had little more than a year of work before retirement, and I was determined to end the rat race whether I had a buyer for the clinic or not. Hope gave me heart to hunker down until the finish line. For me, the spiritual aspect of physical therapy that I would miss the most was the touchy-feely body work, especially if the receiver was silent and receptive. It invariably brought me, with ease, into the here and now of space time. It was also fun to impart my passion for body and physical movements to my sedentary patients who rebelled at the mention of exercise. They would receive a soundbite of my philosophy that life = movement, and no movement = death. My other peppy soundbite was "Breath is life."

"In breath" is the first critical act of a baby, and the last out breath is a goodbye. Breath is the bridge that connects the inner with the outer world. So, breathe consciously, breathe in sync with movement, and breathe gratefully that you're alive. A lot of patients habitually tended to fritter away their time with me by talking trivialities. It was a challenge to have them bring their attention to their bodies, which most had ill-treated and were now lugging around! Above all, what ego doesn't love to dispense advice to the needy and get handsomely rewarded for it, not only emotionally but also financially?

It was hard to hang on to my existential angst in magical Maui with the cool blue Pacific at my beck and call. I could depend 100 percent on Sunday snorkeling in the ocean to refresh my overburdened soul. The ocean was my boundlessly open and ever-changing watery cathedral, where I regularly praised existence for its playfulness and its attention to details. Here come two Picassos (fish so called because of their delicate designs and colors) with the poetic Hawaiian name of Humuhumu Nukunuku apua'a. Their kissy mouths are painted blue. Really! Behind a rock, I spy a trumpet fish looking just like a trumpet watching a baby seahorse. The supreme celestial artist, abiding above all the earthly time zones, standing in eternity, joyfully paints bright red lips on a luminous parrot fish. Lavishes another with purple polka dots and paints a sour-looking mouth on another fish and then covers it up with yellow gold spines to protect it from predators.

"Hello, sir, your planet is on fire, and much like the extravagant Roman emperor, Nero, you're happily busy decorating and ornamenting these little creatures."

Yeah! Existence is so — so non-serious! An indomitable player and a super gamer. Time to move on to the next item on my fluid playlist: float in the water on my back with my eyes closed. My body would get very still and lose its boundaries. It would merge with the ocean and let the currents of the water purify and recalibrate my energy field. I would emerge from the ocean wobbly but wonder-filled, my energy tanks filled to the brim to meet next week's challenges.

During my final phase in Maui, my nephew and his wife were visiting, and we spent a weekend in Hana hiking and bathing in waterfalls. Earlier, I had noticed silver lines in front of my right eye. Since I was wearing contact lenses, I assumed it was related and when I took them off at home my eye would be okay. We were homeward bound and my nephew was driving; I was sitting in the backseat. I closed my eyes and started to practice a Shiva meditation in which you relax and allow your body to move in sync with the moving vehicle. I used to practice it daily when I lived in downtown Vancouver, Canada. At the time, I didn't know it was a Shiva meditation. We had one car, which, at the time, my husband used. The public bus started outside my apartment and took me right to the hospital where I worked. The bus would start off virtually empty at both ends. My favorite seat was the long one at the very back. Eyes closed, mind relaxed and alert, my body would be moving in rhythm with the bus. By the time I got to work I felt fluid, flexible, and super energized. But no such luck for the super exhausted and totally drained person who got into the bus at the end of her workday.

I was enjoying my Shiva meditation and being driven, a rare treat these days. When I opened my eyes, I noticed the trees were wavy, the lamp posts were wavy, and as a matter of fact, there wasn't a straight line anywhere on the road for me. Nothing changed when I removed my contacts at home. I tried reading, but everything was wavy as if I were reading under water. At work, I couldn't read a statement from Medicare, which uses the tiniest print. And I had been fine before the Hana trip. I went to my optometrist, who got me an urgent appointment with a specialist in Honolulu. The diagnosis was myopic macular degeneration. The treatment was an Avastin injection right in my eye. Back on Maui, I started acupuncture treatments. Within two weeks, all the distortion had cleared up, and I could read Medicare statements as before.

Meanwhile a physical therapist who was working with me started to show interest in purchasing my practice. Celestial freedom music to my ears. I started to dream of a seamlessly smooth transfer of management. I loved Maui like no other place ever before, but I knew I had to leave if I was really serious about my enlightenment. I had my mind set on Kona. I was also looking at Goa in India, but my family discouraged me. Too many drug-related crimes and rapes. A friend suggested Mexico, which triggered intense disgust on my face.

In Maui, the demographics were changing. The original Filipino immigrants were moving on to white collar jobs, and Mexicans were coming from California to fill the vacated positions. Most of them spoke very little English, and new patient information gathering was hell for me. Also, somehow, more patients started coming in late for appointments and the no-shows were hard to tolerate.

A noble friend from my spiritual group suggested Mexico, which had come up once before from another friend. Her advice was to do selfless service for Jed McKenna since I so deeply valued his *Enlightenment* trilogy. It's true, I had a confusing crush on him, but to clean his floors and make his bed, which I could barely do for myself—mission impossible! My friend corrected me and said she meant to help him with editing his books. What if he kicked me out, calling me a loser who couldn't write her own books? Almost everyone who had read his books grudgingly and laughingly admitted to such a remote possibility from crazy wisdom guy Jed!

The official day of my retirement came, and at last, the door opened to my final freedom from the great rat race. I sold my practice for a song to my very deserving colleague. My solid survival structure, laboriously built for more than forty years, having served its purpose, was free at last to crumble and collapse. For at least three months after my retirement, my dreams just prior to waking were usually of me still sweating it out in the clinic. I would wake up in the mornings, confused and depressed, not knowing how to start my day. Solution: drink water, put on the walking shoes, and hit the road. I was sure to return home bright and optimistic.

I started the spiritual autolysis process, which Jed describes as "journaling on steroids." It wasn't easy. While meditating deep and relevant thoughts but with pen in my hand, nothing but unwelcome silence and emptiness. So, I decided to write some book reports to overrule my unruly mind.

At this time, my eye trouble started again, with the same right eye, everything wavy and difficulty reading and writing. Back to the eye specialist for another shot in my eye and more acupuncture treatments. No luck! My right eye was declared legally blind. I was gratefully amazed at the functional timing of my tragedy, immediately after retirement. No more work statements with sadistic tiny print. No more driving at night on dark winding roads. I was still functional but unable to drive at night. Great good luck, at least one eye works!

On the social side, a few friends thought I was depressed since I was no longer willing to participate in social scenes and rituals that had excited me before. Depressed? Certainly I wasn't. And I ought to know since half my family members suffer from it. The major push to leave Maui was provided by the health care insurance companies that I had done business with. They wanted me to reactivate a patient's file that had been defunct for a couple of years. I was required to refund the money and make a fresh claim to the newly determined insurance company. My response: go fly a kite at Waikiki. I was still focused on Kona and wanted a place with a covered patio, where I planned to do all my writing. I had a friend in Kona with a robust network of connections, whom I had asked to look for such a place. Several months passed, but no luck. Then another insurance company called with a similar problem. I saw the writing on the wall. I had to make a move.

I had a *Conde Nast* travel magazine sitting on the countertop. I aimlessly opened the magazine. Pages after pages of glossy, vibrant, colorful, eye-grabbing photos of Mexican culture, seducing, persuading, and convincing me to "Go Mexico." I started to sweat and hyperventilate—an unprecedented reaction from my body. Feeling unsettled and shaky, I decided to lie down. The message was written in blindingly bright and loud neon lights. Denial not possible, not anymore! My next step was shown to me again and again, but I had been resisting it with all my might.

Within less than half an hour, I had booked my ticket to Guadalajara and given thirty days' notice of vacancy to my landlord. On the internet, I started to look at the rentals in Ajijic, Mexico, and, voila, found something appropriate for a month. A ladder had dropped from heaven in my Hawaiian limbo. I was out and about, downsizing and de-sentimentalizing my life. My landlord discouraged me and asked, "Who is going to come and get rid of the famously huge Mexican cucarachas for you? Here you throw a hissy fit on seeing a harmless sugar cane field spider. There they have giant tarantulas, flesh eating insects and vicious wasps. Who are you gonna call? Not a good decision. Go to Virginia Beach. At least you'll be close to your family."

A friend who used to roll my joints, with a worried and anxious look, asked, "What're you going to do about your *pakalolo* habit? Who is going to roll joints for you in Mexico?"

My ex-colleague warned, "You don't have good karma with Mexicans. I'm worried for you."

My answer was, "I feel I'm being expelled from my warm tropical womb irrespective of my choice."

P.S.

Ancient battle of the wills. Life is pointing to Ajijic, Mexico, but I'm unconsciously insisting on anything other than Mexico. Reality wins. Only always! It has been a great struggle to not only drop my puny will but celebrate with joy and gratitude the will of existence.

Chapter 24

Viva la Mexico

He believes his problem is caused by her. But it is caused by attachment to his story.

—Byron Katie

I T'S APRIL FOOL'S DAY, 2010. I'm in my rental casita in Ajijic, painfully unimpressed with the town at first sight. Dusty, dry, and squalid. Certainly several cuts above similar towns in India, but compared to Maui—super lush and super luxe, I felt sick to my stomach. What have I done, and for what exactly? I don't know a soul here.

The owner of the casita and his wife had welcomed me warmly with hugs and a Mexican-style aloha basket of goodies. Casita had a sweet private garden with lovely rose bushes that seemed to be sending me fragrant and rosy messages from my future. The two ancient and august trees from the villa next door, separated from my casita by a wall, seemed to caress and console me. They promised protection by gently swaying their branches above me. And I wasn't even stoned!

On my cell phone was a message from my friend in Kona reporting a minor miracle. She had found me just the place I was looking for. Too late! So sad! On my laptop computer, several articles from a friend warned me that the state of Jalisco, where Ajijica is, was the most dangerous place in Mexico due to brutal drug wars. Too bad, so sad! How do I know I'm not supposed to be in Kona, or Goa or Virginia Beach? Because I'm not. How do I know I'm supposed to be here? Because I'm here. Reality rules. Thank you, Byron Katie (a well-known spiritual teacher) for making life so simple. My confoundingly complex mind is addicted to molesting me at any chance it gets. My new job description in my newly adopted country is to free myself fully from the suffocating chokehold of my ego. Hello, who is bound, and who is going to be freed asked my inner bitch, laughing defiantly!

My next-door neighbor, a retired Mexican American with a beat-up Benz, was instrumental in familiarizing me with the town, getting me a used Nissan, a miracle in those days, scoring marijuana, and helping me find the place where I have now lived for a decade. I started Jed's process of spiritual autolysis of writing to look at my new anxiety about having time, and nothing but time, on my hands. I usually wrote for several hours in the morning. In the past, during my journaling days, I had noticed how compulsively and furiously I would express my excruciating emotions. Positive emotions and events were just not that compelling. If people were to read my journal, their unanimous conclusion would be: A pathetic and a deeply tormented soul perpetually harassed by hellish furies.

I occasionally wondered if I was strengthening my melancholic madness, my overly fragile ego, and my rabid rage by giving them my single-pointed attention and enshrining them in written words. Were there benefits to steadying and unraveling on paper the dark, roiling miasma of my mixed-up emotions? There certainly was the undeniable relief and restoration of function, if not resolution. Then I created a horrible humdinger that would require months of unpacking, processing, and writing.

Here is how it happened. I went to the bank in Ajijic, designated by the property manager, to deposit my rent check. It was an old-fashioned bank with an English name, somber and dark, mahogany decor inside. The bank tellers' stations were covered with bulletproof glass with an opening below for transactions. For the sake of efficiency and to minimize errors, I was in the habit of filling out all the bank statements at home. There was only one person ahead of me in line. Fifteen minutes passed. The client and the bank teller were still engaged in discussion. I was getting antsy, but I comforted myself with the thought that when my turn came, I'd be done in a couple of minutes.

For crying out loud, how long does it take to deposit one friggin check? A long time in Ajijic, baby!

When my turn came, the teller returned all my paperwork to me and said their banking system had changed. I needed to go to a teller inside, fill out a new slip of paper, and then go to another teller for deposit. I couldn't believe my ears. After filling in the new slip, I stood in the designated line. A little old white lady with her Mexican translator was being attended by the teller. I was next. Ten minutes passed, and the trio looked no closer to finishing their transaction. I was getting irritated, but instead of neutralizing my irritation, I unconsciously poured gasoline over it. I was chanting ceaselessly to myself how I hated waiting and how exhausted I felt. I was fanning the fire by looking at my watch again and again muttering silently to myself, "Another 10 minutes gone, another five minutes gone." Six to seven employees in the bank and only two clients, including me!

Overtaken by a monstrous internal agitation, I burst through the nearest closed door and erupted at the woman sitting behind the desk. My mouth turned machine-gun, attacked the poor woman ruthlessly. "Is this a bank or seniors' comedy club?"

She picked up my hot debris and threw it back at me. She screamed how demanding and impatient we expats were and that we should go back if we were so unhappy here. Then she snatched the papers from my hand and walked away. She was back in less than five minutes with my receipt for the deposit. On my way out, I noticed that the trio still hadn't completed their transaction. Is the old lady buying the friggin bank or what!

I was all shook up. In less than two months, two people had told me to go home, wherever I had come from. Such a thing had never happened to me during my many, many years of stay in Canada and the United States. Merciless conflict in my head was steaming up my brain. One side was shockingly embarrassed and humiliated and wanted me to run back to the woman and apologize with flowers in my hand. The other side was unrepentant, arrogant, and righteously wrathful. The latter ruled for a few days. Days and days of autolysis revealed fathomless depths of self-loathing and violence. Meditation, marijuana, and walks would pull me out of my hell temporarily, but then the super-sized monsters would swallow me again. I was a breathing and walking terror! I was terrified of my mind and the beasties living there. I knew in my head I wasn't my mind but am the consciousness that is observing my thoughts and beliefs. My as yet nascent skill of witnessing my thoughts was impotent against my wrathful bitch, made of ancient unquestioned beliefs. After all the spiritual work, years and years of it, the wall made of thoughts and beliefs seemed to not have budged an inch. It all seemed so meaningless, and suicide seemed the only way out. More violence! Truly violence does beget more violence. Yes, I'm violent, I shamefully confessed to myself. I would think nothing of killing myself by hurling from my terrace in a fit of despair.

I was using my cherished image of me as a gentle, compassionate, and civilized person to deceive myself and others. Could I kill somebody? Maybe, if pushed to the extreme by my thoughts and emotions. I hadn't done that ... yet! Luckily, I didn't have any weapons on hand. Fresh veins of violence continued to throb in the bottomless depths of my psyche. Despair darkened by my habitual thoughts moaned that everything, including myself had failed. Not only that but seemed to have made it worse. It took me a couple of weeks to swallow my shame and guilt and fully accept my violence, which I hadn't acknowledged before. My formidable bitch spat out memories of me being mean, petty and cruel, not only in action but also in thoughts. My self-image as a compassionate, kind, peace loving meditator and pothead was irretrievably shattered. *Peace is all you want? What a lie*, sneered my bitch. *Aggressions, arguments, conflicts, and bloody dramas are closer to truth*, she reminded me in no uncertain terms. My know-it-all ego, the seeming navigator of my life, had been mortally wounded and deflated for the time being. A blessing!

The bit of practical, immediate wisdom that emerged from this banking humdinger was to outsource, for the time being, all my dealings with the Mexican government and institutions to an English-speaking Mexican. And I knew such a person!

Chapter 25

Is This Truth?

"I was meant for soup, salad, maybe chili. And the trash! I'm not a toy. I'm litter."

—Forky cries out, grappling with its existential crisis
in the movie, *Toy Story 4*

ON THE PLUS SIDE OF life, my Mexican penthouse apartment, with killer views from all sides and extremely generous pacing-to-and-fro areas, never fails to uplift and fill me with super-sized gratitude. And my rent here is so low that what I paid in Maui for a small, two-bedroom cottage alone covers all of my Mexican rent, utilities, and food. I am floating in abundance!

Late one late afternoon I was standing close to the door facing the mountain side of my apartment. An unimaginably sweet bird tweet floated in through my right ear, making it shudder with orgasmic delight! An auditory orgasm! It felt so good, almost criminal!

"Oh my god! Are you flirting with me?" were the words that spontaneously came out from my mouth. The ecstasy factor made my legs tremble. I wasn't stoned, but I was in the process of getting my smoking paraphernalia together for my move to the terrace.

"God flirting with you, what nerve!" cried out my all-knowing inner bitch, my stern teacher. The sonorous bird tweet seemed to have released wonderfully blissful chemicals in the auditory portion of my brain.

After a few tokes, I was transported to the past: Hilo in Hawaii, when I was working with my dream team. I was sent by my company at a very short notice to replace a therapist who was on family emergency leave. Since it was my birthday the next day, I requested a Maui-Wowi joint and ride to and back from the City of Refuge, known for its spectacular underwater world. Wish granted! At the end of my workday, the receptionist at the office drove me to a secluded spot with huge rocks. She assured me that my dive from the rocks was sure to be amazingly dramatic compared to the sandy tourist entrance in the front. The legend of the City of Refuge is that die-hard criminals would be pardoned provided they reached the refuge city. They were thrown into the Hawaiian waters from high cliffs and must survive the sharks and other perils of the deep. Perched on the rock with no one around, I finished my joint, put on my mask, and fins and quietly slipped into the water. I was greeted by a seemingly divinely orchestrated scenario: a gigantic school of yellow tangs circled and swam around me. Underwater, their yellow/gold color, luminous in early evening light, dazzled my eyes. And such a crazy abundance of them! I momentarily closed my bedazzled eyes, and there was the unimaginable vibrational delight of my optic nerves in my brain. A visual orgasm!

Now, standing in my terrace in Mexico, I noticed a cascade of feel-good chemicals with recall of all varieties of positive emotions. Delicious and digestible, like peaches and cream! With maturity, I learned to welcome the negative emotions, too, though hard to swallow and frequently causing smelly and embarrassing burps. Ultimate maturity is to see it all for what it is—simply content, transient, and meaningless, on my journey. I knew this mentally but not existentially as yet.

I continued with spiritual autolysis for several hours each morning. I went for my walks in the late afternoon, along with swimming in my apartment pool. Smoking weed and playtime were for the evening and night due to my eye condition. I frequently did the *neti neti* (not this, not this) process to disengage from my thoughts and emotions. I'm not my emotions, not my thoughts, certainly not my body, not my breath, not even my attention, because they can all be observed just like the objects on the outside. What is left is content free consciousness, or Truth, totally naked of concepts. All that was wonderful, but the seeming doer, my ego, was behind it all, in total control, creating an illusion of tremendous forward movement.

One afternoon I was watching a *Dr. Phil* show on TV, which I occasionally did to get the distinction clear between child and human adult. Dr. Phil certainly represented the human adult, and most of the participants were locked in at various developmental stages of the human child, revealed by their lack of responsibility and blaming others. Today, there was a middle-aged man on the show who had fallen, perhaps in the bathroom, and hit his head on the floor. His head was suddenly emptied of all his memories. He couldn't recognize his wife or remember where he worked. Naturally, the victim was deeply despondent over the sudden, unwished-for wipe-out of his memory. The medical profession didn't have any options left except to put him in a hyperbaric chamber or some such stuff.

I started to laugh uncontrollably, imagining what if the enlightened master Jed McKenna fell and hit his very empty head on the floor? Would that be an event for a man already free from the self and its memories? What if I fell and lost all my memories? Would that be the end of the doubt-filled melancholic seeker of enlightenment? Yes, and the end of much more, but not the misery, because the man on the *Dr. Phil* show was suffering from intense psychological pain. His ego, source of all misery, seemed to have survived the fall.

At this point, I shut off the TV but continued sitting in the chair and looking unconsciously at the blank screen. It occurred to me the blank screen is likened to pure consciousness in non-dual tradition to aid the disciple in getting the hang of the nonconceptual, pure consciousness. My mind, which was still hanging on tightly to its ultimate authority over my life, went into befuddled alarm.

"So, this is truth! That which cannot be simpler."

Nothing left to lose or throw out. And I'm supposed to sit with my eyes closed, groove on the empty screen of consciousness, and write about it? Is this what I'm trying to do with spiritual autolysis? Get to the empty screen? There's tons to write and play with the images and thoughts on the screen of consciousness. Aren't movies, TV shows, and books all about content? But my gurus and guides have called it illusions, *makio*, fleeting sensations, and soap bubbles. The empty screen/empty consciousness is the reality of existence.

WTF! No, no, the movie of your life, of everyone's life, is being played on the empty screen of consciousness, my inner voice cried out. *You and everyone else are identified with the movie running in our heads, completely unaware of the pure consciousness that is the very source of the movie.*

Unimpressed, I stood up in a huff and declared my situation to be a flaming disaster!

P.S.

My attention was undeniably enchanted by the concepts in my mind. My mind had taken possession of the notion of emptiness, which created grievous misery for me, for a time. Now it is clear that Emptiness as the ground of being, is my very essence. Nowadays, I consider myself supremely blessed to be luxuriating in the empty screen of consciousness, which is the silence of the infinite.

Chapter 26

The Silent Generation

> Writing allows you to be your own teacher, your own critic, your own opponent. By externalizing your thoughts, you can become your own guru, judging yourself, giving feedback, providing a more objective and elevated perspective.
>
> —Jed McKenna, *Spiritual Enlightenment: The Damnedest Thing*

AFTER MORE THAN TWO YEARS, the magic number mentioned in the *Enlightenment Trilogy* for reaping the rewards of spiritual autolysis and exultantly declaring "done," had so far eluded me. There were vast swaths of peace and well-being and, yes, bliss too. But "done" wasn't my reality. So far, I have been writing and writing without editing, just putting on paper whatever showed up in my mind. Upon revisiting my fresh writings, I noticed a remarkable increase in my anxiety level as I passed the two-year mark. Autolysis wasn't working, at least not yet! There seems to be no point in continuing with it. I felt as stupid and confused as ever.

The bottom line of all anxious outpouring was "What's going to happen to me? Not yet enlightened! Perhaps never, not in this lifetime. What shall I do with the remainder of my life, of which perhaps not much is left due to my age? Who shall I turn to for help? Wish I was dead—still the theme song of my life."

I saw my mom's image, chronically anxious, nail-bitingly anxious!

Not only for herself but others, her entire family, her clan and country. It was a deep-seated habit, not only hers but also of my siblings. But not my dad, who seemed relatively more relaxed and laid back. Or perhaps he was pretending. The neurons in my brain were whirring themselves into an anxious frenzy. How is it possible that a person, a cosmopolitan globetrotter, brilliantly intelligent, financially independent, able to think for herself and voice her opinions boldly and loudly, turned out to be her mother's clone? How hard I labored to carve a destiny radically different, not only from my mother, but from all the blindly obeying women of my tribe and country! Here I was, just as incompetent as any uneducated woman of my culture when it came to managing my future and my life. If not enlightenment, then I needed at least a man to bring some spring into my life. If not that, at least a likeminded friend, just one. Slumped over, head low, all by my lonely self, I tried to figure out my major missteps.

My upper-middle-class family had fled with a few suitcases filled with expensive items and clothes on a ship from Karachi (now Pakistan) to Mumbai during the partitioning of India. We lived in a refugee camp for a few days, when we were rescued by an uncle who had come from Africa to help his tribe. He had rented a two-story ocean-view bungalow, a vacation house of some Maharaja, right on one of the finest beaches of Mumbai. The entire house was occupied by the refugee clan, except a small room with a portable stove still available at the back of the house for my family of six. My family, my entire Sindhi clan, all refugees, were shell-shocked and mortally confused. Perhaps they suffered from PTSD (the concept didn't exist then), which they had to swallow unacknowledged in order to move urgently forward as demanded by existence. My parents' generation, pre- WWll, and my generation, born post- WWll, are both called the Silent Generation in the West. By god! Silent they were, which was forced on them not only by the current dire situation but also by the old-world authoritarian culture. They forcibly quashed their children's rebellion and resistance by physical abuse and punishment. At this time, I was nine or ten years old and starting to lose my vision. Neither I nor my family nor my school noticed the loss. My family decided I was a low-grade moron because I would frequently miss my bus and train stops. When asked to bring sugar, instead, salt would show up, and a host of other weird behaviors that my mom interpreted as personal annoyances. The little girl I was was petrified with anxiety, trying to protect herself from the next onslaught of physical and verbal abuses.

My brother, three years older than me, was also the generous recipient of the collective anguish and repressed emotions of the adults. Besides violent verbal abuses, he got slapped with heavy slippers, so savagely fierce as to leave bright red imprints on his very dark-complexioned face.

In my tween years, my art teacher at school figured out that my eyes needed to be examined. Around that time, a friend of mine had gotten glasses and we were at a movie theater. I asked to borrow her glasses, and I was astonished by the crispness and details of the images on the screen. I had hated to go to the movies and wondered why the public was so fond of them; I had accepted the fuzzy and nebulous world of porous boundaries as normal reality. I got my glasses and became dazzlingly brilliant overnight.

We were now living in an upper-middle-class hood in central Mumbai. My brother, an avid reader, would bring home books about Perry Mason, Agatha Christie, stacks of comic books, *Archie and Veronica*, *Tubby*, and lots of *Mad* magazines. I would devour everything he brought home. A visiting uncle asked me what my future plans were.

"To be a doctor," I replied. One look at my stack of murder mysteries and comic books, and he went into a tizzy. He warned me and my mom in no uncertain terms that I was going to be a murderer not a healer because of the crime books I was reading. He advised me to read edifying and elevating books, like biographies of Swami Vivekananda, Ramkrishna, and Mahatma Gandhi, which I never did read.

My generation had started the shift from British to the trendy American culture of Hollywood movies, books, Sears Roebuck dress catalogs, jam sessions to the jukebox music of "Jailhouse Rock" and "Love Letters in the Sand," and so on. We blew bubbles from bubble gum, trying to imitate American cool! TV hadn't been birthed yet. We had just gotten our first bulky radio, with a bunch of knobs on it. My brother and I listened to the Voice of America, while my dad, an Anglophile at heart, was all for BBC, Shakespeare, George Bernard

Shaw, and Oscar Wilde. Little did we know that my brother and I were unconsciously being groomed to someday immigrate to America.

My mother, deeply conditioned by Hindu culture, believed that a woman's true place was at home. Marriage and making babies were the ultimate fulfillment of womanhood. My mom was supremely skilled in the art of homemaking. She labored to teach me the art of making chapati (Indian unleavened bread) which most Indian women could do in their sleep. Instead of perfect rounds, no matter how hard I tried, mine would be pentagons, hexagons, or sometimes Minnie Mouse, with two ears sticking out. Mom would sigh in despair and chant her favorite mantra: "Who is going to marry you?" which had pierced and poked my psyche growing up with fear and self-loathing. On my inner journey, most of the time, I felt grateful and blessed to be single.

My mother had been dead for several years, and I, myself, am sitting in death's transit lounge. Yet, her inherited anxiety was still driving me at the deepest layers of my being. So far, it seemed I had succeeded only in pruning the leaves and the branches at the top of the trees, while the roots were still intact and growing in the dark depths of my psyche. I still believed my thoughts, as I had believed her thoughts about me, and I had put an all-out effort to prove my worth to her and to the world. The results so far: absolutely abysmal, both in the material world and the spiritual world. I warned myself to expect more gut-wrenching anxiety and misery moving forward.

P.S.

I wanted to explore the depths of my addiction to my mind and its matchless talent for manufacturing misery. I wanted to untangle the robust thread of my belief that nothing was working out for me—from drugs to meditation to writing, as the cunning survival ploy of my ego.

Chapter 27

Demands of Enlightenment

> "In order to break with one's false self, one would have to break with … everything," Julie says. "Family, friends …" Her voice falters as she considers the ramification. "Everything. Everything you are … everything you know … everything … Really everything."
>
> —Jed McKenna, *Spiritual Enlightenment: The Damnedest Thing*

I HAD COLOSSAL AMOUNTS OF TIME, all the time in the world, for my holy pilgrimage. The outside world, including existence itself, seemed to have forgotten I was still alive in a humble corner of the universe called Ajijic. My phone at home seldom rang except at appointed times. My friends from Maui never called. Other than the occasional call or email from Canada, my social life in Ajijic is zilch. My brother from the US calls every Saturday morning. I call my sister in India one or two times a month, more frequently if she is ill, and such is the case now.

I have stripped my life naked of all non-essentials. I cook a huge pot of veggie curry once a week and eat that for lunch and dinner for the whole week. I usually eat when absolutely starved. That way, I'm eager and grateful to have something to eat, even though I have eaten the same curry for several days. I have an old-fashioned bulky TV that I watch for about three hours a week, tops. I rest a lot—a lot! Perhaps I'm one of the few super-well-rested adult humans in our frantically frenzied, hyper-connected twenty-first century. I recently saw Arianna

Huffington, cofounder of *Huffington Post* and author of fifteen books, on the Bill Maher show on YouTube. She had been working very hard and had been so sleep deprived that she collapsed on her desk and fractured her facial bone.

My well rested jaw dropped, and my well rested eyeballs nearly popped out of their sockets. OMG! We are both at the extreme poles of existence! She is one of the most successful female icons of our time and a powerful role model for us striving females. She seemed to have temporarily gotten disconnected from existence and her body by her relentless drive and ambition to succeed in the world of media. Now she is a passionate crusader for sleep, armed with scientific knowledge about the brain and its workings. Another OMG moment! We need sleep specialists in white lab coats to teach, and persuade us, to sleep!

My sister in Mumbai called for my help, as she, exhausted by constant knee pain, had planned to have a total knee replacement. I asked for two days to decide on my departure date. It was too sudden and sharp a turn for my well rested brain, floating in limbo. I didn't want to go, but I felt terrorized by the word "no" and its consequences. Broken hearts, betrayal, and endless shame! If it were a celebration, it would have been easy to say no. If I were working, I could have said no. I had no excuse except paralysis, caused by existential angst, with which my sister is fortunately not familiar, at least consciously.

For guidance and clarity, I read and reread the chapter, "Let What Will Befall" from Jed's book *Spiritually Incorrect Enlightenment*. Captain Gardiner from Herman Melville's book, *Moby Dick*, begged Ahab for two days to help him search for his young boy, whom he had lost in the whale hunt. My sister had asked for help for two months. Both stories had to do with the human heart, wrapped and tied in strings of love and attachments. My nephew, my sister's only child, now living in the United States with his family on work permit, begged me to go. He had applied for his green card, which after eight years of waiting and much money poured into it, was still in the distant future. If he answered the call of his heart, it was all over for his future. The exit door from the US was fully open, but his reentry would be nearly impossible as he would need a new work permit and another brand-new application for the green card.

"Yes, I'm coming to help," I reluctantly said to my family after much inner turmoil, driven by a shameful sense of duty. They were relieved, even more so because of my solid medical background. That I was in the throes of my egoic death, to be followed by my rebirth as spirit, would be certifiable crazy talk to my family. Spiritual sleep, waking up, enlightenment, and self-realization are not part of their daily vocabulary or life. In all fairness, most of humanity is unfamiliar with these concepts. In Maui, too, only a minority knew of these concepts, and even a smaller number was interested in them. It's the same here in Ajijic.

My family is into popular religious practices, such as being humble, kind, and loving and especially going to the temples, praying, worshiping, and philanthropy. One thing was for certain: I would return from the trip with my ego bruised and battered, hopefully dead or on life support. My sister was my teacher. She knew precisely but unconsciously which dark corner my ego was hiding in, seducing it to come out so she could then beat the shit out of it. If only I wouldn't resist and welcome the assaults, it would be party time forever. Dream on, girlfriend! But the meals were going to be astonishingly delicious!

I was shaken to see my sister looking so weak and feeble in less than one year. It brought out my tenderness and love for her front and center. I could have but wasn't willing to destroy the slender thread of attachment to my family because of the overwhelming burden of restlessness, shame, and guilt. Jed has said in his books, "The price of Truth is everything." I was in agreement but not yet ready to pay the full price. Was I betraying his teachings? Maybe! Nothing new. That, too, was a pattern—betraying my gurus and guides and their teachings. I didn't care. It was my life! If no enlightenment was in my future, only permanent dark sleep, then so be it.

Chapter 28

Death Is in the Air

India has 2,000,000 gods and worships them all. In religion all other countries are paupers; India is the only millionaire.

—Mark Twain.

TWO DAYS BEFORE HER SURGERY, my sister had an appointment with a specialist. She was clear she didn't want any help or support from me in order to walk. I continued to hover behind and around her due to her poor balance. With the doctor, she wasn't her clear and bright self, and so I stepped in and asked questions she was forgetting but would remember later. In her younger incarnation, I saw her providing similar services to my ailing parents while I may have been frolicking with dolphins in Hawaii, and my siblings were doing their thing in the United States.

On our journey home she had a sudden burst of energy and barked at her driver to stop the car. The street was teeming with people. The cacophony of car and truck horns, which Indians feel compelled to use while driving, was terrorizing my brain with confusion. The driver skillfully weaved the car out of traffic, and we were outside a very busy, non-stop-loud-bells-ringing Hindu temple, densely packed with devotees. My sister informed me that it was the Divine Mother's temple, and she was going in by herself. I got out of the car before her and insisted on accompanying her. There were waves of devotees going in and out of the temple, jostling and pushing each other for Ma's *darshan* (viewing). The temple floor was wet, sticky, and slippery from the water of smashed coconuts, which devotees were offering to the Divine Mother. I was anxious for my sister's safety, and mine. She talked to a temple employee who went and fetched the head priest. He led her by the hand, as the crowd parted like the Red Sea, and took her to the altar of the Divine Mother. She did her holy Hindu ritual and deposited a wad of bills in the donation box. Then she pleaded and beseeched the priest to pray for her swift recovery because the Holy Mother seemed to pay attention to his prayers more than anyone else's. He assured her that she was blessed by the Divine Mother and her full and speedy recovery from surgery was certain. Devotees again moved aside for the priest and made a narrow clearing for my sister and me. In the car, my sister was reflecting on the blessings of the priest and how just one look at the beatific face of the Divine Mother had filled her up with peace and joy. She indeed looked peaceful, very relaxed, and much more animated. Dear Karl Marx, methinks the religious opium perhaps works better than the opium of your Communist ideology. Band aid, of course! When hemorrhaging life force, any help, any relief, even momentary, is welcomed. And yes, the wad of bills; it works with the divine around the world, but more powerfully in India.

The day of admission to the hospital, my sister fainted in her bathroom. She was semiconscious but totally flaccid and unable to help. I had to get more manpower to get her up on the bed. I called her orthopedic surgeon and cancelled the surgery, which was rescheduled for the next morning. She was quickly admitted to the hospital for a battery of tests. More than a year earlier she had developed an undiagnosed chronic lung infection, which had been unresponsive to the latest and the strongest antibiotics. A round of steroids was the only medicine capable of suppressing her relentless cough. The price for that relief was the demineralization and weakening of her bones, especially of her spine. Now her kidneys were misbehaving, requiring aggressive treatment. My silent diagnosis of her to myself: very toxic chemistry due to drugs, which was going to get even more toxic, but there was no other solution. By the time she was stabilized, she was too weak to undergo the knee surgery. At home, she was slowly recovering, and it was time for me to return to Mexico, as my air ticket was expiring.

After about eight months, she recovered enough to make her last trip to the US to see her son's family of two grandchildren, whom she adored. There I saw firsthand the power of human attachments. Her ravaged body was propped up by the steroids and vitamins, but mostly by the energetic cords of her desire to see her grandchildren one more time. My question: how long could she hold on like this?

Death continues to be a cultural taboo in varying degrees in almost all societies. In India, the very mention of death is considered unlucky. I had a few private talks with her about her impending death and the finality of this trip to the United States. I also repeatedly talked to her about urging her son not to leave everything and rush to his mom's deathbed in India. As is human, she was so close to death, and yet, she was in death denial, along with the rest of the family. She, along with some cousins, considered my advice on the end-of-life choices and arrangements to be inauspicious. They all wished I weren't so rigorously honest. They wanted me to live with them in their soothing and comfortable death-denial bubble, like the rest of humanity. One of my cousins got upset with me and urged me to give up my dooms day death narrative and speak the pure, sacred, optimistic, and hopeful language of life. Alas! It was too late for that.

Within several months of her return home, she was admitted to ICU. My brother-in-law was devastated and confused and needed help urgently, especially in making decisions about her care. This time, there was no inner turmoil and conflict. I left the next day, ready to meet the challenges that awaited me.

Chapter 29

A Cultural Clash

We forge the chains we wear in life.

—Charles Dickens

I ARRIVED IN MUMBAI IN THE early hours of the morning and asked my brother-in-law whether we should head for the hospital. He said it was too early and we wouldn't be allowed in the ICU. Meanwhile, in the car, I gathered as much information as my brother-in-law was able to provide. All very grim! She had been admitted for excruciating abdominal pain, and a hole in her stomach had been diagnosed, caused by the steroids. Catch 22. Without steroids, she had a fierce, unyielding cough, and with it, her body was deteriorating rapidly, despite an entire host of specialists working diligently to heal and control it. Sharp pangs of despair better left unexpressed.

Later, back at their home, I fell asleep and was woken up by loud banging and panicky exhortations from my brother-in-law. We needed to rush to the hospital, which had just called to inform us of my sister's worsening condition. She was unconscious and covered in a network of tubes, connected to various machines, all doing their thing to keep her alive. Her blood gases were out of kilter and becoming increasingly toxic. My brother-in-law's signature was required to perform an immediate tracheostomy.

So started my more than two months of this daily daytime vigil, mixed with end-of-life consultations with anxious and grieving relatives in a tiny ICU waiting room. The protocol was that one family member of the patient had to be present 24/7. Various medical specialists, with godlike, omnipotent and omniscient demeanors, surrounded by an entourage of students and interns, went in and out to see their patients from 8:00 a.m. to occasionally past 8:00 p.m. If they were seeing your family member, your name would be called, and then only you could go in. The mighty ones would mumble some medical mumbo jumbo and would fly away, leaving you on earth, drowning in dark confusion. I noticed that these made-in-India but Western educated el Supremos responded better to humble, lowered eyes, a beseeching and suppliant demeanor. They seemed offended by eye contact and queries that questioned their authority. Most of the nurses, some of them still in Florence Nightingale caps and crisp white dresses, sweet and sheep-like, would be dancing around their gods in white lab coats, calling them sir. "Doctor, please sign here, Sir-Doctor, please, this way."

I politely asked one of the nurses why this double whammy of power, Sir-Doctor or Doctor-Sir. With the sweetest, soft, feminine smile, she said, "That's our way, isn't it?"

The patriarchy is robust and rules here because that's our way and has been since ancient times. And you corrupt, stupid thing from the West dare to even think of questioning it? You're going to be crushed and crumbled. Do you want that?

No, certainly not on my sister's dime, I silently assured myself, willing to toe the Indian cultural lines.

There were several people in the waiting room with whom I made friends. There were a couple of brothers whose dad seemed to be the only patient recovering with hope of possible discharge. All the brothers were smartphone wizards, and they were willing to help with any unanswered questions or misunderstood answers from the doctors, as well. I, myself, had only an iPad that wouldn't work in the waiting room for lack of WiFi connection.

There was also an elegant Indian Christian lady, usually dressed in gorgeous sarees, a professor of English at a college. Her husband had a computer software business, and whenever I saw him, he would be dressed in black polyester shirt and pants. Very sweaty and dizzying optics for me, especially in the crowded wait room. The two had four children. The youngest, about two years old, was acting up and acting out the unexpressed anxiety and grief of the parents, who were mostly either at work or waiting at the hospital. The woman's mother was in bed right next to my sister, and she didn't look good at all. According to me, it was unfortunate she had survived a massive stroke that left her speech center dead. Most of the time, either she was unconscious or, when awake, she would loudly moan and groan or scream as if being chased by hounds from hell.

Sitting in the waiting room, every now and then I became aware of silent conversations between me and my sister. I would be urging her to let go of her prematurely worn-out body, to which she was clinging with rapidly dwindling threads of attachment. Once she opened her eyes briefly and acknowledged me and became unresponsive again. On another day, she opened her eyes, and I could see she was struggling hard to figure out where she was and what was going on. I tried to orient her but her eyes remained anxious, searching and scanning for something, I would never know what, since she couldn't speak due to tubes in her nose and down her throat. Then, the cardiac monitor of the patient in the next bed started to beep and screech, and the resuscitation team came running with their crash cart and defibrillators. They brought her back to life and her family was overjoyed and relieved. I was stupefied by their selfish blindness and their mortal fears, which those present in the ICU waiting room interpreted as their undying love for their mother. That shriveled up woman in agony was a caricature of modern *Star Wars* medicine of extraordinary measures, not their mother they had known. However, she still at least resembled the mother they had known.

I wanted to draw a line and not allow one more procedure to prolong my sister's life, which was clearly getting ready to depart. The ultimate decision rested with her husband, not me. I explained to my brother-in-law the vicious circle in which his wife was locked, from which only death, not the resuscitation procedure, was going to liberate her. To my surprise, he agreed she was in agony, even though doctors were assuring us she was slowly getting better. He was willing to sign the do-not-resuscitate order. We were informed by her nurse that the process had to be initiated by the lead doctor. When I saw him the next day, I informed him of our plans, and he went ballistic on me. He accused me of losing faith in him and his treatments and how the Indians coming from abroad think they know everything and are constantly interfering and making a nuisance of themselves. He urged me to leave all the medical decisions to him and for me to pray fervently for my sister's life. Yes, I assured him I was praying assiduously, but I still wanted no-resuscitation for her. I told him, gently touching his arm, that I thought he was the best doctor in the world, better than most American doctors, and my sister certainly thought so. Flattery and feminine charm worked! I interpreted his explosion as a sign of disappointment and despair at the increasing certainty of the death of one of his favorite patients.

I remembered a scene from the previous year, when I accompanied my sister on a visit to his office, she in her colorful clothes, with a chiffon scarf trailing behind, bedecked in her beautiful daytime diamond jewelry carrying a designer purse, smelling of expensive French perfume. She would flirt with him and he loved it. When we left, his next patient was a Muslim woman in a burka, accompanied by an elderly-looking man with dyed orange beard. Several sickly-looking men and a conservative Hindu female sat waiting for their turns. I felt her doctor's resistance to my demand was born out of helplessness and defeat in the face of death, which doctors-in-training were taught to look at as something good doctors were supposed to cure. At this point in her life, according to me, death would seem a clear victory for my sister, and for her favorite doctor, a spectacular defeat.

Chapter 30

A Global Spiritual Scandal

No amount of intellect or education can grant one immunity where matters of heart and faith are concerned.

—Gail Tredwell, a.k.a., Gayatri *Holy Hell: A Memoir of Faith, Devotion, and Pure Madness*

I'M AT THE HOSPITAL AND eager to read the weekend religious/ spiritual section of the *Times of India* newspaper, called *"Speaking Tree."* I have struck gold: the mother of all religious scandals. There's a several-page book review of *Holy Hell: A Memoir of Faith, Devotion, and Pure Madness.* There were photos of "Amma, Divine Mother" and her personal attendant, her right hand, a dedicated devotee and the writer of the book, *Gail Gayatri Tredwell*, who is from Australia. I had known Amma for a little less than two decades. She had come to Santa Fe, New Mexico, when I was living and working in Farmington. My friend from Taos had visited Amma in Santa Fe. She was so inspired and uplifted by her meeting, that she called and passionately urged me to visit Amma on the weekend in Santa Fe.

I stood in the long, snaking line for more than an hour for my turn to meet her face to face. This was my first look at her, and she was sitting on a sofa, dressed in a dazzling white cotton saree, her head covered and Hindu *tika* on her forehead. When my turn came, I knelt in front of her and very gently she placed her two hands on my cheeks, bringing my face very close to hers. She gazed in my eyes silently, lovingly and tenderly. My heart melted, releasing tears of pure love, joy, and gratitude trickling down my cheeks, which she wiped ever so gently with her hands. Then she put her arms around me and hugged me with my head resting on her ample bosom. She released her arms around me and looked into my eyes—*ah!*—so tenderly, so softly, and then kissed me on my forehead. And just like that, my love fest was over. From there, I was led into a big room, where her devotees were singing *bahjans* (soulful songs of devotion) in Malayalam, which I don't understand, not even a word. On a big table were glossy black-and-white and a few color photos of Amma, dressed in silk goddess garb with a cardboard cutout of a crown covered in silver glitter on her head. There was another of Amma dressed as Krishna and dancing. All the commercial stuff was too kitschy for me. There was another table with pamphlets and literature showing the philanthropic and humanitarian efforts of Amma, who opened schools, orphanages, and hospitals for the poor in India.

By the time I got to my hotel the radiant glow of divine love had faded and it was time for a joint to reignite the divine connection. I had enjoyed the love experience, but WTF. It was so finite, so ephemeral! I had gotten up early, driven for several hours from Farmington. I stood in line and would be spending the night at a motel and would have to drive back home the next day. For what? "High investment, not much yield," said my personal economist! My friend in Taos was deeply smitten by Divine Mother and her Divine Love and had bought a photo of Amma for her altar. The soulful intimate contact that Amma made with me and a thousand others was undeniable! A couple of years later, in Maui, I would meet Amma's high-powered devotional fan club of chiropractors, doctors, and professionals who met every Sunday to groove on their Divine Mother and sing to her in a language they didn't understand. I was invited to a Sunday session by a chiropractor who used to refer patients to my clinic. I politely refused on the grounds that for several years, I had acknowledged the ocean to be my live temple. There I worshipped the vast formless energy, genderless and religionless, frolicking in front of me in myriad forms, always new, always fresh and spontaneous. I didn't exactly use those words but spoke in much simpler terms more in keeping with my professional image.

Upon reading the article, I was deeply shocked and unsettled to see Amma's dark side, violent, vicious, aggressively abusive, despotically demanding and entrenched in primitive fundamental Hinduism. Gail was Amma's first Western female devotee, when Amma was known mainly in her little fishing village in the South of India. Gail had escaped Amma's thrall after more than twenty years of serving her guru with one pointed devotion. During that time, Amma's brand had become an increasingly powerful global phenomenon. Gail, at the time of writing her book, was safely settled in Maui, Hawaii, and had received extensive psychological treatments. The purpose of her book, she says, is to complete her healing and to provide a realistic image of Amma to her guru-struck and guru-smitten devotees, who were eager to lay their minds, lives, and money at her divine feet.

I believed Gail's honesty and sincerity one hundred percent, since I, too, had been on the receiving end of angst and confusion with Osho. However, hers is top-of-the-line, five-star disillusionment. What to say of the heartbreaking devastation of her faith and devotion! I was overwhelmed with gratitude that she had the courage to expose Amma's shadow for the world to see and understand. I also believed the American family who accused Satya Sai Baba of being a pedophile. Both Westerners! No Hindu in the past had dared to do such an expose because of an extremely deep-seated belief in guru as god. I remembered singing devotional *bhajan* (songs) about guru being your mother, father, friend, and lover. The devotee asks only to sit at guru's lotus feet, wash his feet, and drink that water. Eew! Too yucky!

Okay, I'm being silly and playful. What's being pointed out is the absolute surrender of the devotee to the guru, who is supposedly one with god or existence. Whatever comes her way, a devotee lovingly accepts it as will of Amma, or god. That was the powerful belief that had bonded Gail and other devotees to Amma. To look at your guru with a critical eye and judge her is to sign up for hell, not only in this lifetime but in all the future lives. Your life is cursed and doomed for eternity. Gail, too, believed in these everlasting threats. She gathered the courage to move forward after realizing that a couple of devotees who had defected were fine and nothing untoward had happened to them. I was pleased to see the generous space *Times of India*, a notably conservative newspaper, had provided for a book that was not portraying the Hindu culture and religion in a favorable light. I was on Gail's side and eager to download her book at home since there was no WiFi in the waiting room.

P.S.

Modern India's ancient intractable belief in omnipotence of authority, divine and secular, as well as patriarchy, is slowly crumbling. A couple of beloved gurus have been imprisoned because of charges of sexual assault of young females.

Chapter 31

Two Faces of the Divine

There's no greater failure in the history of mankind than the spiritual quest, the search for truth, and yet everyone continues just as everyone always has, using the same maps and directions.

—Jed McKenna, *Notebook*

A T HOME, I IMMEDIATELY DOWNLOADED Gail's book, *Holy Hell*, feeling grateful for the positive aspects of modern technology. My head was swirling with images of Amma all tender-hearted in public, now known globally as a "hugging saint," slapping and smacking her female devotees. Maybe I should call them selfless slaves, cooking her fastidious Indian meals, painstakingly ironing six yards of her cotton sarees for hours with loving perfection, feeding her by hand, and massaging her legs. Their sins of omission included being late with her meals, being late in running an errand for her, not having her room ready when she wanted it, and so on. The ancient belief in India is that it's a sacred privilege, great, good luck, to be slapped or beaten by your guru, the divine one. As a devotee, you should receive the physical abuse as a gift and use it as a ladder toward god and freedom.

I started to see Amma as Janus-faced, a victim of Jekyll-and-Hyde syndrome. Unconditionally loving publicly and mean, wrathful and childish privately. For the first time, I began to scrutinize the concept of enlightenment, which casts off the identification with the body, mind, and persona as *not me* because of their constantly changing and shifting nature. What is left is immovable, unchanging, and indescribable pure consciousness, without distinctions. If I would abide one pointedly, in pure consciousness, all the flaws and foibles of my persona and body-mind would spontaneously resolve themselves. There is no such thing as progress, improvement, or learning in the non-conceptual world of enlightenment, which is changeless and already perfect. Ego is a ghost, a shadow, impossible to improve.

I saw Amma's persona as deeply dyed in orthodox Hindu culture, which she had swallowed unquestioningly, and she demanded the same of her devotees. On the very top of Hindu pantheon sits Lord Shiva and his lingam, or penis, the big dick energy of rigid Hindu patriarchy. Amma, like a devout Hindu, worships penis power. Gail writes that she dotes, pampers, and schmoozes her male devotees, calling them "my sons" while publicly insulting and privately abusing her female devotees, her selfless slaves. Gail, after years of service, was still living in "a wee spot" "amid shelves of steel dishes, pots and pans," while men had "stylish pads" and one with an expensively carved teak door. Gail writes in the book that she had to beg for milk for girls when they were sick. Once, Amma, seething with anger, grabbed Gail by her throat, dug her nails in, scraping her skin. Gail would hide the bloody scratch marks with her saree. According to her, Amma never ever touched or criticized her male devotees.

An orthodox Hindu is conditioned to hate the body as evil and dirty, especially the female body, because of monthly menstruation, the most evil and impure thing in god's sacred world. The gods and enlightened ones don't sweat, or their sweat doesn't smell offensive like that of the mortal creatures. The goddesses don't suffer from humiliation and ignominy of monthly periods. A myth was in circulation at the ashram that Amma doesn't get her periods and "she's ever pure." During that time of the month for Amma, Gail's job was to shadow her as soon as she stood up from her chair. Occasionally, her clothes would be soiled, but no one besides Gail noticed. And Gail wasn't going to tell the world, as that would weaken and shake their faith in Amma. Gail believed with all her heart that Amma was god herself and faith was a virtue, to be cultivated and nursed. Once, Amma had abdominal pains when she was in the West. When the gynecologist asked her when she had her period last, the attendant with her told the doctor she didn't get her periods. The confused doctor looked at Amma, who then told him the time of her last period.

Back to the humble and squalid beginnings of Amma and her disciple in the smelly little fishing village. No running water, sanitation worse than gross! Like the locals, Gail had to clean her butt with her left hand, sleep on the floor, and eat with her right hand. Gail writes, "All I wanted in life was to know god. I believed through devotion and surrender as Amma's personal attendant I could achieve such a goal." Meanwhile, when Gail got her period, she had to move in with a neighbor who had a separate hut for the menstruating females of their family. Until she was pure, she absolutely couldn't stay in Amma's house because there was a temple in the house. These imaginary defilements and impurities are at the heart of Hindu religion. The human body, an absolute wondrous miracle of nature, is secretly despised. If only it didn't have to poop, pee, sweat, demand filthy sex with its gooey smelly fluids, and worst of all is the female body, which bleeds once a month. If only babies arrived resting peacefully in the middle of giant lotus flowers!

I, too, was raised in a life-denying Hindu household, and my mother, minus the "magnanimous hugs" of Amma, was a gentler version of her. There seems to be a mold for creating a perfect Hindu woman, and my mom was a perfect fit, along with my younger sister. Try as she might, my mom succeeded only partially with me. As Gail was chided by Amma not to talk so loud, not to laugh and giggle loudly, and not to run, so was I, and I was told it was for my own good and protection. When Amma catches Gail laughing, she scolds her, "Women shouldn't be heard laughing like that. There are men in the next room and they might take it for sexual flirtation." And they would because they are unimaginably sexually repressed.

Chapter 32

Sister Love

There was plenty of time, hours and hours of it, and the
thing that was to happen would happen — there was
no hurrying it.

—Mark Twain

IN THE ICU, MY SISTER looked worse, though there had been no
victory for death in the two days I had been immersed in the cosmic
Amma scandal. Her limbs seemed to be more swollen than before. I
hadn't realized dying was such hard work, perhaps as hard or maybe
harder in some cases than being birthed. I shouldn't have been surprised.
My own ego, despite my best efforts, was dying at snail's pace. For a
couple of years, I had been doing nothing but cutting chunks of my
ego, chewing and digesting them by writing. But more seem to grow
like tumors out of nothing. No wonder some masters have called ego
the cancer of the soul. My soul, clinging to the egoic cancer for its life
and identity, is in no way different from the clinging inhabitants of this
mini kingdom of death.

A couple of days later, I was at home nursing a cold while my
brother-in-law was covering my shift. Late afternoon, I received a call
from him informing me that the lead physician, my sister's favorite, was
away on a medical convention. There was a new doctor, very concerned
about her erratic heart rate. This was a new development since morning,
and he wanted his signature for new medication and procedure. My
brother-in-law wanted to know what he should do. I asked him if she

looked uncomfortable and in pain. His reply was no. I advised him to tell the doctor that we didn't want any further intervention and I was coming over right away. I was grateful that the hospital was following our no-resuscitation order.

My sister looked the same, still unconscious, although her cardiac monitor was going wild. I tried talking to her, whispered in her ear, kissed her forehead, screamed at her. No response. Her best friend had come to visit, and they were willing to allow two people to stay but not three. So my brother-in-law volunteered to stay in the waiting room. I had my one eye on my sister and the other eye on her cardiac monitor and my ears reluctantly available to her friend's chatter. She was talking about their enduring friendship and how she always helped her pack her suitcases for her trips abroad. Her cardiac monitor continued to beep wildly, in keeping with her abnormal heart rhythms. And then a flat-line, continuous beep, which brought her nurses running to her bedside. In a flash, in a nanosecond, it was all over. The intense bitter struggle of more than two months ended faster than the blink of an eye. She was gone, gone beyond. I ran to call my brother-in-law, who got only a couple of seconds with her because the nursing staff needed to do their procedures. My brother-in-law I and her friend hugged each other and cried and hugged some more.

I was silently congratulating my sister for managing to free herself from layers of imprisonment, the final layer of imprisonment being that of her devoted doctor and the netted jumble of ICU tubes, wires, and pipes. I was silently celebrating her as a champion and kissing and hugging her in my mind, wishing her good luck going forward and upward. We were thanking each other for sister roles, well played and fulfilled. My brother-in-law handed me a list of people to be notified of her death. I fully realized then that death was for the living, who had to make myriad arrangements on behalf of the departed and freed.

First on the list was her lead doctor, and I had a sneaky suspicion my sister was able to exit due to his absence. I thanked him from my heart for his impeccable care and compassion. He was silent for the longest time and then thanked me for personally calling and informing him. My brother-in-law was busy receiving advice and making arrangements for the funeral services with the help of proper orthodox Hindu relatives.

I was feeling so effervescent inside that I was having fantasies of celebrating freedom of her soul with French champagne at Sea Lounge in the five-star Taj Hotel. I wasn't going to do that or even share my fantasy with anyone for fear of being condemned as cruel and shameless.

Her cremation was the next day, when relatives were going to pour in from all over Mumbai. I had a calming talk with myself to comply and cooperate with long and detailed rituals of death ceremony, so typical of Hinduism. Our wedding celebrations last a minimum of one week. The death rituals are equally long and fantastic.

When I woke up in the morning my brother-in-law had already left for the hospital to bring home her body for the last rites and rituals. On that day, Mumbai, the Maximum City, was totally out of kilter due to a marathon race and a funeral of a religious Muslim leader. The main roads were blocked off, and the side streets were jammed with unmoving traffic. My brother-in-law called to say that since he was in the ambulance, he had been allowed to go, but most people wouldn't be able to get through for several hours. At home, the phone was ringing constantly from people stuck in traffic. Luckily, the priest and some relatives lived in the same town and showed up at the appointed time.

Sitting on the floor beside my sister's corpse, looking at her grayish pale death face, undecorated and peaceful, I remembered how fiercely organized and time centric she used to be. On her final day, the final few hours of her dead body on earth, there's maximum chaos and commotion in the Maximum City. Everyone was disturbed to some degree or the other, but my sister looked unconditionally undisturbed. Absolutely unperturbed! Isn't that how Truth, or Brahman, is described in the scriptures? Are Truth, Brahman, or death the same then? To experience Truth or Brahman, death of the ego is a necessary requirement. Yes, her story, her time centric personhood had died, but her essence, immortal, and unconditionally unfazed is what I was sensing. Truth, which I had been seeking with laser-like focus, at that moment seemed creepy, and I felt justified in shunning it as a deadly disease.

Just then, a childhood friend of my sister, who was in Mumbai from America, called to say she had been stuck in traffic for a couple of hours and wanted to know the address of the crematorium. She was determined to say farewell to her friend and asked if I could meet her there. I agreed, as I was having a sparkling idea à la Jed to take a small container of her ashes to the US and have them transformed into a diamond as a gift from me to her son's family in the US, since they couldn't be present due to immigration issues. I slipped a medium-size steel container in my bag.

At the crematorium more ceremony and chanting. Her friend arrived with a garland for her, meditated, and prayed, and then her body was slipped into a dome-shaped oven. I walked up to the chief attendant and explained my needs and he said it'll be done. I told her husband that I was taking her ashes to the US for their son for a mini ceremony of closure for them. The orthodox members jumped on me and said not to bring ashes home as it was bad luck. I was okay picking up the container on my way to the airport.

Chapter 33

Them Bones

The forest of delusion is treed with concepts, and all concepts amount to the same thing—you're still in the forest.

—Jed McKenna, *Spiritual Enlightenment: The Damnedest Thing*

I'M FLYING HOME BUSINESS CLASS, enjoying champagne and gourmet appetizers with great gusto, which I couldn't enjoy during the arrival part of my journey due to waves of anxiety and worry. Now I felt so relieved, light, and free that I could have flown on my own power. I am feeling enormously grateful to life. It had put obstacles in my way, one after another when I was desperate to sell my physical therapy practice after reading Jed's two books on enlightenment. I was fully fired up by his description of his own first step in *Spiritually Incorrect Enlightenment*: "(I) set fire to my life and went to war." I know of few other enlightened men who dropped whatever they were doing to answer the call of the spirit. I had tried to imitate their muscular moves, but life blocked me like an insurmountable wall. Now it was pampering me for obeying its unique design for my life. When presented with a feast, enjoy; that's all that is required, and I'm good at it. I swallow champagne slowly with awareness, as if it were liquid gold, feeling astonishing delight in my mouth and throat. I silently toast to my sister for the good times and many sweet, shared memories. The creamy goat cheese with compote tastes heavenly on my tongue. I am drooling with delight, imagining my encounter with the rolled joint when I am finally all the way home in Mexico. Amazingly, I hadn't even thought of it until now. I played my character, my persona, my roles, with total immersion, accepting and living both positive and negative aspects. Since the layers of the personhood were relaxing, I could perceive the stark contrast between "person" and "no-person." Person, composed of thoughts and concepts, comes into existence in response to *The Other* and the world, which is also composed of the mind stuff. No person is no-mind, devoid of thoughts, and in my mind no person is connected to meditation and cannabis. I cherish cannabis because it lets me go away from it, this time for three months and in the past a maximum of two years, without desperate yearnings or toxic side effects. Is this a denial of my addiction? Isn't it a good time to kick the habit since my body had cleansed itself completely of cannabis?

Is this my ego speaking? ever eager to do, to cleanse, sacrifice, suffer, discipline and punish herself seemingly for the sake of spirit but in reality to maintain control over my life. My body, used to moving and stretching, had been sedentary, with just the necessary amount of standing and walking. It hadn't complained. The future, replete with play, free and structureless in my ultra-spacious apartment in Mexico, was warmly welcoming me.

But before that, I'd have a brief visit with my distraught nephew and his family in Virginia Beach. He had shaved his head, that being the Hindu custom required of a son. After sharing the various details that he wanted to know about his mom's death, I brought up my suggestion to immortalize her in a diamond, since she was so fond of diamonds and "pretty lies." The latter part, unspoken, was only for me. The entire family was speechlessly stunned. They hadn't heard about anything like that from their wealthy Indian or American friends. Where and how had I learned of this process?

I replied in a shaky, tentative voice, "From a spiritual book." I could see visible confusion on their faces—a spiritual book talking about transforming human ashes into a diamond! They seemed sure it wasn't a Hindu spiritual book. *So what spiritual book is this?* was their next question. An American spiritual book written by an enlightened American master. No one was impressed, not even the youngest member of the family, born in America. After reading more on the internet and consulting with his wife, my nephew agreed.

Next day, they had scheduled a mini ceremony at Chesapeake Bay, which would be attended by family members living in Virginia Beach. Our plan was to take out a little bit of ashes for the ceremony and mail the rest to the lab we had chosen. We three adults got together and opened the box while one of them was chanting Gayatri mantra. The box was filled mainly with bone shards, with very little ash. They both looked at me in dismay and confusion, and I looked back at them in horror and utter confusion. The crematorium manager had nodded profusely, Indian style, but hadn't understood me. I declared that I was going to drown myself in the Chesapeake Bay, holding the steel can of her remains after all the meaningless commotion I had caused in Mumbai and here. My nephew and his wife both hugged me and said, "*Maasi* (aunt), it's not meant to be." I wasn't going to argue with that.

Chapter 34

A Sacrifice

"(Disciple) Are there ways for gauging one's spiritual strength?"

"(Master) Many."

"Give us one."

"Find out how often you become disturbed in the course of a single day."

—Anthony de Mello, *One-Minute Wisdom*

HOME, SWEET HOME, WITH NOBODY to welcome me except my joint and my few plants, my silent and organic friends. I renewed my bond with my sun-drenched and sublimely silent apartment, where the phone and doorbell seldom rang. The street I live on is a dead-end street, very quiet, with occasional noisy gasoline and delivery vehicles. The neighbors are blissfully non-partying and great at minding their own business. The name of the street is Calle de Mina, meaning mine street because of there being gold mines in the past. Nowadays, I think the most appropriate name would be Calle de Ermitano, the hermit street.

With the first few tokes of *moto* (Mexican slang for marijuana) on my open and airy terrace, I felt fully released and cleansed of remaining molecules and memories of the hell of heat and humidity, cacophony and chaos. And above all, a sea of people in Mumbai: the others, everywhere, confining, defining, and limiting me as they had done to themselves. My first breath was so deep and expansive, as if I had sucked the planet of its total supply of oxygen! My soul, bubbly and effervescent, did a few skippy-do flips inside. I decided to step up my smoking and meditation but go easy on writing and reading. Trial and error resulted in two and a half to three joints being the optimum per day. Any more than that irritated my throat and lungs and caused a disgusting surge in mucus.

As for meditation, sitting even in half lotus was no longer possible due to age-related arthritis, especially in my knees. Sitting in the chair for more than ten minutes made my upper back tight and achy. So I decided to meditate in the corpse position, frequently practiced post-Yoga as a cool down. I however, would be, lying on my back over the soft down quilt on my queen bed. That worked well for me since I was always well rested and so almost never drifted off into sleep. As my mind became quiet, presence would reveal itself more and more, and yet it provided no immunity against the intermittent violent attacks of my mind. For months, there would be deep peace, joy, and silence, although with the subtle, barely conscious, and perplexing sensation of "is this all there is?"

Eventually the discontent would explode into a shit storm of anxiety, anguish, and tears. Was I spiritually asleep? No. Was I awake? Maybe, but not fully? Was I enlightened? LOL! Although ego had lost much of its deadly hold, it was still in control of my soul. Long and luxurious vacations were officially allowed, but the leash was still in the hand of my jailer, my boss, my ego! The belief that something was wrong with me and with my journey had deep roots in my being. I was still seeking, still desperate!

At the Ajijic market, at a stall of used books in English, I came across a Jewish religious book that opened up on the page where Lord god is commanding Moses to sacrifice his one and only son, Joshua, the apple of his old eyes. I read those few sentences a couple of times but didn't feel like buying the book, as it seemed the message had been delivered. Moses's love for Joshua was the attachment that was hindering his union with god. What attachment was blocking me on this journey? I didn't have to look too hard. It had to be my attachment to cannabis. Classic egoic ruse! Perhaps I was terrified of full freedom! Is that what was being asked of me—to once again give up ganja for god? I needed to do something to calm my lately awakened deep insecurities.

I was reminded of an Osho story of a Sufi mystic Rabia. She was searching on the street under the lamppost. A passerby asked what she was searching and if he could help. She replied she had lost a needle. Pretty soon, there was a mini crowd looking for her needle. Eventually, one frustrated man asked where she had lost the needle. She replied in the house. The frustrated crowd asked in chorus why she was looking for it on the street. Gleefully she replied, "Because there's more light here." Moral of her story, she told the crowd, was that they were all searching for god outside because there is more light and more help, but he dwells within us. My distorted spiritual calculus demanded I sacrifice my bag of dope by giving it away. I hoped this time, recovery would stay for good.

What to do with all this time in my cave in Kailash, freed from most distractions of normal life? Weed took a good chunk of my day—rolling joints and smoking, pacing and playing, stretching and unwinding my body and then resting. I took up writing again and started to read what I had written before with the intention of shaping it into a book. I was aware my sacrifice was truly trivial and trite compared to the sacrifice of Moses. But this time, I felt very sour parting from my buddy cannabis.

More than two months passed with me walking regularly, swimming in my pool, writing and reading. I also continued with my corpse meditations. During this phase, I noticed that while resting in bed, my hand would automatically drift to the back of my head, just above my neck. It was as if I had discovered a new erogenous zone! It didn't feel like that, but the spot felt unexplainably magnetic!

Chapter 35

I Fall

God is at home, it's we who have gone out for a walk.

—Meister Eckhart

LATE ONE AFTERNOON, I WAS walking home from the hairdresser and was five to seven minutes away from home. In my town, Ajijic, I have to be very mindful while walking, as there are booby traps everywhere: potholes in the cobblestone roads, a sudden slope up or down, a sudden step or two. Most of the traps had become familiar over time, especially in my neighborhood. I was walking on the flat level pavement, and then came to a rise of about a foot and a half outside someone's black garage door. I slipped off of the foot and a half rise as I was about to place my other foot on it. I fell backward like a cement block and the back of my head, where I had been placing my hand frequently, was the first to make contact with the cement pavement. I lay on my back with my eyes closed, shocked and stupefied. My skull and my brain had received the most impact of the fall. My neck and low back were hurting already even though I hadn't moved a bit. Surprisingly, no human, not even a car or dog, passed by me on this moderately busy street. I wasn't sure whether I was alive or dead, fractured or intact. I opened my eyes and saw a sliver of blue sky between the roofs of two houses. Yes, I was alive and able to recognize the sky and the color blue. I slowly stood up and took a few steps. There was pain in my entire body, but I had no headache, a good sign. Perhaps no hemorrhaging of my brain, at least not yet. All the limbs seemed fine. I started walking home, and a memory bubbled up from years ago. English actress Natasha Richardson, wife of actor Liam Neeson, had fallen backward like me on a ski hill in the USA. She stood up fine, but several hours later, she died in the hospital of brain hemorrhage. Memory impeccable? Check. The specter of doom said, *She fell on snow and ice and perhaps had a ski hat, while you fell on merciless pavement on your hatless head. You're doomed, make no mistake!*

I was thrilled to recognize my home, and I was able to unlock doors and climb up the stairs. The pain in the neck and lower back was increasing, but no headache yet, a blessed sign. I wondered whether to call a cab and go to a clinic or self-monitor and follow my reliable strategy of icing and Ibuprofen. I chose the latter for the time being. Here is when my indomitable inner bitch, after many months of absence and peace, resurrected herself. She rolled and stretched her bloody red tongue, goddess Kali style. Her fiery and ballsy monologue of complaints against existence, against god, went something like this: "WTF am I doing in this miserable town? I came here to find enlightenment and peace everlasting. Now it looks like death from silent bleeding, most probably when I go to sleep. Perhaps my last night on earth! Perhaps the last few hours of my brain functioning normally. What a relief that would be! I'll have my peace and rest at last. That's the great good luck scenario. But I don't feel lucky, not after that fatal fall. A fall that never should have happened! How well do I know the terrain? How many times have I successfully climbed that friggin cement rise? Almost every day for several years. The pain in my neck is getting worse. Feels like a grade-three whiplash injury."

She continued her diatribe, "Worst of all, I was present and alert, more than ever before, during the walk. I didn't even have my iPod on, which is a surprise. No one can blame me for walking mindlessly, singing and dancing to Bollywood tunes. For the sake of spirit I gave up my wonderful social life and the bright and blue beaches of Hawaii. Lately I have given up the magic of marijuana and this is my fucking reward: a brain possibly bleeding itself to death or paralyzing stroke with a drooling speechless mouth." She became frantic as an image of a middle-aged patient of mine, who had sustained a sudden cerebral hemorrhage while playing a card game of bridge, presented itself.

That was decades ago! Memory is super fine! The patient's right side was paralyzed, and her language center, located in the left brain, was totally wiped out. Besides grunts and groans, she could speak only one word, "god" and she used it mostly to express her inexorable frustration. Irritation was low level utterances of "god, god ... god." Frustration and rage, loud, aggressive, and rapid yelling of "god, god ... god." If she was in pain, piercing and agonizing screams of god ... god, god," which, as she tired, became "got, got ... got!" When she was happy, which was rare, she would be quiet and maybe even smile.

My robust bitch was terror-stricken by the specter of losing her speech, even though she seldom used it these days. Suddenly words felt sacred to her and language more or equally precious as the meditative silence. Did her unchecked zeal for the silence of being need an adjustment?

Then the image of her appeared as a dependent drooling moron lost in another, deeper explosion of rage. She screamed into the air, seemingly at god, "Is this your plan for me? Is this why you brought me to this god-forsaken place? After all the sacrifices I have made to see you, to know you, to be with you. That's all I have yearned and longed for. That's been my one and only desire for several years. This single desire for you has eaten up all my other desires. Do you even know how awful it is to have no desire and yet still be alive? You feel dead. No future. No excitement! No dreams! Nothing to look forward to! Why bother! You have no ears, certainly not for me."

Although weakened and exhausted, she still had more to say. "Do you know how weary and disgusted I feel with myself for having started this stupid spiritual journey to nowhere, with no signposts and no markers? Despite my ferocious struggle, you remain vague and foggy. So often, you don't even seem to exist. Yet, I know you alone exist. Too crazy-making for my battered brain! No wonder George Harrison of the Beatles soulfully complained, 'I really want to know you. I really want to see you, but it takes so long, my Lord.' No wonder you have such few real lovers. To me, you seem quite happy with throngs of fake and hypocrite followers. While I, who has stripped herself naked of everything, has been sitting neglected for years in the limbo. Undoubtedly unfit for the world of humans! But worthy only of receiving a bloody brain-crushing blow from you. Am I supposed to say thank you, please send me another?" Calculating, or should I say quid pro quo skills of my mind? Excellent, check.

Exhausted and mostly emptied, my inner bitch slumped in the chair and rearranged the ice packs. I shuddered at my bitch's shenanigans and her vile mouth. She had been allowed her full space with no judgement, criticisms, or repression. I had noticed anxiety at her frantic fieriness. If the fall didn't traumatize my brain, it seemed her free-flowing rage might. I had been simply present as silent awareness, an observer for the first time ever, and that's who I and everyone else really is. I felt deep gratitude for the purifying release of rage.

Feeling somewhat relaxed, I remembered seeing a joint that had been stuck in a crack behind a shelf a couple of weeks earlier. It had insisted on showing itself even though I had been looking for something else. I had let it be stuck there since I no longer had a relationship with it. God had spared Joshua even though Moses had been ready to slay his attachment. My translation: you too have passed your test! Go ahead and smoke the sacred joint that has been allowed to slip away and hide from you.

P.S.

Attention is separating itself from the mind although still easily seduced by thoughts. In the Advaita tradition, it's said that an enslaved mind will open the door to all and sundry (any and all thoughts) from a salesman of used carpets to one selling used underwear. Translation: the mind is deeply habituated to getting mixed up with useless and unnecessary thoughts.

Chapter 36

I Chill!

Smoking helped put me in touch with the realm of the senses.

—Hugh Hefner, magazine publisher, *Playboy*

IT'S TWILIGHT AND PLEASANT IN my lovely terrace, where I haven't spent much time since my recovery phase. Deep breaths feel silky and expansive. Cool, fresh air mingled with fragrances of flowers with a bottom note of organic spicy aroma greeted my nose. I need to be fully present and thoughtless in order to delight and revel in these subtle heavenly fragrances, which, in the past, I have poetized as coming from transcendental gardens of god. Such is my state now. The silence of pure consciousness is breathing me, smoking and pacing. Very gently, I start to massage my scalp, neck, and shoulders. The back of my head feels very tender, but I continue working on it, making slow small circles. Within an hour, the pain has decreased by 20 to 30 percent, with much improvement in mobility. The specter of doom has vanished. I see neither death nor crippling stroke tonight or in my immediate future. I'm amused by the gut-wrenching drama created by life. My psychological mind had weakened significantly. The memory, deal-making abilities, and deductive-reasoning skills of my mind fortunately are still in robust shape.

So far I had been at war with my ego, but now I am appreciating its survival value. When I had started my spiritual journey I was pure unconscious ego, chattering ceaselessly like a child with unacknowledged spirit in the background. Over time, the shift has been completing itself with spirit in the foreground and ego in the background, receding, showing up mostly on demand. Ego, in service of spirit rather than spirit serving the ego, ubiquitous paradigm.

The book *My Stroke of Insight* came to mind. The author, Jill Bolte Taylor, PhD, thirty-seven years old, lost her personal self, her ego, totally and completely in the space of a few hours. She sustained massive hemorrhaging in her left hemisphere, caused by the congenital malfunction of blood vessels in her brain. She's a brain scientist and taught brain anatomy to Harvard medical students. In the book, she writes that she had a front row seat to witness the meltdown of her acquired and accidental ego self. Talk about a sudden, total, and unwanted death of the ego! She is stripped naked of all that's accidental and learned. At first, she could not read, write, speak, remember who she was, walk, or even recognize her mother. Because her language center is drowning in a pool of blood, the ceaseless chatter in her brain comes to a sharp halt. She finds herself in the abyss of no-mind, of infinite silence and effortless peace, uncreated by her and always here. With ego, her separate self, offline, she experiences her essential oneness with the universe. She exults in the insight that she doesn't have life but rather states, "I am life." Having clearly seen the distinction between her essential and accidental self, she writes, "I wondered how I could have spent so many years in this body, in this form of life and never really understood that I was just visiting here." What has blocked her understanding is her ego, which covers existence with the network of concepts and words. She is having her first taste of pure existence, of peace that passeth understanding.

Pre-stroke Jill was a hardcore scientist, and following her stroke, she is transformed into a natural mystic. She sees her personal self, which she has lost and which we all are so terrified of losing, as a product of her "neurological circuitry," a figment of her imagination. Some of the default attitudes of the personal self, which resides in the left hemisphere of the brain, are anger, greed, jealousy, fear, possessiveness, loneliness, and hunger for approval. Freed from all that, she finds herself soaking in unconditional love, joy, fearlessness, oneness, innocence, and compassion of her essential self. Jill, as a scientist, is learned identity, ephemeral, which can be put on and off, like a role or a robe. Jill as a mystic is her essential self, unlearned, uncreated and unchanging.

She didn't practice compassion or learn unconditional love from holy books. Nor did she create peace with rigorous religious rituals or experience oneness with existence through meditation marathons. No, none of that. All that happened was a cerebrovascular accident that erased her accidental so-called personal self, thereby revealing her limitless essential self, unbound by American, Christian, female, anatomy professor, daughter, sister, or even victim-of-stroke identities. Since she can't talk, sit, or roll in bed unassisted, or even remember her past, she should have been miserable and wretched. On the contrary, she feels unconditionally happy and deeply peaceful, which she never experienced when she was identified with her small, separate self. It's the love and compassion she feels for the humanity lost in the convoluted complexities of the personhood that inspired her to have brain surgery. She is eager to share with suffering humanity the simplicity of peace and freedom she gained from suffering. Her mantra is "step to the right," in other words, step into the consciousness of the right hemisphere, which is nonverbal and supremely silent.

After her surgery, it took her about eight years to resurrect her personal self and regain the knowledge she had accumulated prior to her stroke. When I saw her TED talk, I found her awesome enthusiasm and excitement to be contagious. She seemed to be dancing gracefully on the stage while reverentially handling a dissected human brain and spinal cord. That year, *Time* magazine anointed her as a global influencer. She is an icon of the victory of humanity over seemingly interminable suffering.

Chapter 37

Decoding of LSD and the Weed World

I have found that often the last thing a really dominating left hemisphere wants is to share its limited cranial space with an open- minded right counterpart.

—Jill Bolte Taylor, PhD, *My Stroke of Insight*

JILL BOLTE'S BOOK HAS BEEN helpful to me after my brutal fall, in accepting the utilitarian value of my ego. I had declared an all-out war on ego as an evil, dark, and destructive dictator, as is the case in most spiritual circles I was aware of. They are not wrong. Ego, especially our "modern" ego, has usurped unimaginable power from existence, resulting in a severe imbalance between the two hemispheres of the brain. The ego lives in the outgoing left hemisphere, filled with conceptual details that help us navigate the external world. It has wrongfully anointed utilitarian science as the savior of humanity. The right hemisphere is an inward movement of consciousness, a treasure house of soul values as well as art, poetry, music, dance, and creativity.

Jill Bolte's amazingly clear portrayal of the right brain has helped me understand not only the cause of my addiction, but also some of my LSD experiences. Looking through this new lens, I see my personal consciousness — my attention — as hyper-addicted to the ego center it has created for survival. It is very ambitious, determined to succeed in the world at all costs and be somebody—preferably somebody rich, famous, and powerful. Gratitude is a hollow word to my persona, with no real emotion behind it.

As an ego, I lived in the past and future like everyone else. I had never even heard of the here and now. I was walking dead, frequently wishing I were really dead. My guess is that my family and most of the world are rooted in the extreme dominance of the left hemisphere. My sibling, who succeeded in his suicide mission, was a brilliant scientist. I have noticed that an ego in tight control of the character would rather kill itself than relinquish its crummy control. Most people, including me, tend to be rather light on authentic gratitude, contentment, compassion, inner joy, wonder, and the optimism of the right brain. I truly can't see any one of us waking up in the morning ruled by one, even just one, attribute of the right brain such as peace, joy, or oneness running in their neural circuitry wanting to shoot himself or other human beings. My own depression, intense self-loathing, and death wish were due to my unswerving devotion to my thoughts. I never doubted my mind, even though I should have. My healing is not due to practicing compassion, peace, or even the attitude of gratitude, but rather to understanding and thus disempowering my ego by not giving it its daily food, which is my attention. In Jill's and my case, it's disengagement from the language center that has resulted in boundless peace, sublime silence, and unconditional joy, which have nothing to do with the others or the world.

My guess is that if Jill hadn't had her stroke, she would have proudly continued being a scientist, separate and isolated, obsessively committed to doing a lot of stuff at a crazy frantic pace. This modern, left brain tendency is universally accepted and lauded. It was only when Jill was virtually forced to surrender to her stroke, when she writes that she "learned the meaning of simply being." Meditation and being were revealed to me clearly and effectively for the first time on LSD. It seems to push the ego chemically aside thus freeing the attention and shifting it to the right hemisphere but leaving the neurons and their connections intact. The mystics and yogis make this shift consciously and willingly with rigorous meditation practice over a period of time. With LSD, the shift is made in minutes, although in my case, it was always accompanied by physiological changes, such as a radical drop in body temperature and discomfort in my chest and stomach. There would also be a strong feel of death around my body, which would last between seven to ten minutes. After that, it was playtime for anywhere between six to eight hours. My left hemisphere knew nothing about play. It knows about games and sports, but they come with rules and regulations as well as the pain and joy of victory or loss.

Jill has experiences of oneness in which she sees all beings as "packets of energy" moving and flowing "en masse" in the ocean of one energy. I have had similar experiences on LSD. I distinctly recall a lot of physical discomfort prior to these experiences of oneness. In one such experience, the walls and floors of the room were breathing and flowing with energy and moving toward me, along with energetic patterns of the sofa and table lamps. I was consumed with terror that I was going to lose my identity and turn into a sofa or a coffee table. I saw thoughts as subtle patterns of energy, flowing in the emptiness of space.

The right hemisphere, she says, is the image maker. On LSD, a couple of times I experienced what later I would discover in a Tibetan Buddhism book as "jewel consciousness." Prepare to die with amazement! Playing with a kaleidoscope on LSD is a fantastic experience but nothing like the jewel consciousness from within, indescribably refined, luminous and electrifyingly dazzling. One after another, astonishingly aesthetic pieces of jewelry—meticulously crafted from diamonds, rubies, sapphires, and tourmalines—were displayed on the screen of my consciousness with my eyes closed. God as the ultimate jeweler! Was I being shown the divine private collection? What a privilege! The Tibetan book aptly called the experience "jewel consciousness." It didn't mention psychedelics but spoke a lot about meditation and chanting and had glossy and colorful pictures of lovely and lithe goddesses with flowing scarves and lovely jewels. My guess is that I had experienced in a couple of hours what these few yogis had spontaneously experienced only after endlessly diligent practices. The effect of the jewel consciousness in my brain was a cascade of sensations so sublime, so filled with delicacy and delight, that there seemed no name for them in our human kingdom—except maybe the generic term "bliss." My poetic description: a lotus garden of luminous colors had blossomed in my head, although temporarily.

Just like Jill Bolte, I frequently experienced effortless deep inner peace, joy, and bliss, uncaused and unrelated to the outer world. Later, I'd see them not as experiences that come and go but as my immovable essence. With the left hemisphere offline, Jill mentions amplification of sensory information—for her, especially hearing and smell. It's the same on acid. While peaking on acid, the ordinary sound of a toilet being flushed can sound like a wild waterfall capable of disintegrating my skull. Jill describes what kept me returning to acid and continues to be the love of my life: "[The right hemisphere of the brain] is kinesthetic, agile and loves my body's ability to move fluidly into the world." I call it meditative movements, or my personal yoga, initiated by stillness of my being. Another noteworthy experience of hers: "My soul was as big as the universe and frolicked with glee in the boundless sea." It's the signature of personal consciousness untethered from the dominance of the brain, floating upon the shoreless ocean of pure consciousness.

In my experience, there is one undivided and indivisible life energy, which is conscious of itself. It exists prior to and independent of the body- mind, its trillion or so cells and manifold programs. Existence, consciousness, and god are all names of this pure ocean of energy, the ground of our being.

P.S.

I consider jewel consciousness and many other sublime experiences on LSD or any other psychedelics, to be illusions in the category of rainbows—they seem to be, but they are not. They provide a brief spiritual uplift, just like rainbows. That's about it! However, the peace and oneness Jill talks about are our unchanging essence, who we really, *really* are. Content of consciousness, even sacred and sublime content, has no seduction for me. Cheap thrills and shiny toys are my last words on them.

Chapter 38

A Gut Punch

Nobody, as long as he moves about among the chaotic currents of life, is without trouble.

—Carl Jung

I CONTINUED WITH MY DAILY WALKS and swims as the injury to my neck and lower back from the fall was healing. Occasionally, I missed my spiritual friends from Maui and my BFF, the Pacific Ocean and its beach culture. If I paid no attention to these familiar thoughts of lack and loss, which were simply sensations inside me, they fizzled away. But every now and then, they would gang up and attack, energizing the victim in me, causing confusion and draining my energy. The human part of me infrequently expressed her grief over feeling extremely lonely, isolated, and friendless. My being was glorying in silence and more silence, aloneness, unlimited well-being, and freedom from the world. I begged the universe to send me a contemplative friend, just one, irrespective of gender, with an interest in the inner world. Its reply seemed to be not yet. From years of walking the same path at more or less the same time, some faces became familiar. Conversations were started, but they never went anywhere. I realized the chasm between them and me was unbridgeable and growing. They were fully immersed in the world, irrespective of age, while I was busy liberating myself from it.

Little more than a year after my first fall, during one of my daily walks, again I slipped and fell on gravel outside someone's garage. I was grateful that my legs were fine, but my left wrist started to swell immediately, a sign of possible fracture. It was diagnosed as a crack fracture, and my wrist was put in a removable splint. I couldn't tie my shoelaces, fasten my bra, or clean my right armpit with my painful left wrist. No walking or swimming but, luckily, no problem rolling joints. My gardener drove me in my car to shop for food and opened my bottles of wine for me. The availability of affordable manpower for old expats like me is a huge blessing in Mexico.

Since I hadn't walked or swum for three weeks, even though I was now fine, I no longer had the zest to continue. I forced myself to go for walks for the fear of deepening my isolation from the world. The walking habit I had cultivated since 2006, hardly missing a day after reading Jed's book *Spiritual Warfare*, evaporated into nothingness, just like that, much to my shock. Due to minimum mingling with the world, the content of my consciousness, too, had dwindled to almost nothing. There was pure consciousness living this life, mostly engaged in the existential activities of eating, sleeping, smoking, pacing, and playing.

I could have taken a trip to somewhere I hadn't been, as I had the money and time, but I had no desire, absolutely none. I was keenly focused on enlightenment, which I was beginning to see as consciousness without content, absolutely undisturbed and unreactive to any input coming from outside or inside. Even though I was living under a rock and my ego seemed to be dying right on schedule, it could still rise and assault me. But me, who? Who is afraid of the ego, since it had been seen and understood to be nonexistent? Frequently, there was no sense of even "I am." How, then, can a "nobody" be terrified of melting ice sculptures?

And then the event came.

My only friend, a former neighbor, wanted to go into our little town to see the newest version of the Ben-Hur movie and couldn't get her usual movie friends interested. I didn't want to go. Mainly because the theater where it was playing didn't like turning the house lights on before or after the movies. I, with my one functioning eye, found it impossible to navigate in the dark and would have to hold on to my friend's arm, but even then I felt unsafe. I had once walked up to the manager and requested, in my poor Spanish, that they turn on the lights. Instead, he brought his flashlight, and I had one of those myself, but he didn't turn the lights on. This time, my friend assured me that she would bring her very strong military grade flashlight and would hold on to me until seated.

After the movie ended, which neither of us enjoyed, we went for dinner. When time came to pay the bill, I realized my wallet was missing. I had the usual precious stuff—driver's license, bank card, and Mexican permanent resident card, along with some money. I stayed effortlessly nonreactive. I remembered how calm and undisturbed my favorite spiritual teacher, Byron Katie, had been when she had lost her handbag. My major anxiety was for my driver's license from the state of Hawaii. It had been issued a month or so before my one eye had been diagnosed as legally blind. Getting the rest of the cards seemed a manageable hassle, requiring mainly time, patience, and a high tolerance for boredom.

I called my attorney in Ajijic and asked him to apply for my new permanent resident card. I remained serene and peaceful inside. All the cards, including my driver's license from Hawaii, were in the mail and I had a fingerprint appointment at the immigration bureau. There were off-and-on buoyant sensations in my consciousness, which I interpreted as triumph over my reactiveness. The morning of my appointment, I quickly grabbed Osho's book *Only One Sky* to read during my wait at the immigration office. The book starts with an injunction to stay "loose and natural." The dissolving of personal self in universal self, Osho describes as a "total orgasm" with the universe. This took me to my own memory of total orgasm with the ocean in the south of India, recorded here in Chapter 13. My name was called as I was sitting, eyes closed, enjoying the most blissful experience of my life from the past. I stood up with the biggest grin on my face as I was led to a small office where my attorney's assistant was sitting with the immigration officer. I was told that the last time I had entered Mexico, it had been as a tourist, not as a permanent resident. Almost instantly, my happy and triumphant face, my memory of total orgasm with the universe, and Tibetan advice to stay loose and natural vanished in vapors. I'm by nature anal retentive and a lifetime of drugs hadn't tampered with the trait. I knew I had filled in my immigration forms correctly and had presented my permanent resident card where needed. It was clearly their fault, the government employees at the airport.

Meanwhile, my temper had risen from 0 to 600 degrees. I was told that to get a new card, I would have to leave the country, go to a Mexican consulate anywhere in the US, get the required documents, and re-enter Mexico. Then I would have to start a whole new procedure to get the card, which I knew was already in their friggin' computer. I also had a copy of the stolen card. No matter how much I raged and how aggressively I blamed the Mexican government, the immigration employee remained unmoved and undisturbed, like pure consciousness. No empathy, no sympathy, no polite "I'm sorry you have to go through this." However, she said I could sue the Mexican government. With fury on my face, I stood up and screamed, "You bet I'm going to." I told my attorney to start the process. He told me that lately there had been lots of cases like that. He thought the Mexicans were fighting back because Trump had verbally abused them by calling them rapists and criminals.

As I was driving home, still raging and fulminating, the very thought of suing — *Kamla Beaulieu v Government of Mexico* — cracked me up. Oldy moldy ant of a woman is suing a giant! It wasn't hard to hear the crushing and crunching of the oldy moldy ant of a woman. My attorney was pleased when I told him I had changed my mind. He informed me that besides costing me loads of dineros, I wouldn't be able to leave the country. At least not until my case was settled, which could be anywhere from a minimum of two years to who-knows-when.

Since life had handed me a lemon, how about a refreshing lemonade! No, a grande margarita, with salt on the glass rim! I started fantasizing about some real adventure. How about Belize, the second largest barrier reef after Australia. Instant soul buoyancy and bubbliness! I called a friend in California, who was willing to join me on my trip. I informed my attorney and asked him to prepare necessary paperwork. He was not at all supportive of my plan. I assured him there was a Mexican consulate there and that I had their address. But how familiar was the Mexican consulate in Belize in dealing with my particular problem? I suggested Ecuador, but he didn't relent. He was strongly in favor of Las Vegas. According to him, they, only, knew what they were doing. How about Sacramento? I would get to visit my friend, at least. No, he hadn't heard good reports about that consulate. His only advice was that sorting out the mess should be my pressing priority. After that I was free to go to Belize or Bermuda to play and have fun. As far as I was concerned, anything but Vegas. But Vegas it was.

Chapter 39

Surrender? What's That?

The saint knows that the spiritual path is a sublime chess game with god.

And that the beloved has made such a Fantastic Move.

—Hafez, *I Heard god Laughing: Poems of Hope and Joy*

DEFLATED AND RESIGNED, I STARTED to make my travel plans. Glitches and more glitches. Everything that could go wrong did go wrong, freely and abundantly, as projections of my dark attitude. The Mexican consulate in Las Vegas rejected the monthly statements of my income as insufficient, while my attorney had declared them to be more than adequate. The head honcho, a *señora*, screamed at me for having a dumb attorney. In a soft and humble tone, I told her how much my attorney respected her consulate for being knowledgeable and efficient. No luck. Proof of more financial assets was needed to qualify for resident status.

I went to the Wells Fargo bank to get copies of my financial assets, but they were experiencing glitches with their computer system. It took them quite some time to prepare the statements. I had arrived at the consulate before it opened at 8:30 a.m., and it was past 1:00 p.m. when I was handed the necessary paperwork, signed and stamped. I could only hope it was all in order.

Exhausted and dragging, I hailed a cab for the hotel. As soon as I was seated, the driver asked me with a mischievous smile on his face, "Would you like to hear some Bollywood music?"

Disoriented and shocked, I leaned forward and asked, "Excuse me?"

And then he, a young white American male, clicked a button. There was Sonu Nagam, singing his most popular and my very favorite song about living life totally, since tomorrow is so uncertain, and life is such a fleeting show. How true! There I was, smiling radiantly, swaying and singing with the music. I was thrilled that our once upon a time humongous world had transformed itself into a global village. I had once hailed a cab in California named Swami Taxi Company. That the universe was playing all the time, whether I notice it or not, became a certainty. Yes, I had lost in the game, but play is beyond winning and losing, it is pure fun and enjoyment.

Sitting in the hotel bar with my mojito, I noticed a review of the entire month going on in my head. Make no mistake, my ego was dying, or was it still only pretending to die? It seemed to have more than the nine lives of a cat. My ego was still in combat mode with life and screaming inside, "This shouldn't be happening, not to me. I was only sitting at home and meditating. I didn't even want to go to the movie. I went out of love. Life is so fucking unfair!"

Surrender is frequently mentioned in the spiritual books, without which, I was aware, there's no hope of enlightenment, ever. Yet when rubber met the road, it was often all about my will be done. How could sweet, tiny old me be filled with so much heat, fight, and aggression? It had all been a useless drain of my precious life energy, exhausting and meaningless. In the past, I had complained how mysterious it was to figure out god's will. Now, I know what ever is, is absolutely the will of existence, standing naked and in plain sight.

I thought of the surrender story that had rattled me to the core from one of my favorite mystics, Michael Singer. The chapter heading "Acceptance, Acceptance and More Acceptance" from his book *The Surrender Experiment: My Journey into Life's Perfection* says it all. He had bought land in Gainesville, Florida, and had built himself a meditation hut. Every morning at 3:00 a.m., he was on his meditation cushion. Pretty soon, a woman named Sandy began walking on his property. Then she asked for his permission to meditate in open air on his property, which he gave her. Next, she asked if she could join him in his meditations. He had lots of mental resistance to the idea but said yes precisely because of the resistance and his spiritual experiment to surrender unconditionally to what is. Then she started bringing friends with her to his meditation hut. Even though I didn't know Sandy, I started disliking her and judged her as an opportunist. In my tribal Sindhi culture, we have a saying: If you give someone an inch, they will ask for a yard. Give them a yard, and pretty soon, they'll be asking for an acre. Sandy's behavior showed me that perhaps those worldly wise are right. However, the world and its wisdom were not what drove Michael.

Now, the cherry on the cake. Michael was away for a few days. When he returned to his property, he was perplexed to hear "the buzz of a circular saw" instead of the usual silence. Sandy, with the help of Michael's friend, was building a little house for herself on his property without even asking him. He writes, "Imagine what that voice in my head was saying." Oh, yes, I can imagine, as my voice in my head went berserk and ballistic and became even more reactive than Michael himself. My pet peeves against life are exploitation, injustice, and unfairness. Michael never used the word exploitation, but I couldn't let it go. In my worldly view, he was kind and generous and was clearly being exploited by this meditating woman. What did Michael do? He went home and meditated, which meant he calmly observed a storm of crazy thoughts generated "by the preference-driven mind." My "preference-driven mind" was screaming, *Not fair. I'm not even allowed to have a good preference, even a selfless preference, which is to meditate for self-realization.*

He writes, "If I had a choice between using this real-life situation to get my way or to free myself from being bound to my way, I would choose freedom every time." I had tears of joy for Michael's spiritual victory when he wrote, "So I went back up the hill, strapped on an apron, and helped them build Sandy's house." I must have repeated the last lines of Michael's full acceptance at least several times to myself to tenderize my own resistance. Even in my fantasy, even after a mojito, I couldn't get up graciously to join Michael's divine construction team. He was clearly choosing to give total value to what is, while I was still enamored with what isn't.

Chapter 40

A Gold Nugget

Thinker and thought don't even exist.
Oh! Mind how can you go on
Thinking so shamelessly!

—Avadhuta Gita

A COUPLE OF DECADES AGO, WHEN I was living in Maui, I signed up for a weekend group of holotropic breathwork with a couple of psychologists who had advertised it as psycho-spiritual exploration of LSD calibration. I was eager, as the concepts of self-exploration and experimentation had been the drivers of my psychic engine for several decades. During the start of the week, one of my family members was scheduled for gallbladder surgery. Everything had gone well, and she was supposed to be discharged on Saturday. On Friday morning, one of my brothers called to say she was in ICU due to a lung infection. I was shocked, as gallbladder surgery, being routine these days, wasn't supposed to go in the critical direction. I never pray, only complain, but this time, I did pray and asked for a dream about her prognosis. I had a mini two-frame dream. Frame one: I see a card table and recognize my dad's back. Frame two: he turns around and hands me a sealed envelope. End of dream.

I immediately woke up, sat upright, and started to cry. My translation of the dream: she's going to die. I didn't know what in the dream led me to this conclusion, perhaps the sealed letter, but there was an undeniably dreadful gut feeling. After I had finished bawling, I found myself becoming irritated with my dad's unemotional and frigid behavior. Couldn't he have said something kind and loving to comfort me. He had been an absentee dad, and I sure had daddy issues. He had been dead for several years and was behaving even more distant and emotionally cold than he had been in real life. It took me some time to wake up fully and realize it was my dream and I was its sole producer, director, scriptwriter, audience, and now bitter critic. My dad had moved on, and I was the one clinging to my past, our past together, all of it nonexistent and dead.

I tried to get some sleep after the dream, but it was impossible.

It was Saturday, the day of my holotropic breath workshop. The drive through lush tropical jungles of Wailuku Valley to the therapist's home was mind-blowingly spectacular.

The two-story house had wraparound porches and lots of windows and glass doors, creating opulently lush optics. I liked the husband and wife team. The husband was very attractive and charming. We were a group of twenty and were paired into breather and sitter. I, as the breather, laid down with my blindfold. My partner was supposed to be present and available but not interrupt or guide my process. I started with my accelerated breathing, as was demonstrated. There was loud African music playing. Within ten minutes, I had shifted into a non-ordinary state of consciousness. Body continued to breathe, but my consciousness was at a high altitude, having a dialogue with the critically ill family member in ICU. Yes, she was dying, but she was at peace with it, even though she was not even sixty. She was tired of living, of the same old daily grind and dramas. She hadn't realized her weariness with life until her health had taken a sudden downward turn. She was locked up in an old-style toxic Hindu marriage from which only death could free her. Now that she had accidentally found herself at death's door, there was no turning back. We both thanked each other for the gift of love and intimacy. I dropped back into my body and continued to breathe and cry. This was no fantasy! I knew that such a communion had occurred between our souls, and I shared it with the group.

In the evening, the moment I reached home, the phone rang. I knew exactly what message I was going to hear. Unsurprisingly, I wasn't disappointed.

Part of doing my first holotropic workshop was one complimentary therapy session. My therapist was the charming male. I shared my daddy dream, which I'd had a few hours prior to my holotropic group. Toward the end of the session, he asked why an attractive and smart girl like me was floating around single and unattached in the world. I assured him it wasn't by choice. He had somebody in his mind for me, his therapy client. I was very excited and couldn't remember the last time I had been on a date. The guy called, and we planned to meet at a beach. He was an ex-Osho follower, like me, an immigrant with a heavy German accent. He used to be a physician in Germany. When he heard the call of Osho, he dropped his comfortable life and ran to India to be with him. Since he didn't wish to write his US medical board exam, he was working as a manager in an upscale shoe store. He was all over me, which I enjoyed very much. We went out one more time, and he suggested that we do a holotropic group as partners. What a lovely new age romantic idea. Oh, how thrilled I was! At last, love had chosen to bless me in this most lovely of all Hawaiian paradise.

When I entered the workshop hall, he was already there, deeply engrossed in a flirtatious conversation with a younger woman. When I walked up to him to say hello, he briefly acknowledged me but continued his conversation without even pausing for an introduction. He seemed to be silently shunning me, and I was at a loss for a reason. I felt very hurt. A few minutes later, he came over to tell me that he had changed his mind and had found himself a partner and I should do the same. I was deeply devastated and took his rejection to heart. When the group started, I tried to distract myself with all kinds of new age spiritual wisdom I had learned, which worked as long as I was the sitter. When my turn came to lie down and breathe, I was plunged into hell almost immediately. I'd had no clue there was so much unresolved emotional pain stored in my heart. All the anguish, insults, rejections, and betrayals I had suffered since childhood were all perfectly preserved. It wasn't tears but streams of hot water pouring down my eyes, soaking my blindfold. So many beliefs came bubbling up: the world is too cruel, everybody hurts me, all the people in my life have hurt me.

With great difficulty, I stood up with a dripping blindfold, a dripping nose, and a throat filled with mucus. I was led by my sitter to the bathroom. When I came out, I was still sobbing and heaving with pain. As a kid when I cried, I remembered my mother complaining that I cried so damn authentically and loudly, as if I were being dismembered alive—over absolutely nothing, according to her. More tears and sobbing over that memory. I didn't want to lie down and do more breathing, which I couldn't do anyway. I decided to lie on a bench in the terrace and see what happened. Both the therapists came to console and hug me, but I remained inconsolable. I continued crying as the repressed painful memories surfaced. I kept mumbling to myself that everyone I knew had hurt me—my entire family, my friends, lovers, teachers, and yes, most of all, god/life. Maybe there was one friend who hadn't hurt me yet, but she wasn't living on Maui, and it was just a matter of time when she too would turn against me.

The second part of holotropic breathwork had ended. We were required to express our experience of the session as a crayon painting, a Play-Doh sculpture, a poem, or a song. Since my torrent of emotions was showing no signs of abating, I decided to leave for home. I drove home through a curtain of tears pouring from my eyes. Eventually, I was done. My heart had emptied itself out of all the angst and suffering, at least for the evening.

Within a couple of days, I was immensely appreciative of my boyfriend of few weeks, whom I was no longer seeing, and of holotropic breathwork, for providing me with incisive insights into my psyche. With great shame and anguish, I admitted to myself that I had created an enormously painful tumor in my heart. I had been selectively focusing on the memories of the others and the world hurting innocent me, who had done nothing wrong to deserve emotional pain and suffering from them. A lie! At the time, I believed I had never ever hurt anybody's feelings. As a matter of fact, I believed that I went out of my way to not hurt people's feelings. Another lie! I realized I had engaged in the black magic Jesus had warned us against: amplifying the flaws and moles of others while being blind and hiding my own petty cruelties and transgressions from myself, never mind the others. Slowly, deeply buried memories started to surface, of how I had hurt people in my life with my words and deeds. I had slapped my younger sister when she was ten years old. Over what? I couldn't recall. I had said tons of mean and nasty things to my ex-husband during our marriage of fourteen years. I realized my twisted belief that "people hurt me" was the cause of my deep seated unconscious paranoia and much of my anxiety. I was constantly scanning the world for next put down, next painful shock, next scathing of my super-sensitive heart, under the cunning protection of my mind.

Some years later, when I would meet Byron Katie and the "The Work," I would dig still deeper into my untrue psychological belief that people hurt me for more balancing truths, which would eventually liberate me from my attachment to my sad, fake, and dysfunctional story. Many, many years later, in Mexico, I would be shown the early chapters of my sad psychic drama.

Chapter 41

A Real Acid Bath in Mexico

There is neither past nor future. There's only the present.
Yesterday was the present to you when you experienced
it, and tomorrow will also be the present when you
experience it. Therefore, experience takes place only in
the present, and beyond experience nothing exists.

—Ramana Maharishi

IT WAS RAINING AND THUNDERING. I woke up in the middle of the
night, my nose blocked, making it difficult to breathe. I took 200
mg of ibuprofen, a rather mild dose. In the morning, I woke up with
my nose fully open and functional. Around evening, my nose was again
in trouble. At bedtime, I took another 200 mg of ibuprofen for good
measure. I was awakened in the early morning by nausea and vomiting
and severe cramp-like pain in my solar plexus, right below my rib cage.
My entire body seemed to be suffused in acid, concentrated at solar
plexus. Was it acid reflux? No matter which way I turned, there was
acid nausea. I decided to walk around. More nausea, vomiting, and then
diarrhea. I wanted to drink water to prevent dehydration, but couldn't,
as it tasted awful and was aggravating my nausea. Somehow, through
it all, I knew not to panic and that it was somehow connected to my
psyche. I kept thinking to myself that Jed frequently mentions acid
baths in his *Enlightenment Trilogy* as being connected to nauseous and
extremely painful death of the ego. However, I was sure that he was
using acid baths as a metaphor, not a freaking reality.

I decided not to seek medical help but kept the emergency numbers handy. I looked up the Google Doctor and found valuable advice: take very small sips of water, enough to keep mucous membranes of mouth and tongue moist. Over time, according to the digital doctor, I'd be able to handle more water. It also suggested chicken soup and saltine crackers, oatmeal, and Pepto Bismol. I didn't have any of those at home. I managed to find a vendor who was willing to make the soup fresh and deliver it to me. Meanwhile I started the "sippy, sippy" game with the water. It took me about half an hour to consume 3 ounces of water, but at least it didn't aggravate my nausea. The "sippy, sippy" drinking of water cheered up my soul, and I was certain I was going to live.

When the freshly made chicken soup arrived, I opened the container with great excitement but nearly fainted from the concentrated smell of chicken, which aggravated my nausea. I hadn't realized that my sense of smell had become unnaturally acute due to my acid condition. There I sat, in a puddle of tears, old, wrinkled, and grey haired, crying for my mom and her comfort foods. My favorite, when sick as a child, was her rice gruel with mustard seeds and cardamoms, known in India as *khichdi*, with a tablespoon of plain yogurt. After a few minutes of airing the soup, I was able to slowly eat it. The big hit was the saltine crackers. I couldn't remember when I had last eaten them, since I wasn't fond of them at all. But on this day, their saltiness and doughy texture held the promise of life. For about a week, I couldn't drink coffee because the smell aggravated my condition. Suddenly, sippy cup, saltine crackers, and Pepto Bismol were my new best friends.

During this time, feeling very weak and bored I turned on the TV. It was only a few months before the 2016 election. Upon seeing Trump on the TV screen, my acid level and nausea took a leap. I had to shut the TV off and lie down. I was perplexed! A few hours later, feeling somewhat settled in my stomach, I turned the TV on again. This time, it was Hilary Clinton on the screen. She too aggravated my acid reflux but much, much less than Trump. Next day on the TV, I looked at Trump again, and my condition worsened notably. Then I noticed thoughts of anxiety such as *What's going on with me? Could this be cancer?* and *Am I getting better or worse?* would aggravate my nausea. I started to call them acid thoughts and acid people.

More than a week passed, but my nausea and vomiting continued, although less frequent and less intense. I decided I would seek medical help only if my condition worsened. A friend suggested fresh coconut water because of its rich electrolyte content. What a great idea! Not for my body! It fiercely rejected the fresh coconut water and started a new round of nausea and vomiting. One day, I was leaning over the sink, vomiting, and from the depths of my feeble being the following video was released: A baby, perhaps six or eight months old, was crying. Her family was distraught because they couldn't seem to sooth and calm her. I didn't see any faces of the family members, but the din of their loud, angry and frustrated voices was terrifying to the baby. She was crying to keep her tubes and pipes open, which were tightening and contracting due to invisible stress particles in the air. The little girl had no other survival tools except crying to keep her lungs from contracting and shutting down. A dark-looking woman in a white saree (perhaps baby's nanny) entered the room. She picked up the baby and rocked her, and the baby immediately stopped crying. Nanny took the baby outside. In the next scene, the nanny opened the door to her home with the quiet baby in her arms. The baby started to stir immediately with agitation. There was a frustrated and disappointed voice, perhaps of her mom, that they were back so soon. The baby started to bawl again.

Here, I was given a feel of the atmosphere in the baby's home, filled with invisible stress particles, much like fine particulate matter present in the air as pollutants. The baby's sensitive body was being choked by the invisible but felt stress particles in the air—finer than finest mist imaginable.

The end of the video. A question popped up: "What would you prefer, this painful and inconvenient psychic cleanse or an all-expense-paid trip for two to Sandals Resorts, anywhere in the world?"

WTF! OMG! You, too! Conducting these crazy, mindless surveys! Okay, I preferred the psychic cleanse now that I was emotionally mature. My previous trips to five-star resorts had been loads of fun but lacked any substance or significance. I remembered just seeing a commercial on TV for Sandals Resorts. Now life was using it on me to give me a clear read of my psychic status.

I was stunned by this video at this juncture in my life. I had done a lot of work on my childhood, such as inner child work by John Bradshaw, codependency workshops, and individual therapy sessions. I had not only forgiven my parents but deeply appreciated them for playing their roles so perfectly! They had been the super agents for my awakening journey. I was grateful for the concrete glimpses of my babyhood and the unforgivable feel of my early family atmosphere.

My prolonged, intermittent acid baths lasted for more than two months, forcing me to change my eating and drinking habits. I could no longer enjoy the bouquet and taste of red Chilean wine, which I used to buy in bulk. Dinner and lunch of the same veggie curry was no longer acceptable to my stomach. Life was demanding that I change my simple and ascetic ways.

I decided to visit Tuesday market, less than a ten-minute drive from my home, known for its offerings of wholesome organic gourmet cooked foods. My first stop was at a table manned by a tall and attractive looking Japanese duo. They offered me a sample of butter chicken curry. The fragrance of cardamom, which was not only part of my mom's comfort foods but also an integral part of her cuisine, created a Proustian moment from his book *Remembrance of Things Past*. The fragrance was warm, sexy, and celebrative, evoking the enigma of memory from the distant past. Eating the sample piece of chicken, generously flavored with cardamom, was an aphrodisiac delight for my still-weak body. No scenes from the past rose up on wings of smell and taste, as they had for Proust, "like the scenery of a theater." Even though the sample of butter chicken didn't reunite my soul with space-time remembrances, it nevertheless came home with me to disrupt my vegetarian lifestyle of several years. The meals at home became a celebration of the abundance of nature and the ethnic diversity of our little gourmet market. They included salads with grilled shrimps and cilantro dressing, falafels, Singapore-style noodles, Szechwan eggplant, tonkatsu chicken, and other yummy dishes.

Chapter 42

Eureka!

Most days my mind was as fidgety as a monkey tied up in a patch of biting ants.

—Gail Tredwell (a.k.a., Gayatri), *Holy Hell: A Memoir of Faith, Devotion, and Pure Madness*

BACK IN MEXICO, ONE EVENING as I was smoking a joint on my terrace, doing stretches and dance moves, my personal consciousness, temporarily freed from its all-consuming devotion to the survival of my personhood, was floating above my head, shooting for the sky. While my attention was engaged in its space explorations, I noticed a deep silence within me. When consciousness returned to my head, there were all kinds of judgements and assessments about her mini adventure. Then the consciousness left again, followed by vast effortless silence. I continued the experiment several times with the same results. Disengagement of the attention from the mind equals peace of mind or no-mind. If I wished to make the kettle of my mind whistle with all sorts of thoughts, then leave the attention in the head, plugged into its most favorite hangout. If I didn't want the rush of thoughts, unplug the kettle by bringing attention to my tummy, feet, or relax my eyes especially the third eye area. If I had some huge crazy mayhem going on in my head, I could dissolve it instantly if I wished by unplugging my attention from the head.

I jumped for joy with my newly found empowerment. Yeah! I had found the off-and-on switch to my mind. The picture of an oriental

Buddha sculpture from a Buddhist meditation album, with the tip of his nose broken, floated up in my consciousness. A baby monkey, soft, sweet, and surrendered, is nestling peacefully in the curve of Buddha's left shoulder. Buddha had successfully subdued the monkey mind. He had done that by sitting in his famous Buddha pose and focusing on his breathing, which has become the popular Buddhist meditation, Vipassana. I had tried that at Osho ashram and at several other spiritual events, but it never clicked for me due to physical issues. Lying flat on my back on my well-feathered bed and focusing my monkey mind on my breathing was clearly the path for lazy ol' me.

Around this time, the word, sucking, started to show up in my consciousness. An embarrassing word. Suck. But what! Then, one day, the whole sentence appeared: when sucking become the sucking. WTF! Even more embarrassing! A useful flash of memory. That line was from *The Book of Secrets*, commentaries by Osho on *Vigyan Bhairav Tantra*, ascribed to Lord Shiva. There are 114 techniques of enlightenment given by Shiva, in the most terse and telegraphic manner. The sutra on sucking simply said to be total in the act, which didn't make much sense to me at the time.

The technique of Vipassana meditation is mentioned, along with several other breathing techniques. My favorite quickly became the one where attention is brought down to rest in the belly button while breathing is going on all by itself. Occasionally, I would perform another technique, a lot more refined, in which attention rests in the tiniest gap before breathing in and another gap at the end of exhalation. I noticed that this technique kept my attention tightly engaged on the task. I could lie in corpse pose with my attention on my belly button easily for two hours and sometimes more. Every time thoughts showed up, I knew the attention had moved back to the head and just that observation would bring it down to the belly button area. It's a scientific fact that attention can't attend to two sensations at a time. In physical therapy, certain electrical equipment designed for pain relief is based on this principle.

My long corpse meditations were the ultimate game-changer for me. Pretending death gave long periods of silent stillness to my hyperactive attention, my exhausted brain, and my stressed body. It also dissolved a lot of unnecessary and dysfunctional patterns of thought due to lack of attention. Any time spent in pure emptiness was nourishment and tonic for my being. Not only was I making friends with my inner emptiness, but I was also enjoying resting in it. A salutary impact on my breathing was unexpected, as I had put no conscious effort in it. My lung capacity improved phenomenally. While witnessing my breath, I noticed the sexy magic of exhalation: very subtle and relaxed sensation below the belly button and in my sex center. Not a full-blown orgasm, just ultra refined sensations of pure delight, barely perceptible. Total stillness is a must for this experience.

One day, another question bubbled up: Between doping and corpsing, what would I choose? Was it a trick question designed to push me into recovery again? I protested that the question was unfair because doping for me is about relaxed activity/play: stretching, unwinding, playing with breath or air, such as singing or simply making spontaneous sounds, and ceaseless pacing. Doping is celebration of the dynamic aspect of life. Corpsing is about no activity except breathing, stillness of body, and silence of mind. To put it bluntly, it's a rehearsal for death. Death, I have learned, is unimaginably relaxing—so silent, so unperturbed! Doping equals life and movement. Corpsing equals deep stillness and unfathomable passivity. To choose between life and death! It can't be done, for they are two sides of a single coin. Can I choose the front of my body, the center of my worldly identity, over the back of my body, which I have never even properly seen? Still, to answer the playful part of me, my inclination is toward corpsing. It's certainly money and hassle free. But my main reasoning is that my attention is sinking deeper and deeper in the fathomless ocean of pure existence, of life eternal. Corpsing is somewhat similar to deep sleep, in which there's no mind but also no consciousness. In meditation, I'm fully alert, deeply relaxed and yet thoughtless. I see the silence and stillness of meditation as the master key for exploring existence.

Chapter 43

I Sing the Blues

There's no mistake in the universe. It's not possible to
have the concept of "mistake" unless you're comparing
what is with what isn't. Without the story in your mind,
it's all perfect. No mistake."

—Byron Katie, *A Thousand Names for Joy: Living in
Harmony with the Way Things Are*

TIME: 2016, PRIOR TO THE US presidential election. I'm watching
CNN's *GPS with Fareed Zakaria*. Sunday is my only two-hour sit-
down-and-watch-TV day while cleaning the bulk brown rice, shaping
my eyebrows, plucking my graying mustache hair, and trimming my
nose hair. It's a ritual that starts with *The Lead with Jake Tapper*. Now
I'm listening to my handsome desi (local, Mumbaikar) boy Fareed,
whose show my girlfriends say, and I agree, makes them feel very
intelligent. My one eye is on cleaning rice and the other on Fareed, but
both ears are available to listen to his talk. Enter his guest of the day, Bill
Maher, whom I don't know. Toward the end of the interview, Fareed
talks to Bill about his passion for marijuana and its legalization. Now
they have more than my eyes and ears. I adjust my glasses and look at
Bill. Fareed reminds Bill of his famous saying: "Say no to god and yes
to drugs." Oh, my god! I'm envious! Maybe that should have come from
my mouth! Maybe not.

I'm impressed. I now have a crush on Bill. Does he have more
sharp and cutting edge sound bites! It never occurred to my fossil

brain to check out his show on YouTube. Instead, I ran to Amazon and downloaded his book *The New New Rules: A Funny Look at How Everybody but Me Has Their Head up Their Ass*. Very witty, sharp, and current. Lots of laughs while my soul fretted about losing her focus and discipline with humor such as "god is a monkey" (true—Hindus have a monkey god, deeply revered. I once scored free dope in his temple), Colin Firth ejaculating Haagen-Dazs, or the photo of a blob fish that he wants to rename as the world's saddest vagina. One of his new rules that stuck in my memory is "There aren't 101 sex tips. In fact, ladies, there's only one—it's called a blow job. Do it 101 times." As the months wore on, I forgot all about Bill Maher's book and his tip to the ladies—blow job 101 times.

One morning, I was in deep meditation—perfect silence, in and out. Absolutely nothing moved inside. Gradually, I became aware of gentle vibrations in my jaw and in my head, which translated into thoughts: blow job 101 times, certainly not in one day, at one time. I'm sure not even a superhero can handle that, even if the giver of blow job was changed frequently. How much pleasure can a human nervous system tolerate all at once? Any research, fellas? Then the image of Ravana, from the ancient Hindu epic *Ramayana*, perhaps the world's first monster, with ten heads, and twenty arms but only two legs and one dick, showed up with his ten bright red tongues, eager for action.

This iteration of Ravana in his American incarnation was inspired by Nina Paley's 2008 animated film *Sita Sings the Blues*. I had seen the film at least a couple of years earlier. Especially interesting to me was the intermission scene, in which Ravana shows up carrying ten treats of popcorn and ten treats of Coke in his twenty hands, each busy feeding his ten mouths. In my meditative fantasy, Ravana, thus liberated by a female American artist, seductively shows up in front of hot and sexy Sita, the faithful and loyal wife of Rama, whom he had kidnapped. The very thought of ten tongues and twenty hands on my body had me trembling with delightful thrill, as well as the fear of being annihilated with pleasure. I was urging Sita in my fantasy to go ahead and give the monster a chance and liberate womankind forever from concepts of monogamy, faithfulness, and loyalty. After all, her husband, the hero of the epic, *Rama*, must have played the field while she was being all chaste and loyal. Let us not forget, Sita, your father-in-law had three legal wives and who-knows-how-many mistresses. Sita, epitome of a good and virtuous Hindu wife, clung to the concept of loyalty and kept chanting her husband's name, "Rama, Rama," to cool Ravana's monstrous passion. In my playbook and in Nina Paley's words, Sita blew up women's timeless "cry for equal treatment."

An increasing inner disturbance forced me to open my eyes. It dawned on me (*duh!*) that my attention had moved to my head and had been busy opening and closing the files of my sexcapades and desires. Who needs movies, TV, or porn when there is a free-flowing awareness in the house? I hadn't been alert, hadn't been conscious, for god-alone-knows-how long. Shame, guilt, and disappointment rose up, but I quickly disentangled my attention from them and let it sink into presence. Once again, peace all around, and I took a few very slow, deep, conscious breaths, which filled me up with gentle bliss. Before I realized it, my attention had once again flown back to the head and was deeply immersed in my old sexual files: How many blow jobs I had given and received, and which were the uncontested winners? Who were the great lovers, and who were the worst in my life? My inner world was spinning out of control! Goliath (my mind) had clubbed David (my personal awareness), leaving it lying unconscious in the bushes. Part of me had derived deep delight from a review of my old sexual files as well as other people's sexual histories. And the other part, the dedicated seeker of higher truths, was ashamed and deeply distressed at her unconscious fall from grace! End of meditation for today.

Consciousness knows deeply that it is not the thoughts, not the mind, that it is the witness of thoughts, just an observer of the movie, not the movie itself. Grudgingly, I admitted my consciousness was still obsessively enchanted and at the same time terrified of her own thoughts. What good is this knowing if the attention still gets identified with and lost in the movie? I reminded myself that sexual thoughts are like any other thoughts except, due to my repressed conditioning, I had given them a hell of a lot of meaning. Obviously, my consciousness had derived much pleasure and delight from not merely watching but getting lost in sexual memories and fantasies. Clearly, this entailed much more pleasure than resting in the ocean of awareness of inner joy and bliss. My holy-moly attitude was shattered by shame, especially after considering my age, which technically should have relieved my mind of all sexual pursuits. That's what even Osho, the "sex guru," had said. I couldn't recall reading or hearing about any other seekers being harassed by sexual thoughts this late in their pilgrimage. Here, I had been walking the earth as if I were already a Buddha, which not only I am but we all are. Had I thought I might even be grander since I had credited myself with rediscovering the off and on switch to my mind? But the switch didn't work this time. The monkey mind had won the moment and consciousness had lost, at least this round.

Chapter 44

Adore Me!

Nothing happens by accident in the divine scheme of things.

—Ramana Maharishi

I WAS AT YOSEMITE NATIONAL PARK Hotel with a Californian: my physical therapy colleague from the distant past. There was some misunderstanding about our bill, which my friend had already paid. We were standing in a queue at the reception desk. When our turn came, it seemed it would take some time to straighten up the mess. I told my friend I was going to the souvenir shop. Within a minute, I got bored with the trinkets and found myself walking to a far corner of the store. On the way, I was pulled like a magnet to a baby stroller. A plump, blond hair and startlingly blue-eyed baby was euphorically engaged in sucking his closed fist.

I said to myself, what a perfect display of Shiva's sutra, "when sucking, become the sucking." When our eyes met, we both lit up like two mini suns on some distant galaxy. He seemed to be saying silently while drooling delightfully, "Oh! How I adore myself! I taste so, soo, good! Here, have a taste of me, and let me taste you." He let go of his wet and dripping fist and vigorously started reaching for my fingers, my hair, anything he could grab and put in his mouth to taste the very essence of life. I teased and played with him by bringing my hand very close to his mouth, nearly brushing his mouth and chin lightly, and then withdrawing my hand. This would renew his determination, and he would reach for my hand with increased vigor and excitement. While playing, I would talk to him in a singsong tone, "My hands are too germy, you handsome little boy. I haven't washed them for hours. Oh, no you nearly got me! You are not allowed to win this battle of germs, because mine are different from yours. Sweet baby prince, there are some distinctions we need to observe, just for survival."

The little boy was exploding with pure ecstasy and joy, flailing his limbs, cooing and gurgling away. Not once did he cry or show disappointment at not getting his way, which was to taste my fingers or anything else he could get hold of. His parents, standing nearby, were distracted by their son's loud squeals of delight and ecstasy and came to join us. His mom picked him up, and I kissed the soles of his soft, plump, blemish-free feet, which he accepted as his royal privilege. His mom said he seldom cried. I looked into his aloha-blue eyes, shining and sparkling like two little mirrors.

"What baby school did you go to before birth? If I had to give a perfect baby award," I said gently, touching his third eye, "it would be you, you sweet thing!"

The kid crooned joyously in agreement. "Of course it's me, the most adorable one in the entire universe."

His parents were chuckling merrily. My friend, looking slightly hassled, joined the team of revelers and worshipers of life. I said goodbye to the little package of pure life and delight and wished him enjoyment while hiking on his young dad's back through the cathedral of gods in Yosemite National park.

In the car with my friend, we talked about the mistake in the hotel bill and how she had sorted it out. Meanwhile, I packed away the memory of sweet communion with pure life in the form of a baby boy, to be unpacked fully at home and savored as a rare delight under the influence of cannabis. I knew if I told my friend that life had gone to great lengths to arrange my meeting with the baby sage and teacher, who was going to demonstrate for me the Shiva sutra, "while sucking, become the sucking," she might have judged me a demented perv. In essence, I knew my lesson was not really about sucking but about living life totally, single-pointedly, at all times as only infants and children are able to do, before we, society, contaminate them.

My friend, entrenched in a Western scientific mindset, wasn't prone to looking towards India for any pearls of wisdom due to their dire poverty and squalor. My friend, being politically correct, didn't say anything like that openly to me. I sensed it when I suggested a simple meditation technique for her progressive dementia. She had been prescribed and was diligently practicing mind games and memory-boosting techniques on the computer. I didn't advise her to stop her mind games. I simply suggested resting her exhausted mind with meditation. I accepted my friend's silent criticism of my poverty-stricken culture as a gift to be opened and unpacked for possible reasons and solutions at a later date.

It reminded me of a Buddha story. A man had been shot in his foot by a poisoned arrow. First responders arrived to help. The man said, "Wait. Before you pull out the poisoned arrow, I want to know your caste, your nationality, your religion, and your zip code. Are you a doctor?"

Meanwhile, the poison is spreading into his body, pulling his death closer.

Chapter 45

A Spiritual Prostitute

Shiva is silence, and it takes deeper avenues of silence to reach the silence of Shiva.

—Editorial by Mohanji

L IVING UNDER THE ROCK IN Ajijic, mostly YouTube algorithms and sometimes TV have been acting as my guides. I was watching BBC India on June 21, 2015. I saw Indian PM Narendra Modi, smartly clad in a white tracksuit, with scarves the colors of the Indian flag, saffron and green, wrapped around his neck. He was opening and leading the first international yoga festival in New Delhi, India. It was a very brief clip. I wanted to scrutinize Modi's outfit and see how he managed the two scarves, or did he even wear them while performing yoga? So I visited YouTube, where, along with the yoga festival in Delhi, there was someone else who grabbed my attention. This was in Rishikesh, on the banks of the river Ganges, in the foothills of Himalayas. It was a black man clad in loose and comfortable Indian clothes. He had dreadlocks and a big red tikka (circle) on his forehead and was sitting in a chair with huge posters of the Yoga festival behind him. I was immediately hypnotized by his presence and clicked on his picture. I was treated to more than an hour of Advita Q and A *satsang* (gathering of truth-seekers). The speaker had an accent that I couldn't recognize, but it certainly wasn't Indian. Yet he looked perfectly at ease in Indian clothes and culture. His clarity, his simplicity, his visceral language, such as the smell of personhood or the ego molesting you, immediately endeared him to me. The spiritual journey, he said, was twofold: from person to presence and then from presence to pure consciousness, or universal consciousness. Then he posed the question: can the consciousness that observes your body and mind be witnessed? It was the ultimate freedom question that immediately led me to universal consciousness. Not that I wasn't familiar with universal consciousness, but the question acted as an on/off switch. I could play with it to my heart's content and unfailingly land in the universal consciousness, the ultimate observer. Wow! And wow again!

I found out the speaker's name is Mooji and he is of English nationality but originally from Jamaica. He is a devoted disciple of Papaji and Ramana Maharishi. In my excitement of my final freedom, I completely forgot about the PM Narendra Modi's twin scarves and yoga day celebration. I'm sure the PM didn't mind. Being a Hindu, he would be happy to hear that his fashion style had helped to send this vain and superficial woman to moksha (liberation). Since then, I have feasted for free on Mooji's YouTube videos. My all-time faves are his meditations on truth, or universal consciousness. I'm deeply intimate with personal consciousness and its friggin undying romance with the mind. Truth, being non-conceptual, is naturally said to be indescribable and ineffable. Mooji talks of attributeless truth in an honest, experiential manner while stripping it of its attributes: you're bodiless, weightless, and ageless. You're not only unconditionally undisturbed but absolutely undisturbable. You have no mother, father, friends, wife, or children. You're alone, forever alone. You're unconditional love and so forth. Repeated listenings to his meditations on Self or Truth were imperative. They helped my personal consciousness, master of flimflam, to rediscover the delight of resting in the absolute simplicity and innocence of impersonal consciousness.

Another teacher, Rupert Spira from the UK, was also brought to me by the YouTube algorithm. The understanding I received from him has to do with the physical body storing old impressions that unconsciously drive us, in spite of our deep understanding of our true nature. He helped defuse loads of frustration caused by failures of my attention to stay in pure consciousness, its home and where it belongs. Instead, my attention liked to smoothly slither away into dark and dreary recesses of my mind and get entangled with dead weight thoughts, those repeat offenders. Rupert's yoga meditations are about gently dissolving the contractions, tightness, and knots in the physical body by becoming aware and breathing. To show that we are already what we are seeking and that our essence is not even an inch apart from us, he asked the standing participants to take a step toward themselves. So absurd! How are you going to do that? On par with Zen koans like "Show me your original face, the face before you were born" or "What is the sound of one hand clapping?" There's no verbal answer to these existential puzzles. Head-scratchers and crazy-makers, they have the potential to free up the attention from the iron grip of the mind.

The physical presence of a guru, teacher, or guide is valued because it provides frequent reminders of our true nature, which keeps us alert and awake. For me, that need is provided by YouTube videos and audio recordings of spiritual teachers that I can repeat again and again as an aid to abiding in the universal consciousness. Ego, too, was painstakingly crafted by daily repetitions of mundane details. I'm deeply grateful to all the members of my personal holy club who are available to me 24/7 with a click or two of iPad, in the perfect comfort of my home.

I have personally benefited from, and perhaps the secret of my success is, my wandering guru eye, which brings me gurus and guides as needed at the time. Life has been my most reliable and consistent guru, leading me to drugs, then to Osho, and subsequently to other teachers. When life brought me, unasked, Jed's *Enlightenment Trilogy* in Maui, I offered the books to my dedicated seeker friends. Most of them shunned the books as if they were dipped in some deadly virus. They already had gurus and teachers to whom they seemed to have taken a silent oath of eternal loyalty. I felt like a spiritual prostitute in their chaste company. I was desperately looking for keys from anyone, anywhere, to open the existential doors behind which I was mercilessly struggling to breathe and keep afloat.

Traditionally in India, the disciples stay with their masters for ten or fifteen years or more and are committed to digging only in one spot until they find pure waters of life, which some do. To my credit, I have dug monomaniacally for Truth, but using different tools, sometimes Indian, sometimes English, sometimes American, and so forth. If I had stayed loyal to Osho, for example, and shunned Jed's books, or clung to my noble Maui tribe, I would have perhaps matured into a happy adult but certainly not fully liberated and awake from the dream. Jed's books gave me DIY exuberance and deposited me in Ajijic. They also helped me to become increasingly single pointed and freed my consciousness from ego through the writing. This book is the fruit of the seed which he planted in my mind.

Solitude, which I resisted and resented off and on, was the alchemical agent that peeled and dissolved my dense egoic layers like an onion, revealing the underlying no-thingness of pure being. Osho didn't approve of renunciation. Especially Hindu-style, in which you renounce the world not because you have had enough of it like Jed's First Step. But because it's believed to be a fast track to god. I was unconsciously and compulsively compelled to move forward through my massive resistance to leaving my helium-high lifestyle in Hawaii. It's all now seen as small potatoes compared to the awesome and incomparable fulfillment of having completed the ultimate existential game.

Chapter 46

The New Woman

The secret (of sex) is that it's a biological natural device to make you aware of meditation. It's through sexual orgasm meditation was discovered. Sex is a natural phenomenon—meditation is a discovery."

—Osho, *Sex matters: From Sex to Superconsciouness*

I WAKE UP IN THE MORNING, and the YouTube algorithm is gunning for sex lessons for me. Besides my usual spiritual videos and music, I discover two TED talks on female sexuality, the first one on clitoral awakening and another entitled "Orgasm: The Cure for Hunger in Western Woman." I save both the videos, to be watched in the evening while rolling joints.

The first video I clicked on was on orgasm and hunger. An attractive young woman on the stage introduces herself as Nicole Daedone. With some hesitation and nervousness, she introduces the most loaded topic on the planet—sex, and in particular, the female orgasm. Her website is called *One Taste*, after Buddha's description of truth like ocean water tasting the same everywhere, at all times. She has my full attention. Her technique is called "Orgasmic Meditation, or OM."

Holy music to my ears. OM, she says, is different from regular sex. She first had a taste of it at a party. A man, perhaps a Buddhist monk but most certainly a meditator, approached her. He offered to introduce her to a sexuality practice. She takes off her pants and lies down while he keeps his clothes on. Absolutely no quid pro quo. Very gently, he is going to stroke her clitoris for fifteen minutes, at the end of which, she is free to go. At this point, she assures the TED audience that she's a good woman. I'm convinced.

She takes off her pants and lies with her legs open in a butterfly position. He shines a light on her genitals and starts to describe what he sees. It's a standard Buddhist meditation of observation uncluttered by judgements or assessments. He shares his observations with her, such as her outer labia are coral and the inner labia have a red tone to them. Nicole says she was so touched by his loving, compassionate, and "clean" observation that she had tears in her eyes. Then, very, very gently, he started to stroke up and down the upper left quadrant of her clitoris. He stroked and stroked, and nothing happened. Her attention, as usual, stayed stuck in her head and was molesting her with usual female concerns. Maybe she didn't look good down there. Maybe she was smelly. Her thighs were too fat. The guy was too creepy and would she marry him and so on. And then, she says, "The traffic jam in my head broke. I was on an open road. Not a thought in sight." She further explains that all that was left was "pure sensation, pure feeling," uncontaminated by thoughts. Plus, she got in touch with her hunger, "a fundamental hunger for connection."

I was so excited that I gleefully shouted vive l'America, where freedom reigns supreme. Could this happen in India, even with holy syllable OM sitting atop? Not a fat chance! China, LOL! Forget the East! Europe? Possible, perhaps at a small scale. But in America, you're virtually on the world stage! I was enormously impressed by Nicole's courage and boldness. I branded her as the New Woman, tuned in, turned on, but not a dropout. She seems a savvy entrepreneur in the men's world and yet looks soft, sexy, feminine, and centered. She meditates and seems to enjoy a measure of freedom from her conditioning and her mind. Osho frequently talked about new man but never a new woman. When questioned, he would say by man he means humanity, which includes both man and woman. I never believed him, he being a man from an extreme patriarchal culture.

I emailed her video to my most liberated female friends around the globe. Then I lit my freshly rolled joint and started to pace on my terrace. Would I have the courage and trust to take off my pants and let a little-known man stroke my clitoris? The thought alone was sweaty and uncomfortable. The fact of her internal dialogue stopping completely even for a brief period during stroking was of particular interest to me. These moments of internal silence are highly coveted on the spiritual path. I saw it as a fun and functional meditative technique for busy millennials of the twenty-first century, wanting a soulful connection with their partner. OM, according to me, had the signature of Shiva and tantric yoga. I needed to find out more about this jewel in the lotus.

At night, when I went to bed, I found myself spontaneously OMing. I loved the idea of bringing my full attention to this itty bitty point and keeping it there for fifteen minutes. If my attention left for the head, I would be shocked! What rotten taste! To leave heaven down under for the smelly stagnant swamp of thoughts in my head. With one session, I was immensely impressed by the direct experience of "pure sensation, pure feeling" in my clitoris. It can be described only as supremely refined and exquisitely delicate. In the morning, I was aware of very subtle relaxation in my pelvic area.

The core philosophy of Tantra is that sex is sacred, and so we were told frequently by Osho at his Pune 1 ashram. But when the rubber met the road, the sex I had with swamis was anything but sacred. Most were sloppy quickies! Osho's only injunction was to be total in the sex act, or any act, to make it sacred. I had no clue what he meant by total. I had my light bulb moment during OMing. Bring your attention down to the clitoris and preferably hold it there to evoke "pure feeling or pure sensation." I understood at last that any act done with full attention thus becomes sacred.

The next day, I downloaded her book, *Slow Sex: The Art and Craft of the Female Orgasm*, and immediately started to read it. I had already been self-OMing and found it very beneficial. Halfway into the book she is asked about self-OMing without a partner. Her "no" answer stunned me, but her explanation made perfect sense. She says OM is designed to give the conscious mind a break by liberating it from the grip of the control freak ego. To be free from mind control, even temporarily, is the longing of all humanity. She compares self-OMing to tickling yourself. Point well made. But what to do with my own positive experience of self-OMing? My entire sacral area has become more alive. Overall sensitivity has grown, and my usual meditations have reached the stratosphere! Why? Because personal consciousness is able to tolerate longer and longer periods of freedom from the chattering ego mind. In the Indian tradition, the sacral, or the tailbone area, is considered the seat of Kundalini energy, or life force. My life energy has been on the move more than ever before. I also enjoy the butterfly position of lying down. Since I can't sit in lotus position comfortably, lying in the butterfly position seems to offer more or less similar benefits of opening my hip joints. I told myself, I have a longer list of experiential benefits than most testimonials in her book, so I'm going to carry on. Although I agree with Nicole that OMing with a loving partner would be a much richer, certainly more fulfilling, and more complete an experience.

P.S.

I absolutely recommend hearing Nicole's TED talk and reading her book if you wish to practice OM, *Slow Sex: The Art and Craft of the Female Orgasm.*

Chapter 47

More Clitoral Contemplations

In the total orgasmic joy of sex, time disappears, ego disappears. That's the greatest longing in you. You're not aware of time, you move into eternity; and you're not aware of separation, the ego is not functioning at all — that's the joy.

—Osho, *Philosophia Perennis*

WHEN I TRY TO EXPLAIN the concept of meditative sex or OM as pure play, free from expectations of orgasm, free from goals and achievements, I don't get very far. Not with my age group of golden girls. They try to convince me that their sex life is or was very satisfyingly orgasmic. I have no argument with that. My point is to show slow sex, or OMing, as a gateway to tasting existence, to heightened awareness, and sex as an exquisite art form rather than mechanical rush for orgasm. Emphasis on slow means the attention is resting in the genitals rather than being busy and occupied in the head, from where we're habituated to actively doing sex. Attention in here and now is present and relaxed. The difference is enormous! Slow sex is the evolution of the garden variety hurried sex of ejaculation-as-orgasm to the highest ecstasy of pure existence.

Tantric yoga describes sex as the most alive thing in us through which life is propagated. If sex is meditative, it can penetrate to the very source of life. During the deepest moment of orgasm, ego and time disappear. Attention is literally pulled down from the head by pulsating and throbbing sensations in the genitals. Freedom from the head means freedom to receive and enjoy the pleasurable sensations of the body. It means freedom from the motor-mouth ego. Could this be the reason for humanity's obsession with sex all over the planet? Humanity is addicted to the mind and thinking and has an unconscious desperate need for relief from the prison of the mind. Enter meditation, which allows us to drop ego and time without sex. Therefore, meditation should be easiest during sex.

OMing brilliantly and beautifully combines orgasm with meditation, especially female orgasm, by engaging the attention in the act. Most females on the planet, especially in developing countries, have no clue about the clitoris or orgasm. To a relatively lesser degree, such seems to be the case also in the West. A friend tells me of an episode from the 2011 BBC hit show *Mrs. Brown's Boys*. Mrs. Brown, an older woman, has six children. A friend comes by with a pamphlet titled, "Women Should Have Orgasms Too." As they are browsing through the pamphlet, distraught and resentful Mrs. Brown angrily accuses her dead husband of giving her no orgasms, not even one, while she gave him six children. My friend and I agreed, if OMing infiltrated the planet, all the exhausted and frustrated Mrs. Browns of the world, in Nicole's words, would be "turned on, nourished and hydrated" wonder women of the world.

But not so soon! I told my friend I was remembering a horrible story of genital mutilation that could have belonged to *The Vagina Monologues*, by Eve Ensler. I had read the story in the *Times of India* newspaper during my hospital watch days in Mumbai. A young girl of little more than perhaps ten years, belonging to a Muslim sect, was being taken out by her grandmother on the pretext of getting her few sweet treats. Instead, the little girl found herself in a dark room with other older women. She was asked to lie down, and the women pinned down her legs and arms. While the scared little thing was struggling, one woman quickly sliced off her clitoris. My friend looked at me with shock and horror. Yes, I added, done in the name of god, the creator of the clitoris in the first place. The young girl, now middle-aged, well dressed, and educated, was pleading with the Indian government to stop the barbaric practice. According to me, not only was the girl sexually mutilated, but worse still, her psyche was cruelly crushed and mutilated. If your own grandma brutally bamboozles you, who can you trust?

I had another more positive story about genital mutilation from the TV series *Nip/Tuck*. A gorgeous African woman whose clitoris had been removed as a child was working as a model in the United States. She was concerned that the US models were obsessed with sex while she wasn't turned on at all by sex. She had come to the famous TV plastic surgeons with the hope of refashioning her clitoris. No problem! They repurposed a lump of nerve tissue from her toe into a clitoris. Surgically she was healed, but the new clitoris wouldn't function. One of the plastic surgeons, single and handsome, decided to take on the challenge of rehabbing her clitoris. No luck. A lesbian nurse in the clinic had the solution for her. She put her in a clinic room and gave her instructions on auto-stimulation and closed the door on her. When the African model emerged from the room, she looked blissed out and announced, "I saw god."

Chapter 48

Yoga Divine

Now let me sit here,
on the threshold of two worlds,
Lost in the eloquence of silence.

—Rumi, "In the Arms of the Beloved"

THIS IS THE MOST DELIGHTFUL chapter of this book for me. Herein is revealed the jewel in the heart of the lotus. All the preceding chapters are the petals of the lotus, arranged precisely to display the divine dazzle of the jewel.

One morning, I am deep in my corpse meditation, head empty and thoughtless. My breathing is very slow and extremely relaxed, almost negligible. Body boundaries have dissolved. Stillness within and without. All-inclusive vastness and openness of silence: birds chirping, neighbor's dog barking, stray sounds from the downstairs apartment and distant buzz of the traffic. My body, my bed, my entire bedroom, is merged in vast boundless silence. All is still. My attention, a dimensionless point, is floating in the infinite ocean of energy. And this motionless pure energy is all there is. No beyond or further here. No inside or outside here. My attention, the only movable point, starts to frolic and explore the invisible ocean of energy. No matter where my attention goes, far away in the cosmos or deep in the bowels of the earth, the pure, silent energy is there prior to the arrival of my attention. There's no possibility, none, of personal consciousness ever getting out of this ocean of energy. It tries all the tricks and techniques, but disconnection is not possible. For attention to believe a thought is the only way to cause its apparent disconnection from the source. At last, it sinks into the ocean of boundless peace, always here. It requires no maintenance and no gatekeeper. There's no time here. Bliss bombs are exploding all around. Attention returns to the mind to utter, "Not two, not two." Tears of joy are streaming down through my blindfold. My energy body, fully exposed as a sensitive neural network of energy lines, is shivering almost imperceptibly with ecstasy and delight.

My attention resurfaces. Like a child gleefully saying to itself and to the ocean of energy, "You and me two, right, you zero, me one. Now, watch me disappear into you to celebrate our oneness. Me a drop of you and you an infinite ocean. I'm no longer afraid of you, of your total emptiness engulfing and overwhelming me, who is but a minuscule drop, a tiny ripple on your boundless surface. Your emptiness only seems empty because I have removed all the conceptual furniture in my mind that I had thought was me. If I were to remove all the furniture in my house, it would look empty too. But your emptiness turned out to be overflowing with unconditional peace, love, joy, compassion, and bliss."

Then my attention disappeared again in the unfathomable ocean of consciousness. What remained was simple, silent self-aware energy, like the sky with no clouds, not even white clouds, for now. My attention did that many times, surfaced and then disappeared into pure consciousness. I was delighted to rediscover experientially the obvious and unarguable oneness of the wave and the ocean, of the personal and universal consciousness. Eventually, it returned to my head and joyfully declared, "I'm free. I'm liberated from my mind, from a fake separate self. If this is not friggin *mukti* (liberation), then what is it?"

My head was buzzing with excited thoughts. "I have voluntarily, willingly and with full consciousness, committed suicide. I'm no longer afraid of my mind or my source or addicted to the illusion of separation from my source. At last! I'm liberated from the sticky, gooey ego that I spun like a spider's web to maintain and strengthen my separate identity. My ego is the cause of my seeming expulsion from the so-called Garden of Eden — a metaphor for oneness with god, or life force."

Here's the joke; To get back to the garden, for decades, I looked outside, in books, knowledge, sex, drugs, gurus, teachers, romantic relationships, selfless service, and travel adventures. Looking within wasn't easy because there was nothing to do but just be. It has been the hardest for me to give up my outbound dynamism, excitement, and thrills for the inbound passivity of being.

And herein is the glitch that prevents and delays us souls from consciously hitching up to the oneness. It is that the total passivity and lack of any ambition, the bottomless silence and stillness, feel like death, despite being the true source of all life. The description of DNA is so apt here. Science tells us that DNA is the most unalive, most non-reactive molecule in the universe. Yet, it is the very source of all life on the planet. Death of the ego holds the promise of life eternal. But it must die voluntarily and consciously!

Gleefully, my inner voice said, "Lucky, lucky me! I did it, and now just to 'be,' to rest in the void of consciousness, is my highest joy. Going inward has transformed personal consciousness, or attention, into Atman, or soul."

The ocean of pure energy, or source, even though nameless and formless, for the purpose of communication has been labeled by ancient seers as Brahman (or god), truth, spirit, or "I am that I am." Some of the nonreligious labels for the source are quantum field, universal consciousness, life force, all that is, or simply "That."

Sparkling with joy, my soul continued. "As source energy, you are free from needs, demands, desires, expectations, judgements, and criticisms. You have no religion. (What? a god with no religion! Time for me to howl with laughter!) You have no nationality, body, or gender. You make no distinction between a pope or a pauper, a president or a prisoner. You know nothing about crime and punishment. You're pure and innocent and free as a newborn child. As such, holy books and the concepts of sacred and profane are meaningless gibberish to you."

Then the attention disappeared again in the source energy. Emptiness stood up and slowly stretched the body.

Chapter 49

A Love Sublime

To fall in love with god is the greatest romance; to seek him, the greatest adventure; to find him, the greatest human achievement.

—Saint Augustine

THIS, I KNEW, WAS SO complete a death of my ego! I could taste her ashes in my mouth. Since my conscious merger with the existential ocean of energy, I have been luxuriating in the limitless spaciousness and silence of truth. These days nothing is more precious than the nurturing rest in truth. My delight is ineffable! Nothing of the limitless can be expressed in words, which are limited and meant for communication mainly with the external world. In the inner world, words and concepts are useless. Silence is the official language of truth, and it is fathomless.

Yet I feel the urge to use words out of the fullness of love and joy. How shall I celebrate my union with the limitless ocean of energy? How shall I relate to the boundless relation-less oneness? Jesus's connection to the source as the Father, indicates that he felt warmly and wonderfully taken care of by pure existence. When in love, especially overflowing love, words such as existence, pure consciousness, or even truth sound like dull and dreary clunkers. The word, god, shows up as the lover's name for pure existence, or truth. The overflowing love which I'm experiencing is the divine wine of the Sufis. Jed seems to have the lighthearted relationship of a playful puppy with the all-that-is. Buddha created no conceptual relationship with the universal. For him, the personal consciousness didn't even exist, being an extension of the universal. He labeled the dissolution of personal consciousness in the universal as Nirvana, the end of suffering. So why bother?

I noticed my mild attraction toward the lover-beloved dynamic to express overflowing love and gratitude. Then I decided I prefer my emperor naked, without any distinctions, not even of Father, Divine Mother, or Lord and servant. Having gained near impossible freedom from the mind, which is nothing but a set of distinctions, I lean toward the silence of one hand clapping. I noticed that the dualistic relation with the divine offers incredible solace, company, creativity, and occasional distraction and laughter. But that too comes and goes, along with devotion, worship, bliss, and ecstasy.

Jesus declared that the Kingdom of god belongs to the children. Why? Because they are free from the duality of the mind. The little children, pure and innocent, are the gatekeepers of the Kingdom. Truth precedes the mind and its sleek shenanigans. Even the distinctions of "in" and "out" don't apply here. Initially, when I was identified with the mind, there was a clear-cut distinction between the outer world of shining things, dazzling ideas, beautiful people, and the inner world of dark emptiness. I believed my inner emptiness was my own private curse. I erroneously assumed everyone else was filled like chocolate eclairs with the yummy melted chocolate of love and goodness. My morbid fear of emptiness threw me again and again into the arms of the outer world, so rich in drama, with so much to do, become, learn, add, grow, change, create, explore, and experiment. Luckily I was awakened by the fatal pain of asphyxiation caused by my hyper-connected, hyperactive mind. The Frankenstein monster of my own creation was sucking my life force and devouring me with gusto and no hesitation.

Oh, how I worshiped my mind! I believed myself to be the creator of all the succulent fruits of the civilization. Such hubris! I believed in science, the brainchild of my most fabulous creation, the finite mind. I once heard on TV a religious person declare science as the spiritual director of this age. I can see science as the director of the material world of objects but of the spiritual domain? Undoubtedly, science and technology have elevated the human condition and are the roaring dynamic engines of modern society. Yet they don't qualify for such sublime honors. Science is focused outwardly on objects, and cause and effect are its foundation. Scientific theories and experiments, once proven, are available to the entire scientific world. It's no longer necessary to prove the law of gravity or the theory of relativity.

On the other hand, truth is the inscrutable, invisible subject that can't be analyzed, examined, and dissected. Nothingness can't be studied or scrutinized. And who will do that? Mind? Fruit of the tree of knowledge blessed by human society. More accurately, truth is the subjectivity of humanity, accessed only by turning the attention inwards. Truth is causeless, uncreated, and indivisible. So are its fruits of peace, joy, well-being, and bliss. A scientist can be the spirit but can't scrutinize and analyze it as an object using her inadequate mind. Unlike science, truth must be realized by each and every person individually, even though there's only one ground of being. Like all existential activities, my full stomach and my deep sleep last night are of no use to you. You still have to eat and sleep for yourself. Similarly, each person must make her own connection to truth.

Since truth is uncreated, Friedrich Nietzsche or any other existential philosopher can't kill it and declare, "god is dead." Truth is not an entity, concept, or figment of human imagination. It alone exists, and therefore, I exist. "I am" is the only incontrovertible and uncontested truth of existence. The myriad labels attached to "I am" are all relative and accidental, mere add-ons that make me somebody with an identity. Naked "I am" is nobody, a zero, one with truth (which, too, is zero). Truth as formless emptiness is too unpalatable, too plain and unshowy for humanity. Since I'm already truth, any efforts and practices to reach it only take me further away from it and plump up my personhood. Like it or not, the paradox here is that to gain life eternal, it's necessary to pass through the death of personhood stuffed with conceptual complexities. To walk with truth/god, it's imperative that "I am" be equally simple and empty.

Have I arrived at some exclusive place where man and god are one? Unsurprisingly, this place, which is not a place, is rigorously all-inclusive as the ground of being of all: saint and sinner, pauper and prince, enlightened and ignorant. I have simply rediscovered and acknowledged my oneness with the ocean of pure consciousness. Verily, now, "In god (spirit), I move and breath and have my being" (Acts 17:26–28). And so does everyone else. I had simply been unconscious of my everlasting connection with truth, which no Satan or science can tear asunder.

Chapter 50

Energy Lines

> It's like I live suspended in a network of invisible lines, and even though I can't see them, I know they are there, and I have learnt how to fit in with them. They are always there, and should the day come when they're not, I'm content to fall.
>
> —Jed McKenna, *Spiritual Warfare*

I'M PROFOUNDLY IMPRESSED! THIS IS friggin deep shit! Why? According to me, it's coming from deep silence, which means freedom from the ego. Jed's mention of the above lines in his book has perhaps gone unnoticed by most of his readers. I can only hope that he and I are talking about the same invisible lines, as it's his one and only mention of them. For me, it has been a lifelong affair of tuning in and playing with them, which continues to this day.

Very early, on acid, I fell in love with my form. Despite how it looked—fat or bony, muscular or flabby—in general, the perceived flaws no longer mattered. What mattered was how my body felt. My attention temporarily freed from the mind, dropped down into the body, energizing and enlivening wherever it rested. At the time, I didn't know it was my consciousness causing the hitherto unknown surge in my well-being and aliveness. Personal consciousness de-focused and relaxed, it felt like some mysterious force was breathing, walking and moving me. It was seeing, hearing, and touching directly through me, without the interface of the mind. I truly didn't have any words to express and understand what was happening. I was simply thrilled to be feeling intensely alive and alert and having so much more energy than ever before. Now I understand it to be the energy released from my head into my body because my personal consciousness was no longer in its customary habitat. The extra energy would sing and dance through my body with joyous abandon. Very new for my hyper-rational, extremely self-conscious, stiff and rigid persona, which abhorred physical movements. I had always felt inadequate and clumsy doing anything with my body, such as sports and dancing, especially with others and especially if I was being watched. To be singing (granted, out of key), to be dancing (granted, like a robot) was a minor miracle for me. For the sublime thrill to run through me uninhibited required my attention in the presence.

Over a period, my body, moving spontaneously and organically from within, with my eyes closed, revealed inner energy lines and vortexes or chakras along the spinal axis. I would later call these energy lines neural networks because of their extreme sensitivity. I have found these lines mentioned as fibers and imperceptible threads of light in several of Carlos Castaneda's books. The sorcerer Don Juan has a sidekick, Don Genaro, who specializes in being able to sense not only his lines but also of the trees and mountains, and leap and twirl and whirl with them. He is described by Carlos to be floating and soaring weightlessly like a kite in space hanging from a thread of light. Yogis call these lines energy threads. To experience these flights and leaps of subtle energy lines, the internal dialogue must be completely off.

Many years ago, during my time at University of Toronto, in the rooming house where I lived at the time, I had two experiences on LSD. These would leave a lasting impression on my mind, guiding me through my spiritual journey right up until now. In one I took the trip solo, and was lying on my back on my bed. There were a whole lot of sensations traveling up to my head from below my navel. Translated into thoughts, I understood: "We know you're blind without your glasses. We have noticed on acid and marijuana your eyes get dry and your vision gets distorted, forcing you to remove your glasses or contacts. Without the visual aids, the objects in the world have no sharp boundaries and bleed and merge into each other and the surroundings. So you have been more or less forced to keep your eyes closed and look inward. We are very happy with that. We're going to teach you to relax. This relaxation is unimaginably deep and ungraspable by your mind, which won't and can't be present during deepest relaxation. We are going to help you to keep all this a secret until the end of your journey."

At this point, there were sensations in my vocal chords and in my closed mouth, as if they were being examined from inside. The invisible "we" was pleased with the success of the operation, which meant I would be effectively mute until the end of my inner journey. During this inner dialogue I was addressed several times, much to my intolerable embarrassment and dismay, as "Daughter of the Ganges." Too Hindu smelling! Too ancient! I was tripping on the most modern, most trending drug on the planet. I believed I was heading where no one, or at least very few men, had gone before, certainly no women. I wanted nothing to do with holy Hindu icons. The whole experience lasted less than five minutes, and I promptly forgot all about it. Much, much later, I would recognize the "invisible we" to be connected to Shiva. "Daughter of Ganges" should have been a dead giveaway. Duh, me! The Ganges River originates in the Himalayan glaciers, the mythical home of Shiva. In sacred art, Ganges is also shown flowing from Shiva's head as the symbol of descent of higher knowledge for the benefit and liberation of souls from their limitations and suffering.

The second experience, again on acid, occurred several months later. I was pacing and stretching my body and found myself in front of the full-length mirror. I felt the urge to remove my clothes and stand naked with my eyes closed. My body was being slowly moved out of its habitual mold and placed in a new configuration, stretched and taller, with a new center of gravity, about an inch behind the old center. The new posture was exquisite in its elegance and alertness, but I couldn't hold it for more than a couple of seconds. I collapsed on the carpeted floor in a heap of painful exhaustion and despair. I cried out in deep anguish, much like Arjuna, who is reluctant to fight the "Big War." He is pleading and beseeching Lord Krishna, who is coaxing and convincing him to fight. "It can't be done. I can't and won't do it," I kept muttering to no one through tears and goobers dripping down my face. I got a brief glimpse of the massive transformation of my body. The impossibility of its attainment and the sheer intensity of commitment and dedication required had reduced me to a ruinous heap of madness. My sinking heart kept desperately chanting, "It can't be done. I can't do it. This is absolute insanity!" No being, no entity beamed down to console and comfort me in the moment of my worst meltdown ever! Didn't talk about this horrendous psychic storm to anybody, not even my husband. The fear was that he would insist I give up tripping and consult a shrink. Thus, the secrecy was maintained effortlessly.

By and by, the extensive work with my inner energy body has changed my posture and my gait for the better. The relaxation that's on the other side of the stillness continues to deepen, no longer on acid but through meditation and marijuana. It involves relaxation of these subtle energy lines, especially in the sacral area, jaw, and back of the head. My physical eyes have worsened, but I continue with my play because relaxation, stillness, truth, and enlightenment are synonymous in my playbook, all pointing to pure emptiness.

P.S.

During the process of reviewing and editing my manuscript, I had an epiphany: what I have been calling energy lines and energy centers are nothing but ancient Kundalini energy. It has been expressing itself through me since my first acid trip and first toke of cannabis, whether I recognized and acknowledged it or not. It is the primal and subtlest manifestation of somethingness. Merely a hairbreadth removed from no-thingness of pure life energy, one with it yet subtly distinct.

Chapter 51

Osho on my Mind

Sex is like an atom bomb. A potent weapon which fascinates and frightens. We're afraid to let it loose, yet we all have our finger on the button.

—Zeena Schreck, *Demons of the Flesh: The Complete Guide to Left Hand Path Sex*

I WISH TO EXPRESS MY LOVE, reverence, and deep gratitude to Osho here as in upcoming chapters, he along with a few other gurus, will be receiving my sustained critical attention. If I stayed on the sidelines I would be sadly compromising my truth, which is not possible from the peak of consciousness where I currently reside. Osho, a die-hard rebel, wouldn't want me to do that. Osho deeply loved and appreciated his favorite icons, Buddha, Mahavira, and Jesus, but he didn't hesitate to criticize them, claiming only he had the right to criticize because he loved them so deeply. Only Lao Tzu, his all-time fave, didn't receive his critical gaze, maybe only a little.

His ashram in Pune and his uniquely profound teachings delivered in his speakeasy style, with wit, humor and dazzling brilliance, packed always with apt anecdotes and stories, are his immortal legacy. That the ashram is thriving deeply warms my heart. It continues to be a global oasis of experimentation and exploration of existence, human psyche, sexuality, freedom, authenticity, human connections, and various ways of expressing truth and so forth. A couple of scenes from a book, *The Pune Diaries*, written by an old *sannyasin*, Anand Subhuti, in the post-Osho phase, highlight my point. He is enjoying a cigarette in the outdoor smoking temple of the ashram. A young woman comes and spontaneously sits in his lap, shares his cigarette, takes a selfie, and disappears. A few days later, an unknown middle-aged European woman approaches him and asks, not exactly in these words, "Voulez vous coucher avec moi ce soir?" His answer was a yes, after the evening meditation and at his place.

I rhapsodically ask, where in the world is an experiment with risqué behavior rewarded with meditative sex in a safe and supportive environment? If I were a millennial with an adventure seeking spirit, I would be heading for Pune. The ashram during phase 1 offered a variety of therapy groups, perhaps the finest and the best in the world and very reasonably priced for us foreigners. A singular characteristic of Osho therapies and groups is that insights, resolutions, and healings happen organically and unplanned. The current internet photos of the ashram, very posh and futuristic looking, convince me that the situation remains just as good, perhaps even better, without Osho—the guru and god of crazy-ass wisdom—at the helm.

Lately, memory of an ancient therapy group scenario from Pune 1 was triggered by a brief video clip on YouTube, entitled *"Conscious Parenting."* The guest speaker was gorgeously brilliant Dr. Shefali, a clinical psychologist and world-renowned wisdom teacher. She was on the *Vishen Lakhiani Show.* He is an entrepreneur, author, activist, and handsome dude. My take-home nugget: a parent's connection to the child must trump correction of the child. Since I don't have children of my own, to me, the show was a creative way to pass the time with beautiful and smart people while mindlessly rolling my joints. But wait! Notice how the unconnected dots from my past surfaced, clamoring to be connected to reveal a global picture of unconscious parenting. I'm pacing on my terrace, smoking my joint, when the following video bubbled up: I'm in a group setting with approximately eighteen to twenty *sannyasins*, sitting in a circle. I couldn't remember the name of the group. We are all in the nude, which represents a lack of pretense and the raw nudity of truth. A veritable mini world sitting together, consisting of *sannyasins* from the entire European Union, few from the US, me from India-Canada, along with one more Canadian, two Japanese, and one

Chinese. The unstructured group became spontaneously focused on the topic of our mothers. Festering childhood wounds were being exposed, waiting to be healed. I was stunned to see the world of diverse cultures and values saddled with same old bags of mommy-centric emotional abuses. The collective airing was done with some degree of guilt and shame for the woman we hated, loved, and adored. Here, I had thought I was the only one with a hard-hearted monster of a mother. But she was small potatoes compared to the global tales of mothers who thought it was their sworn duty to raise rigidly responsible and serious, lifeless adults. When my turn came, I was speechless. All I could mutter was that my old lady wasn't all that bad, relatively speaking. Looking at the group with the new Shefali lens, I clearly understood that all the global moms had unconsciously, not knowing any better, emphasized *correction* over *connection*. We were paying for it with existential angst of being worthless, undeserving, and fundamentally wrong. Our rigid life sucking personas had choked our souls and denied us full expression of life. The global child rearing belief in correction over connection, of not only our generation but also the preceding generations, tenderized my heart with compassion toward my mom. My relationship changed dramatically with her, for the better. Her zeal for correction, resulting in a mountain of misery, was in many ways responsible for the success of my inner journey. She was a perfect mom, flaws and all, to keep me company on my ascension to the highest peak of human accomplishment. I wondered what my destiny would have been raised by conscious parents. I could not imagine. I will be looking at the gurus in the upcoming chapters with Dr. Shefali's lens of parental overcorrection so typical of the old world. Also, the authoritarian upbringing of millions of their disciples makes them susceptible to authoritarian control and abuses of all sorts from their gurus. That it's for their own good, repeated since their childhood, is a song they expect and with which they are thoroughly familiar.

I cherish all my experiences with Osho, good and bad, equally. However, the bad ones delivered more spiritual gold. I gratefully accept his wisdom — the parts which work for me — and discard the rest. His priceless contributions toward my growth and awakening have been an introduction to Shiva, his definition of meditation, his stand on sexuality, and his love of laughter and rejoicing. Osho's commentaries on Shiva's meditation techniques, recorded in *The Book of Secrets*, have been of immense value to me on my journey. Without the book, I might not have been able to fully complete my journey. The technique of focusing my attention on my navel initially and then refining it, is blessed by Shiva through the mystical agency of Osho. Meditation in its purest form, Osho said, is not concentration but defocusing and relaxation of attention. It's not a doing, although initially it may not feel like it. Understood correctly, meditation is effortless being. Contemplation is different from meditation as it requires focusing attention on a thought or an object, therefore not totally relaxing, but a sort of doing. Similarly, visualization is a subtle form of doing. Osho's definition of meditation as the ultimate relaxation with infinite depth has been of tremendous help to me. I now see meditation as the destination itself, which is contentless consciousness. If truth is that which cannot be reduced further, then the contentless consciousness or no-mind is the same as truth/god/enlightenment. Having reached the irreducible truth, Osho remotely encouraged me to move deeper and deeper into the stillness until *sat-chit-ananda* (truth-consciousness-bliss) is reached. The bliss he is pointing to can't be directly pursued. It is an outcome of deepest relaxation and immense silence of being.

I appreciate that life pulled me away from Osho in the early part of my journey. I was to discover that I didn't need proximity to a guru or a guide or a group or a commune to find that which can never be lost. Yes, without the Prozac of communal emotional support, it was terrifyingly treacherous at times but not impossible. Solitude, a frighteningly bleak beast to embrace initially, delivers generous rewards. Once my personal consciousness had freed itself from the mind, my entire life became effortlessly meditative. Somehow, I don't think I would have been able to liberate myself in Pune 1, even if I stayed there for years, even if I were a member of the inner circle. This was totally out of the question in the American phase, where hard unpaid labor 24/7 was rolled out not as work but worship.

Another of Osho's bold experiments was with human sexuality. He declared Tantric sex to be sacred, meditative, and the highest of art forms. It's different from the standard sex routine of mere ejaculation, which is taken to be an orgasm. Tantric sex demands unwavering attention to the sexual act, great sensitivity and freedom from the desired outcome of an orgasm—in short, total freedom from the mind. That is the supreme ideal. Besides, perhaps Osho, most of us were light years away from such an ideal.

Lately, I have been questioning the value of Tantric sex as a pathway to enlightenment. Is it a bait-and-switch operation? Osho's acceptance of sex, drugs, and rock 'n' roll certainly attracted counter-culture freaks in droves. Most certainly, my husband and I would have run away from the old ascetic set up of an ashram, guru, and meditation. Look at me now, not a Tantrika (sexpert) but certainly a meditation champ. I'm wondering whether Shiva, the original Tantric master, also used sex as bait-and-switch maneuver. In my experience, pure consciousness is sensitivity itself. And meditation is one way to befriend it. If you're sensitive, sex is sure to be magnificent! If your sex is glorious, then meditation will deepen, with a strong possibility of a merger with limitless consciousness. Osho's poetic description of the union of the personal with the universal as orgasm with the whole is gloriously apt! To me, meditation and sex are cozy cousins because of glimpses provided of the silence of pure consciousness. The ultimate goal is to make all existential activities meditative, from eating, walking, and breathing to pooping, by bringing your attention to them.

The problem with free sex, however, is that it is not only emotionally complicated, but physically, the threats include unwanted pregnancy and STDs, including AIDS. With all the sexual freedom, such as some having none to little sex and others having sex three times a day, as well as the Tantric practices; did anyone get enlightened only through the medium of sex? By enlightenment I mean freedom from the mind, living in and as pure, contentless consciousness. Osho's personal secretary, Sheela, had many lovers and wrote in her book that she enjoyed champagne truffles after sex. Is she enlightened? According to me, nope. Awake, yes! Osho's inner circle of beautiful people got lots of sex. Did anyone get enlightened? I don't know. According to me, sex is too sticky, seductive, and addictive to allow full freedom from the dream state. Another reason Osho encouraged free love, and lots of it, was to satiate the sexually repressed *sannyasins* so they would turn their backs on it with ease when the time came to become single pointed in their search. Such was the case with me. However, that could be rare. Desire for more sex and with different partners is perhaps more common. According to me, meditative or Tantric sex can give glimpses of truth, but only glimpses. Enlightenment, however, demands a grindingly painful death of the ego, which fiercely objects and resists truth. There's no other way.

Chapter 52

Failed Gods: As Shadows Noir

It will be western women who will change the world.

—His Holiness, the Dalai Lama

D URING MY SOLITUDE IN MEXICO, I deeply contemplated four personally disturbing books on guru-and-disciple relationships gone sour, ugly, and toxic. I also encountered guru worship disguised as authoritarian mind control to keep the disciples crippled and dependent on the guru. Two books have been written by the inner circle of Osho. Both authors are women, and both had to serve prison time for their blind guru devotion. The third one was written by a devotee of Amma, whom I have already scrutinized to some extent in the early part of the book. The fourth whistleblower is also a woman exposing the guru worship cult of Tantric Buddhism in the US and sexual abuse of the Western women by their gurus and lamas. I'm also going to include a fifth book, which is a lovingly written, honest biography of UG Krishnamurti, known as an anti-guru. I am deeply grateful to all of these writers, most of them Westerners, for throwing the bright light of truth on the ancient Hindu guru-disciple relationship. According to me, it seems to be in dire need of healing in the twenty-first century. Without their courageous expositions, we would not have known the shadow side of their gurus' personas, so adroitly hidden from the public eye.

Why am I willing to descend into the ancient swamp of Hindu guru-disciple relationship? First of all, like the gurus, I, too, have completed my inner journey. Also, I was an Osho follower, although I remained on the periphery because I couldn't get sufficiently infected by the Osho devotional virus. Perhaps my overall average worldly profile and enchantment with drugs made me immune to his irresistible charisma and charm. I was born and raised in India by my orthodox Hindu mom, who had been conditioned to revere and respect all manner of *sadhus*, saints, gurus and holy scriptures. But I have spent the bulk of my years in the West and was married to a French Canadian. I deeply cherish the Western values of freedom of thought, expression, and gender equality. I love that no one is above the law of the land and no one needs to bow and prostrate to authority, secular or divine.

I'm unable to deny and instead wish to openly celebrate in my book the brilliant work of these spiritual giants, some of whom have scaled the highest peaks of consciousness known to man. They are all mega-spiritual influencers. They have inspired millions. And also have damaged many. According to me, they seem to still be carrying small bags of rocks in the form of hard baked beliefs, which have resulted in needless spirals of ruin. I'm going to look at their psychological shadows, taking into account the complexities of their super-sized lives. Current American society is similarly engaged in coming to terms with high powered worldly men and also priests, who have unacknowledged shadows of archaic male entitlement and privilege resulting in sexual abuse.

I'll be looking at Osho, UG Krishnamurti (henceforth UG, as known to his disciples) and a bunch of Tibetan male gurus and lamas whose Tantric cult has roots in India. Amma is the lone female guru, deeply dyed in Hindu patriarchal culture and guru worship. Her path is of the heart and devotion to Hindu gods, especially Krishna and goddess Kali, both of whom she is known to channel.

One of the heavyweights of Hindu pantheon is Shiva, who represents death and destruction as well as sexuality and regeneration. In Hinduism as well as Tibetan Buddhism, only the false is destructible. That which is real can never be destroyed. Shiva, representing sexuality, is worshiped as *lingam* (penis) and Shakti, his consort, as *yoni* (vagina). Lingam as an erect penis looks dynamic and potent, like a missile or a rocket ready to launch into the cosmos. Yoni as a circle around the base of the lingam is hardly visible and therefore hardly noticed by the worshippers. I, myself, saw it only when shown. Together they form the godhead, or existence. Maybe a Hindu male gets his attitude of male privilege and entitlement from lingam worship. All current societies are patriarchal and are now in various stages of being toppled, especially in the West. A typical Indian male is still fiercely hanging on to his superior authoritarian role and his male entitlement. Man alone can become enlightened, only he can joyfully utter, *"Aham brahmasmi* (I'm the ultimate)" is deeply embedded in the Hindu psyche, although that's changing in modern times. From childhood, as a girl, you're conditioned to respect and bow to male authority in all areas of life. Although much has changed, the cultural atmosphere is still suffused with vibes of female subservience. Women to this day in orthodox Hindu families are programmed to believe a husband is like god, but "like" is unimportant. Woman's goddess power is limited to temples and rituals and is subservient to god, her husband. He is god, and that's what he and she believe. If she argues with him or burns his dinner and he (god) beats her up, both the parties feel the beating is justified, with the woman begging for his forgiveness.

Another meaningful characteristic of Hindu culture is that since ancient times, India's ruling ambition has been to know oneself. It's in India that existence first asked profound questions about life and death and then answered them for itself. In its single-minded quest for truth, India has renounced all and staked all. Perhaps this is the underlying cause of its national economic poverty. Buddha and Mahaveer, both royals, renounced their kingdoms and manifold comforts and conveniences in a sincere search for truth. The basic act of renouncing all tremendously increases one's status in the Indian society. Even the richest man and the most powerful politician will bow to the renunciate. Truth realization is considered the highest accomplishment of humanity, bar none. Self-realized and enlightened beings, mostly males and a few females, are supremely glorified and portrayed as gods, goddesses and superheroes. Formless truth or pure consciousness or god are seen to be synonymous. The divine attributes of all-knowing, all-pervading, and all-powerful god are generously projected on the truth-realized guru who happily embraces and absorbs and even encourages these projections.

Guru and god being equal, by surrendering to guru, you're surrendering to god. Surrender to guru, or existence, means your life is no longer yours. You have offered your ego with its likes and dislikes, along with its distinctions of right and wrong, to your guru and are willing to do whatever the guru deems necessary for your awakening. This gives the guru great power and unlimited prerogative to create situations from tender to tough—capable of delivering necessary shocks and jolts to stir the disciple's comatose brain. Without the utterly necessary step of surrender, either to guru or truth or life, which is actually a process, no spiritual progress is possible. Lyrics of an ancient, extremely popular devotional song by Mira Bai make the concept of surrender ruthlessly clear. The devotee will sit wherever she is asked to sit. She will eat whatever her beloved Krishna provides. Should the beloved choose to sell her, she is willing to be sold. I ask myself, am I willing to be sold by existence in the marketplace as a menial or sex slave in return for enlightenment? My brain freezes and my heart stops! Luckily, such is not my fate. In Pune 1, many Western *sannyasins*, including the whistleblower Jane Stork, cleaned ashram toilets 24/7 for many months. In the culture of the commune, it is seen as a privilege. All of the guru's commands/demands must be carried out happily and joyfully. Resistance and resentment, questioning and cross examination, are not tolerated because of the surrender pact with the guru. My own surrender was to life, which allowed me to fight and resist, hurl abuses at it, and move forward, kicking and screaming, until I saw the light for myself. What is, or the will of existence, or "Thy will," is seen to be, again and again, not only supremely powerful but perfection itself compared to my puny and blind will-crafted by society.

But why not surrender directly to god or existence? Gurus declare again and again that a very rare human is able to surrender directly to a formless and nameless energy with no attributes, humanity being heavily addicted to form. Since guru equals god, it's a sin to speak ill of your guru or leave your guru. If you do leave, you are doomed for eternity. You are urged to seek the company of holy men and saints above all. It's the seeker's privilege to look after the physical comforts and needs of her guru to accrue his blessings, which are considered the most potent, priceless, and indestructible currency. Who has broadcasted these divinely imbued statements? My guess! Gurus themselves. They have managed to convince us that we absolutely need them. Neither am I denying that we don't need them.

The last critical factor is how the gurus relate to their body-mind and persona. Body-mind and persona are seen as fake by the gurus because they are constantly changing. I can't remember the thought and feelings I had an hour ago. My body and persona have gone through and will be going through innumerable mutations from birth to death. Humanity is sealed and fused with the ever-changing body and mind, taking that to be its identity. This unstable identity with its ceaseless stream of thoughts is labeled as sleeping, dreaming, living with eyes closed or living unconsciously.

Mind is the only obstacle to truth or god realization. Mind's main function is survival and therefore it must go outward. A guru, using various techniques and himself as an example, breaks the outgoing conditioning of the mind and turns it inwards upon itself. It's a gigantic feat, fraught with terror and torment because it's going against the deeply familiar outward movement encouraged by society. The guru and his commune provide much needed guidance and social and emotional support during the pivot, which otherwise could be accompanied by treacherous loneliness and suicidal self-doubts. The pattern of going from outward to inward is the same in both East and West. Jesus declared the kingdom of god is within, not without. An Indian guru's experience of the kingdom within is of pure, impeccable consciousness, free of thought content. Uninterrupted peace and joy are its inherent nature. The guru has transcended his limited human identity and taken on a new identity as limitless pure awareness and a new abode in pure awareness. As such, she will witness her thoughts but will not get mixed up with them because of her experiential knowing that she is not her thoughts. Truth, we are told, is the fire that burns everything non-essential in its way. It sounds so clear and simple in theory! In real life, there are times when the guru's pure consciousness seems to get entwined with old and ingrained beliefs. This creates bloody emotional chaos—not so much for her but for the disciples, who are still deeply entrenched in their dualistic minds.

With these principles of Hindu spiritual tradition iin mind - that man's a superior being, truth is the apex of human attainment, one who has attained truth is equal to god, and guru's total disregard and disidentification with her body and mind — I plan to look at guru-disciple dynamics in the next few chapters.

Chapter 53

Failed Gods: As *Enfant Terrible*

"A whistle is to make people jump."

Ruth Krauss, *A Hole Is to Dig*

BREAKING THE SPELL IS THE tell-all book written by Jane Stork, an Australian and a former deeply devoted disciple of Osho. I found her book to be heartbreakingly honest and factual. No vindictive agenda except to heal herself through writing her incredible story of disillusionment, losses, grief, and struggle. Her exposure of Osho's dark side had a seismically devastating effect on my cherished spiritual concepts and ideals. Osho, raised in the repressive Indian and Jaina culture, had a deep-seated tendency to criticize and provoke all the religious and authoritarian institutions of the world. He thrived on making enemies. In the United States, he stepped up his game! He threw conceptual firecrackers and projectiles at Christianity, the Pope, the state of Oregon, politicians, the locals, the US government, and, more or less, the entire Western culture. His stated purpose was to shock and jolt them into awakening from their collective slumber. The smell of blood was in the air, especially since the ashram had its own mini retaliatory militia of weapon-touting and gun-wielding *sannyasins*. Jane Stork writes that Osho was asked how far they should go in protecting him from hostile and outraged Oregonians. His reply: if ten thousand or more must die to protect him, the rarest flower of existence, then so be it. Should there be an attempt to seize him, his people were to form a "human shield" to defend him. *Sannyasins* believed themselves to be super privileged to have a live Buddha in their midst. No one asked why their living god, with such a peaceful and joyful demeanor, was so belligerent in his wake-up maneuvers. Also, why bother waking up the Pope and the Oregonian and their politicians. Unlike his followers, they hadn't signed up for "The Wake Up with Osho" program. Osho was aware of his chronic habit of exposing authority and poking his nose in the business of others. I heard him say that once, his chauffeur in India pointed out his habit of unnecessarily getting involved with other people and useless causes. Osho tolerated no questioning or criticism of his authority or the commune. His stunts and flash made him a publicity magnet and also an object of vitriol, especially to the locals and the politicians.

Osho passionately championed meditation as the savior of a humanity which seems determined to commit suicide. Yet he also leaned very strongly toward love, surrender, and devotion to the guru (i.e., to him), as the express route to enlightenment. The dark side of the culture of surrender and guru worship is exposed by all the whistleblowers except UG, the anti-guru. Osho in his discourses said that truth attained through meditation is dull and dry. Buddha, one of his favorites, was later condemned to be too drab, too otherworldly due to too much meditation. Buddha, according to him, needed a few shots of earthy energy of Zorba the Greek from the eponymous novel by Nikos Kazantzakis. Enlightened Buddha dancing, laughing, drinking and partying with abandon of Zorba was his dream of the 'New Man' he implanted in his sannyasins.

Truth in the service of love, he said, especially guru worship and devotion, is so, so very juicy! So excitingly alive! There was an intense fever of devotion around Osho. Thousands of mainly elite Westerners believed it to be a privilege to be dedicated disciples in egoless surrender to Osho/the living god. Ditto for Amma and Tibetan Buddhist gurus and lamas. Only with Osho, everything is super-sized, including his misdemeanors and his blatant flouting of the laws of the land. Who paid for the criminal karmas initiated and instigated by him for the higher cause of creating an immense Buddha field to relieve humanity of its suffering? His sweet and surrendered minions, who believed he would take responsibility for them in case of legal consequences.

Osho's godly vibes of purity and peace and his profound discourses were his seduction tools of surrender for his *sannyasins*. Osho used to laugh at the mind-numbing obedience of soldiers in the army. When commanded to turn right or left or march in single file, they unhesitatingly and unthinkingly obey. So did his followers. Their goal was to protect Osho, who was gleefully throwing conceptual explosives at the cherished American institutions. Few of his *sannyasins* were really involved in a plot to kill the attorney general of Oregon—their perceived threat to the deportation of Osho. An event recorded in Jane's book clearly highlights the extent to which he controlled the will and minds of his devotees, who unthinkingly obeyed him and did illegal stuff because it was indirectly demanded of them. Ashram had borrowed a large sum of money from an American *sannyasin* who wanted her money back. When Osho was informed, he had a hissy fit. He refused to return the money, claiming it was a gift. His legal department advised him to return the money, but he had no use for their advice or anyone else's advice, being god himself. On the contrary, he advised them to alter the writing on the legal document and go to court to defend him. They did exactly that. No questions asked, no resistance, no moral fight. They believed Osho is god and god is omniscient. Jane was dressed for court in proper clothes from a special closet and was handed the fudged legal document but wasn't told of the alteration. In the court, when she looked at the document, she instantly realized the fakery but insisted as instructed that the document was authentic and untouched. The ashram lost the case and had to return the one million dollars along with $700,000 in fines. Time to clap! god was judged in a *Judge Judy*–style court and lost. And justice was delivered on earth in America. Intrigues, scandals, secrets, Watergate-style wire tapings, deceptions, denials, and lies at Osho's US ashram, along with his insistence on himself as "one-man government" of meritocracy, never fail to remind me of President Trump and his White House.

Osho is portrayed by his diehard devotee and personal secretary, Sheela, as an enfant terrible living behind the role and reality of brilliant eloquence and memes of compassion, meditation, and profound peace. In her book *Don't Kill Him*, we see that in the US, birthplace of the affluenza virus, the enfant terrible has grown into a monster due to

Sheela's own pampering and coddling. She fears he may destroy his own teachings, his vision, and his new commune, built painstakingly by her. I sense her resistance in exposing him while he viciously and vindictively threw her into the lion's den to save his precious ass. She protects him wherever she can and also protects herself from further legal and social consequences. According to Jane Stork, Sheela, in the prison cell, incessantly talked of her unconditional surrender and love for Bhagwan, her god, her master. That he is still her god is evidenced by her use of uppercase His and Him in her book. However, according to me, she seems to be having a hell of a time integrating his dark persona, his human side, with his timeless teachings. His persona is extremely demanding, ridiculously impatient, mean, vindictive, violent, insanely cunning, and crafty. Osho is a master of manipulation and exploitation. He will massage a wealthy *sannyasin*'s ego publicly, so he is likely to empty out his wallet for him. Then he would send Sheela to set the egoic donor's head straight. All the mean, nasty, and obnoxious stuff was handled unquestioningly by Sheela. Because of that, she was later shunned by *sannyasin*s as an evil bitch who was the cause of destruction of the US ashram. Being needy, the *sannyasin*s clung to their enlightenment blinders. They were unwilling to see the Svengali-esque Osho behind the curtain, pulling Sheela's surrendered strings. Thus, he maintained his perfect godlike demeanor, forever exuding serene perfume of spirituality. He performed these operations with such exquisite skill and refinement that the public would not have even got a whiff of them had Sheela and Jane not been forced to expose him. The straw that broke Sheela's back was his demand for thirty Rolls in one month, although at the time, he had more than ninety Rolls already. Why the humongous greed for Rolls? He said that it's his device to destroy the pride of America, the richest nation on earth. It's his prankish ploy to arouse jealousy, from the US president to evangelical clergies with private planes, and Silicon Valley billionaires. To sink vast sums of money and human energy in a prank! Did he succeed? I don't know. In the end, they all perhaps had a good laugh upon seeing him being paraded on national TV in irons.

The entire commune blissfully believed that the master is god. He not only knows what's best for them, but certainly what's best for

America—nay, the entire earth—and he has no self-interest at all. They trusted him totally with their wives, their wealth and children, their minds, and lives, believing that he would take care of them. Both the books portray him as insanely greedy for money as well as luxury diamond watches and pens. Is he a mercenary, or is he playing some high order game? He throws a hissy fit if his personal demands are delayed or denied because the commune is in heavy debt. Only Osho and his inner circle lived in royal luxuries. Meanwhile, Jane's young son, also a *sannyasin*, went around in cracked and battered sneakers because of lack of funds for the drab and unsexy necessities of life. It's hard to forget the image of Osho leaving his crumbling empire, clutching his jewel box, which would soon be confiscated by the US authorities, in his private jet with his inner circle. With no safety net, the minions on the ground were left to fend for themselves.

Amma's enfant terrible aspect, expressed as physical abuse, especially of her close female devotees for minor mistakes, has already been discussed. Her inner circle of devotees, including Gail herself, is hypnotized by the belief "she (Amma) is my guru, so it (beating) has to be for my highest good." As Gail wakes up from her trance, she writes, "I began to see her (Amma) as someone who exploits people's inherent desire to belong, to be loved, to find meaning in life." With a heavy heart, Gail describes Amma's selfishness. "All that Amma worries about is her image. Everything picture perfect. Not a drop of concern for the individual, for me." Similarly, Osho showed no outward concern for Sheela or Jane or other devotees who went to prison for illegal activities instigated directly or indirectly by him. At Amma's ashram, she and the male devotees got the cream, while the watered-down version was given to the female devotees. Her selflessly serving female devotees are described as having "ashy skin, sunken eyes, slumped posture and thinning hair." When Gail escaped from Amma's euphoria-saturated devotional prison, she described herself as "the walking corpse"—her reward for decades of selfless service and surrender.

UG Krishnamurti, lovingly described by Louis Brawley in his book *Goner: The Final Travels of UG Krishnamurti*, is an incarnation with a relatively milder vein of cruelty, although with a wicked and raunchy mouth. UG loved playing slapstick kind of goofy theater with Louis, who writes that he was like a two-year-old who loves to be spun around again and again. Sometimes UG would pour water on him and tell his audience that he was facilitating his spiritual progress. Louis was UG's court jester, with a mandate to make his audience laugh. While he was figuring out new comedy material, UG would unleash "fresh beating on him." Overall, Louis enjoyed UG's attention as if it were "gold."

In the following incident, according to me, UG crossed the line and became a full-blown enfant terrible (or a terrible father—I can't decide). In India, UG had a sore throat, and a juicy question was put to him with a potential to launch him into a harangue. Louis, mindful of UG's ailment, got upset with the lack of sensitivity of the questioner. The "little old sage" walked up to Louis and slapped him three times, calling him "filthy bastard" and forcefully screaming at him to keep his mouth shut. Louis was rightfully shocked, but the Indian devotees assured him that it's a privilege to be beaten by your guru. That's the eastern conditioning. Louis got the "unmistakable message" never to interfere, even though it was out of concern for UG's well-being.

In his book, Louis extols UG as the most compassionate and sweetest man he has ever met. I don't doubt that at all, but UG had an inconsiderate and shockingly uncouth aspect to him. Louis writes that a woman receptionist at NBC asked UG for his opinion on ecology. He reminded her that she was still wiping her ass with toilet paper after shitting. Ouch! According to Louis, during car drives in Europe, he would toss out the window the used cups and napkins, along with his spit, on the "immaculate highways of the world." If a driver in the passing car gave him an evil eye, UG's insouciant response was, "You clean it up, then." I was stunned to notice that UG's gross Indian behavior was rather endearing to his Western fan club.

Don't get me wrong—I hold UG in high regard. I value his clear and concise enlightened statements: "If you want one thing, you will surely get it. Or your job in life is to shut up." This is 100 percent truth, delivered accurately and efficiently. I know that no good is going to come out of my hissy fit, since gurus/gods—as UG, Osho, Amma, or Tibetan Rinpoches and lamas—are truly not open to being shown they are wrong. The pervasive and pernicious belief is that gurus don't make mistakes because their actions come from the non-duality wisdom of emptiness. Since ancient times, gurus have rejected duality as illusory, which it is, although there's no world without it, not even of guru and disciple. I would most certainly be given a collective stink eye emanating death rays by their devotees and ceremonially expelled from the fold for expressing my truth. It would matter naught to me because, in UG's immortal words, I have found the "courage to stand alone."

Chapter 54

Failed Gods: As Dictators and Misogynists

The things in the world that we think are terrible are
great teachers.

—Byron Katie

THE GROUNDBREAKING BOOK *ENTHRALLED: The Guru Cult of Tibetan Buddhism* is written by Christine A. Chandler, MA, CAGS. After almost three decades of mindful meditation and one pointed guru worship, when at last her devotional fever breaks, she feels she has "broken out of a glass prison for the mentally ill." I noticed in her book that Rinpoche Sogyal always showed up with a train of epithets such as "misogynist extraordinaire, an alleged sexual predator, the alleged sexual and physical abuser of hundreds of western women, a spiritual fraud," and so on. I don't know Rinpoche Sogyal but any mention of his name in her book would invariably cause a disturbance in my psyche, as if I had heard of him or knew him from somewhere. Pretty soon, a powerful click, and I ran to open Jed McKenna's book *Spiritual Warfare*. There he was, Sogyal Rinpoche, his wise and memorable words as the introductory quote in one of the chapters in Jed's book. I have found the following piece from Sogyal, quoted by Jed, as an extremely powerful wake up aid that I have myself read several times and I have read it aloud to my seeker friends. Sogyal Rinpoche writes,

> "Perhaps the deepest reason why we are afraid of death
> is because we don't know who we are. We believe in
> a personal, unique and separate identity—but if we
> dare to examine it, we find that this identity depends

entirely on an endless collection of things to prop it up: our name, our "biography," our partners, family, home, job, friends, credit cards …. It is on their fragile and transient support that we rely for security. So when they are all taken away, will we have an idea of who we really are?

"Without our familiar props, we are faced with just ourselves, a person we do not know, an unnerving stranger with whom we have been living all the time but we never really wanted to meet. Isn't that why we have tried to fill every moment of time with noise and activity, however boring and trivial, to ensure that we are never left in silence with this stranger on our own?"

Who writes like this? Who speaks like this? A sexual predator? An abuser who beats men and women with a stick! According to me, it's someone who clearly knows who he is, someone in touch with his deepest essence—so rare. Someone who is enlightened, someone who has taken the inner journey. Yet I believe Christine fully. But what to do with Rinpoche's dark side? My mind hobbled for days from extreme cognitive dissonance. Sogyal, a millionaire monk according to Christine, has a harem of devoted and loyal, professional Western women. He sadistically beats and humiliates them and occasionally has them wipe his ass to prove their devotion to him as their guru and living Buddha. Most of his female devotees cover up for him thus enabling his sexual abuse. She writes that a few woke women have complained, since there exists a Canadian documentary of his sexual and physical abuses (*In the Name of Enlightenment*). There are few lawsuits against him but as yet no criminal charges. According to Christine, the reason for this is the support from high places, such as the Dalai Lama, along with Hollywood heavies, billionaires, friends, media outlets, and powerful professional devotees, all praising and endorsing Lama Sogyal. Why? Because, according to me, Rinpoche is intimate with the "unnerving stranger," the ground of our being, the immortal one, beyond life and death. They all long for a taste of That, of Heaven; all of humanity does. The main reason for humanity's disregard of guru's dharma shit is the existential terror of meeting "the stranger" directly. They all hope and believe that the guru will magically connect them with their Being, thus liberating them forever from earthly worries and concerns.

She calls Tibetan Buddhism a "guru-worshipping cult," disguised as "master-slave dynamic" of the most nefarious kind. I would like to put the Indian gurus under my current scrutiny, Osho, UG, and Amma, along with Tibetan heavies Sogyal and her "perfect guru," Lama Trungpa, in one basket and label it "enlightened dictators." I'm using Lama Trungpa's words from Christine's book. Osho hated democracy and promoted meritocracy, which turned out to be a one-man dictator government, such as his ashram, especially in the USA. The ashrams of these gurus and most spiritual groups seem still to be based on traditional authoritarian models. Christine describes Chogyam Trungpa, her teacher, as exceptionally charming and charismatic although with "a despotic vein of cruelty." UG's biographer, Louis Brawley, writes that in the lobby of a Parisian hotel, he was looking for UG. The concierge said to him that your "dictator" is in his room.

All of them are sexually promiscuous, except UG, with "movie star looks" but "a shriveled penis," which he blamed on enlightenment. Osho definitely followed the Tantric trend described by Christine, of offering a special audience for the female students whom the guru fancied. It was Sheela's job to bring in the evening, the hot chicks who turned on Osho, wearing a robe, sans underwear, to keep the energy undivided and circulating freely. When I read in Gail's book Amma's sexcapades with her boys, whom she calls her sons and proudly presents to the world as celibates, I was thunderstruck. The sex between guru (representing the authority and unconditional love and caring of a mother and father) and the disciple has a noxious incestuous stink for me. Guru exists only to free the disciple from the chains of the ego. I can't see how mingling of the so called supernatural and divine body fluids of an enlightened being with a disciple, who is blinded by devotion, can bring about the disciple's spiritual development. According to me, even consensual sex with a worshipful disciple is exploitation. What to say of non-consensual sex with disciples and innocent children!

In her book, Gail rationalized to herself that Amma is doing it perhaps to contain the male sexual energy in her ashram. Can I see

Amma's immeasurable compassion and unconditional concern for her male disciples in her sexual encounters? It's a stretch! But it is possible, if I bring into consideration the extreme repression of sex by orthodox Hindu society, and its extreme exaltation of celibacy, especially as applied to the female sex. Most of the gurus publicly present themselves as celibates and preach celibacy to their followers as an express route to the divine. Privately, on the other hand, some of them are fucking their brains out.

Christine is a social worker with a graduate degree in psychology in sexual abuse and trauma. Yet she was so effectively mind controlled that she would deny and rationalize her guru's and other lamas' sexual and physical abuse, as did the rest of her group. They called this treatment "blessings" offering a most coveted "glimpse of a state of non-duality." Nonetheless, a heavy price was being paid for these glimpses—by the psyche in the form of denial and a slipping into deeper and darker egoic states.

All the gurus have amassed vast wealth. Osho was perhaps on the top of the heap as the richest and most flashy and flamboyant guru ever to grace this illusory earth. The least among them, with the smallest following, was UG, who had nearly a million dollars saved up in Swiss banks. Amma is sleeping on the bed of money and gold jewelry, according to Gail. The Tibetan gurus have titles such as Shambala king, regent, earth protector, and they live like royals in the United States.

Christine, under the Tantric spell, would learn to see herself and the cult members as special and "superior to the whole human race." According to me, this divine arrogance (from which I too suffered briefly) was one of the causes of lack of cultural sensitivity and the downfall of Osho's ashram in the United States.

Once Christine started waking up from her nightmarish story, she saw the Tantric cult as an "opiate addiction" and would say, "Guru worship is a hard addiction to give up." Even Louis, the follower and biographer of the anti-guru UG, with a bristle tongue, rhapsodizes over the "charm of his (UG) company" and how "being a junkie, you could never get enough of him." A reminder that Louis was slapped by UG for a minor mistake and yet he writes that he was determined to hang on to him "no matter what."

Like autocrats, all the above gurus love praise and adoration and despise doubts and disagreements. Buddha's timeless attraction has been his insistence on thinking for yourself and "[being] a light unto yourself." But when the reality is laid bare, adoration and blind obedience are the required attitudes with all of the above gurus except UG. According to Christine, followers are urged to frequently repeat to themselves, "My guru is the best." "How amazing are his teachings." How amazingly lucky we are to have found these living Buddhas. The followers take vows to protect their lama's secrets, or else they will go to hot and cold Vajra hell for eternity. According to me, both the victim and the perpetrator are displaying their dysfunctional conditioning of secrets, sins, and punishments. Christine was so deeply indoctrinated in the guru cult that for decades she didn't leave her home without the locket containing a piece of Trungpa's hair and his ceremonial robe.

But is there a difference between a political dictator and an enlightened dictator? Is there a difference between an ordinary pedo, a sexual and physical abuser, and an enlightened abuser?

Chapter 55

Failed Gods: As Magicians

Allegiance to any spiritual teaching or teacher—any outside authority—is the most treacherous beast in the jungle.

—Jed McKenna, *Spiritual Enlightenment: The Damnedest Thing*

VISUALIZE A TRANSPARENT GLASS FILLED with sandy, murky water. Let it sit in a corner, undisturbed, for a couple of hours. All the muck and sand will have settled down, leaving clear and pure water. This is an apt metaphor for meditation. The crap in the glass settles down all by itself. Meditation, in its purest definition, is a non-doing, a simple, effortless being. Sounds easy, huh! It's the hardest concept to grasp. It is naturally rife with misunderstandings, requiring years of sitting silently, waiting for the crud floating in the mind to settle down. When this happens, it's a tectonic shift that burns up the individual's attachment to the mind. Sediment at the bottom of the glass is the ego, or personal consciousness, which consists of dualistic concepts: I/ you, up/down, and so on. Universal consciousness, the pure and clear water on top, is free from thought content and is the ground of being, not only of humanity but of the entire universe. Nothing was done to attain universal consciousness or to purify and clean the muddy water— absolutely nothing—except allowing the crud to settle by itself.

All the gurus in the last chapter, which I have put in a box labeled "enlightened dictators," have developed a singular knack of disentangling their personal consciousness from the crud of the mind. They immensely enjoy resting in the indescribable void of pure consciousness. This cool knack is the majestic masterpiece of the guru, commanding awe and the deep devotion of the devotees. It's the ultimate freedom as well as rest and relaxation, unimaginable but deeply yearned for by humanity.

The brutal dictators Hitler and Lenin, politicians and pedophiles, and physical and sexual abusers, live submerged in the dense murkiness of the mind, identified with their thoughts and concepts. Their power comes from outside. They know themselves only as egos and slavishly and indiscriminately obey their dualistic minds. Their singular knack is that of seeing the false as real and the ability to convince humanity of the validity of their divisive concepts. Humanity, already mesmerized by its identification with body-mind, easily falls under the spell of the dictators and abusers. None of them have a clue that they are not their thoughts but are the awareness itself.

The gurus are identified neither with their personas nor with their thoughts. They observe their personas and thoughts as though they belong to someone else. They are identified with the subject, the watcher of the thoughts, the invisible "unnerving stranger." Thus untethered, they dissolve into the boundless field of silent aloneness, widely known as enlightenment. Slavish devotion to god or guru is our chintzy attempt to dress up the eternal aloneness which is believed to be a terrifying black hole by humanity. Guru becomes the superhero, sweeping and swooping the sky of emptiness like an ethereal eagle. Their awesome powers come from within. The perfume of serenity, unconditional love, and compassion, which they effortlessly exude, intoxicates and pulls humanity like a magnet. Seekers yearn to be close to such a rare flower and some of them are willing to pay the required price.

Guru, when she returns back to earth from the great beyond, is going to need a persona to function in the world. Her earthly persona is in disrepair because of her identity and romance with the void that contains everything. Since she is able to observe her persona and is able to slip in and out of it, she sees it as fake and meaningless but also as a necessity for her guru work. Guru, then, is an inescapable black hole, lightly disguised as a human being. On the other hand, most of humanity is unconsciously identified and fused with shiny, functional, and well-fitting personas. Their dressed and decorated exteriors hide and guard their inner black hole from themselves and from others. The Guru is nearly inhuman and godlike, and the rest of humanity is all too human! Now, imagine the misunderstandings and mistakes, frictions and fireworks, between the two. But the guru pays no heed because she knows of the transient nature of all turbulences.

The personas of my gurus, which also include Tibetans, have roots in Indian soil. Patriarchy, authoritarianism, male chauvinism, and the child-rearing culture of over-correction and under connection continue to shape the psyche of India. Amma chided Gail, raised in relatively freer Australian society, not to talk and laugh loudly for the fear of sexually arousing men in the next room. This shows me how Amma was raised and is imposing similar restrictions on her female followers. UG, slapping his biographer, indicates the violent culture of control in his childhood. Violence from Osho, dripping and oozing soulful grace and love, shredded my sanity. The event is recorded in Jane Stork's book. He slapped his English girlfriend of decades with his slipper, giving her a black eye, because of her chronic fits of jealousy. Does his enlightenment transform what looks essentially like an act of violence into a gift of grace? I have heard sages and mystics say that when you're thoroughly dead (i.e., totally egoless), you're free to do whatever you want. But could Osho have momentarily slipped back into reactive darkness? His relationship with his girlfriend was a toxic brew of problems that made Sheela, his secretary, painfully aware that he had "many weaknesses of the ordinary man."

They were raised with the concept of nonviolence and reverence for life. Osho's discourses on reverence for life could melt a stony heart. Christine talks of physically abusive lamas on the East Coast purchasing the caught lobsters from the fishermen and releasing them with compassionate flourish back into the waters. While I was growing up, my mom would tenderly pick up a spider and deposit it gently outdoors but wouldn't hesitate to beat the shit out of me for some misdemeanor. She didn't see her behavior as violent because of the centuries-old collective societal belief in punishment as necessary to raise obedient children and good citizens. No one did because they were all culturally fitted with similar lenses and filters.

I see the same dynamics at work with all the aforementioned gurus. Beating and abusing disciples and occasionally driving them to mental and physical collapse for the sake of their spiritual growth has been the way of the enlightened masters since antiquity. Does verbal or physical ego-busting bring about freedom from the ego, or does it frighten the ego into darker density? I have seen more recorded examples of the former. My personal guess is that the latter group may be much larger but has gone unrecorded due to fear of divine retribution.

The old-world personas of my gurus still seem to be acceptable in the East but are causing them grief in the West. Their deeply ingrained unexamined beliefs are reflected in their behavior of sexual and physical abuse, as well as substance abuse. Their thunder, their laboriously attained at-homeness and coziness with the pure consciousness, can't be emphasized enough. It clearly sets them apart from most of humanity, but their misdemeanors can no longer be justified on the ever-changing global platform they have chosen to influence.

I took a major leap into maturity when I realized meditation alone and resting in truth might or might not clean up my mind of the lingering untrue thoughts that were tripping me up in the world. Enter Byron Katie, a fully homegrown American enlightened master carrying the existential gift of "The Work." In her book *A Thousand Names for Joy*, she writes that if the thoughts are only watched, as in meditation, but not investigated, they "retain the power to cause stress." Having suffered enormously, I agree with her totally. "The Work," says Katie, unpacks the beliefs, revealing that they don't match reality. Take the still-robust ancient belief that man is superior to woman. This may have been true once upon a time, but in the modern Information Age, it's a lie. "The Work" connects us to the body and shows how it is affected by an untrue thought. In this case, it puffs up the believing male ego and gives him caveman swagger and an attitude of entitlement. As a woman, I feel deflated in my chest and have the resigned, stooped posture of an inferior human.

According to "The Work," by reversing the original belief, I arrive at a new belief, that women are superior to men. Equally true. But more importantly, I have liberated my attention stuck on the polarity of male supremacy. Questioning the belief makes future gender equality experiences possible. "The Work" exposed my deeply troubling belief that reality should be different from what it is. The whole human race is wedded to this belief including my gurus, to some extent or the other. Osho fought against the bureaucracy in India and fulsomely in the US because of immigration issues. He was a crusader for one world free of borders and passports, nations and races. A noble vision but not yet the reality.

Unfortunately, in this space age, Amma continues to honor the untrue Hindu belief that a woman is impure during her menstrual periods. Not only that, but her Hindu culture believes that a truly divine woman of Amma's caliber has transcended the physical ignominy of menstruation. The society considers itself very religious but seems to be silently screaming at life/god, "You don't know WTF you're doing!" It's not enough that Amma has the rarest knack of silently, nonverbally stirring the human soul and connecting it to the timeless being within five minutes or so. The culture demands a pure body, free from periods and smelly sweat and absolutely zero sex drive for both sexes, as well as several other inhuman requirements. So the gurus get in the habit of hiding their human frailties and using the disciples as a cover from the judgments of society. Such grand hypocrisy!

Gurus need to look at their definition of surrender and bring it into the modern age. Nonconsensual sex as requirement for guru-surrender is a punishable crime in most modern societies, including India. As a result, two very well established and revered gurus are doing prison time. I'm thrilled to see the millennial Indian females kick ass and break the ancient female mold of meekness, obedience, and submission to authority.

Another belief—the guru as god, which confers godlike powers that are then abused by some gurus—has been courageously exposed by whistleblowers perhaps for the first time in human history. I don't doubt that the guru lives and breathes in god/truth, but she is still in the body, with a mind shown to contain ancient uninvestigated beliefs. The human part of the guru is inarguably small—let us say less than even 10 percent—and her godly part is not only more than 90 percent but rather infinite. Now, think of a tiny mosquito. So small, and yet it has the power to cause not only intolerable discomfort but life-threatening diseases. The five books I have mentioned have given voices to the victims of their bites and stings. I see an urgent need for the gurus to clean up their beliefs, meaningless from the perspective of infinite being, but vicious and demeaning from the human perspective. Humanity, too, needs to grow up and take responsibility for their life rather than abandoning it at the feet of the guru, like a child. In my opinion, unkind acts or words, whether by parents, a guru, or a government, show only one thing: that thoughts of separation are being believed. In the entire universe, there is nothing faster than believing an untrue thought that can disconnect us from uninterrupted peace and joy of being, which is our human birthright.

Chapter 56

The Mommy Spell!

> To be enlightened—just to take the First Step on
> the actual journey toward enlightenment—is to be
> henceforth and forever excluded from the whole human
> thing.

> —Jed McKenna, *Spiritual Enlightenment: The*
> *Damnedest Thing*

MY FRESHLY FREED FEARLESS ATTENTION, having lost most of its ability to stick to thoughts, decided to revisit several thousand handwritten pages of spiritual autolysis. My purpose was to hunt out any emotional beasties still struggling to survive. There was only a page or two devoted to indescribable and inexpressible truth, although I had spent and continue to spend an incalculable amount of time soaking and swimming in it. There were times when my ego treated truth as some emotional ideal to live up to. At other times, ego itself, the grand problem, is frustrated as it looks for truth, which is impossible to lose, thus revealing its undying passion for drama and problems. The more dramatic the situation, the gnarlier the problem, the more I felt like a super woman. My consciousness merrily went on these topsy-turvy rides, having neither the full clarity nor the confidence to reject them as not-truth.

Pages and pages recording my ambiguous relation to the aloneness of truth. Initially, I had met a single retired guy in Ajijic, and I fell for him. He was kind of a dick. The motive behind my sure-to-fail romance was to be saved somehow from the vague and uncertain spiritual journey I had embarked upon. Luckily for me, he soon left for a beach town. The needy and nervous human in me was occasionally desperate for contact. But it was seen as an escape from the inevitable pain of unscrewing and shedding more of the nuts and bolts fastening me to my mind. There were times when the longed-for silence of truth would drive me bat-shit crazy. Too much silence, too much peace, too much death of personhood. The notes clearly revealed that it wasn't truth but my belief in my thoughts about loneliness, my belief in the story that I needed human contact, love, and friends, that was driving me to despair.

There were times of clarity, when these anguish-filled thoughts were seen through as fabrications of my struggling ego, the bully-in-chief, deeply attached and committed to creating misery! Stacks of notes exposed my mind's addiction to conflict and being always right, recorded events of Ego's lust and thirst for survival! Then, there would be several months of peace and no drama, but also no writing. It became progressively clear that no attachment to thoughts meant no suffering and therefore no writing. Attachment to a thought, especially a negative one, would promptly plunge me into hell, followed by fast and furious writing to escape from hell. At such times, a whole bunch of well-armed gangsta thoughts would unite and urge me to open my eyes and see that nothing is happening, absolutely nothing! I had lost everything and gained nothing, zero. How many more years did I intend to stay in self-imposed solitary confinement, from which truth would not liberate me since it obviously didn't have such powers? Many times, my attention, realizing these were only thoughts, vaporized legions of them in an instant. One special thought mocked me; that I was fake and was doing nothing more than pretending my suffering away. I was asked with the confidence of Dr. Phil, "And how's that working out for you?" I had recorded lumps of burning pain in my throat and heart—a sign of continuing slavery to my mind.

A few pages down, I had written about some sexual feelings I had noticed for a younger woman here in Ajijic who could have passed for my daughter. It struck terror in my heart. Am I a lesbian and may be a pedo? My mind had sent me its best punch so far. I was wobbly and disoriented. I was so terrified that I stopped writing for a few days.

Soon, I realized that I had been seduced once again by the smooth operator—my ego. On examining the sexual thoughts further, since I hadn't gone deep enough due to fear, they turned out to be lifeless duds. The woman of my interest had loads of emotional issues that I wished to lighten because I thought I had the necessary skills and endless compassion. Actually, I was yearning for a hit of psychological Prozac (i.e., being needed by somebody). In reality, it was my ego's chilling strategy to survive.

Many months later I wrote about a mini video released by my subconscious during deep meditation. My mom, dead for more than a decade, showed up in her crisp lily-white sari, her thinning white hair pulled back tightly in a bun. I was with this young woman and told my mom, "Meet my wife." My mom was visibly confused and horrified, knowing nothing about lesbians and same sex marriage. The end! My mental video lasted no more than two to three seconds. It was the end of my meditation too! I had recorded how the vision caused my old body to tremble uncontrollably from deep inside. Vibrations of neural networks were out of control. It all happened so fast I had no time to remind myself that I was the glorious watcher, unmoving and unchanging, rather than the one being watched, who comes and goes. Ha, ha!

I wrote in my notes that I didn't know what to do with this waking nightmare which had revealed itself in my meditation. Am I a lesbian? Is that the end result of my all-consuming spiritual search of "Who am I?" Howling laughter! No, it can't be my essence, which was here before the appearance of this seismic thought and still is here, totally unfazed and undisturbed. My attention, feeling bone naked, had allowed itself to be mesmerized by the possibility of a new identity as a lesbian. I had played with lesbian identity off and on since my university days in Canada and had rejected it again and again as ill-fitting. My mind had donned it once again, perhaps out of loneliness and deprivation—not only of male attention but of human contact and connection in general. My terrified mind had created this scenario to avoid its certain death from the near-total social isolation of my seeker lifestyle. It was another brilliant trick of the mind!

What about the ghost of my moral mother haunting me when I, myself, was sitting in death's transit lounge? Why did I come undone at my mother's stern gaze of horror at meeting my imaginary wife? What am I really afraid of? Really, really! I had been unconsciously and skillfully hiding the answer from myself under a mountain of recorded pesky thoughts and feelings. In reality I was paralyzed by fears and immense resistance to exposing my addiction to drugs, sex and rock 'n' roll to my family and the world. Yet how could I write about my spiritual journey without mentioning my intimate encounters with drugs and sex? I couldn't see how. What would I say? There are scatterings of fearful thoughts about how my conservative family and my orthodox country of birth, India, would receive my still unwritten book, which would challenge the Hindu society that is entrenched in ancient patriarchy.

Months later was recorded the brutal killing of young and gorgeous Pakistani model, Qandeel Baloch, known in social media as Pakistani Kim Kardashian. She was strangled by her brother, who, in turn, was harassed by society for violating its cultural and religious norms. Luckily, my only surviving sibling, my brother, lives in America and has dropped those shitty, suffocating values in favor of relatively liberal values. Most of my close family also live in America, and a few are married to Americans. They may be shocked because I have tightly concealed, so I think, the wild and rebellious side of my personality. For security reasons and to gain respect, I had projected the safe and stolid persona of a professional; reliable, independent, and in control of her life. Further down the page, I saw a question: Imagine you have the complete book in your hand. How would you feel about presenting it to your parents if they were alive? Sweaty and turbulent! It was about the same psychological reaction as when I introduced my imaginary wife to my mom: crushing shame and guilt for ruining the family reputation. Revisiting the notes lit up a lightbulb in my brain. An ancient mommy spell ("What'll the people say!") had been passed on to me unbroken by her. The fear of others had been her guiding light and first principle of morality. To her credit, people often do say vicious things and do gruesome deeds, as shown by the death of Qandeel Baloch, mentioned above. What are some of the vitriolic pronouncements I fear from my conservative clan, dead and alive? "There's absolutely no need to have written such an embarrassingly foul-smelling book! That, too, at her age, before dying! Who reads such shit? Delusional old fart, comparing herself to enlightened Buddha! Lock her up." And much more. Nonetheless, as an American citizen of the twenty-first century, I plan to lay all my cards on the table, regardless of consequences!

I perused the notes for more trails of breadcrumbs to the ancient house of shame and guilt. I found a couple of paragraphs from my days of slavery to my mind. The question being asked: Do I consider chemical mysticism to be immoral cheating, an unethical shortcut? A vague *perhaps* was my answer. Spirit, or universal consciousness, is impervious to everything from mind altering drugs to cyanide, including super deadly viruses, bullets, and bombs. They work only on the body-mind. No small thing! I have repeatedly described attachment to the ego as the only obstruction to truth. In my case, the drugs temporarily deactivated my ego and repeatedly shook my stone solid worldview. They provided me not with glimpses but with huge vistas of truth, but I couldn't sustain my encounters because of my unchallenged ego. Cannabis helped many times to mollify inherited suicidal thoughts by deflecting my attention to breathing, which was enough to break contact with my ego-gone-berserk. I had hoped that my solitary sojourn in Mexico, devoid of social and marketplace stresses, would cure me of my drug addiction. Then I would write my squeaky-clean spiritual masterpiece, in which vanquished sex, drugs, and rock 'n' roll would be a mere footnote. Ha, ha! Dreams within dreams! On the contrary, endless self-imposed solitude stirred up deeply buried anxieties and terrors that, due to lack of distractions, I had to face head-on. Currently, I consider myself irretrievably healed of my primary addiction to my mind. Yet I continue to enjoy my gentle explorations of drugs and my brain chemistry. Did drugs ever really save me any time? I noticed that where the answer was written the entire page was rough and crinkly from puddles of my dried tears. How to rate a journey which started around age thirty and is still continuing after seventy-eight years? It should perhaps be judged as a cautionary tale by the future seekers of the spirit! There were times when I saw my inner journey as a moronic ride of circuitous and meaningless meta twists. Who in their right mind would volunteer to take this journey? Would I do it again? Heck, yes! Call me insane!

With or without drugs, it's the destiny of all humans to sooner or later acknowledge and realize their undying connection with non-dual spirit prior to and beyond the mind. My favorite part of the journey? The end! Body alive, vibrant, and super sensitive, and mind empty of thoughts, yet alert, sharp, and brilliant floating, peacefully and joyously in the shoreless ocean of truth! It is the peak of human fulfillment! Flamboyant wealth, devoted family, fulfilling marriage, legions of loyal friends and fans, rewards and accolades of a successful career—nothing, but nothing, in my playbook, trumps the rest and relaxation of the silence of no-self. Death, which greedily gobbles up all, can't touch the sublime satisfaction and fulfillment of completing the existential cosmic game of realizing my ego-less unity with the ocean of pure energy.

Chapter 57

A Miraculous Success

"Play gracious one." Shiva to his consort Parvati.

—Osho, *Book of Secrets*

THIS CHAPTER WAS INSPIRED BY a New Yorker article called "Sweet Smell of Success," dated November 4, 2019, written by Carina Chocano. Star of the story is middle aged Suzy Batiz, a spiritual seeker. In this, my favorite spiritual scenario, she finds not only the kingdom of god within but also without. She made "Forbes's list of America's richest self-made women." I'm thrilled to meet spiritual seekers who are glowingly successful in both the worlds. Some of them, like Oprah, Michael Singer, Dr. Deepak Chopra, all of them Americans, come dancing to mind along with Suzy Batiz. Suzy ascribes her flamboyant business success to her spiritual evolution. She sees herself not as an entrepreneur but a spiritual explorer "whose medium just happens to be business." My interest in Batiz's story is related to her golden product, which is a toilet spray made from essential oils creatively labeled as "Poo-Pourri." Its job is to take the smell out of shit, which it must do extremely effectively to anoint her as one of the richest self-made women in America.

I'm not interested in eradicating shitty smells, but in the shit hole itself. Henceforth I'm going to address it respectfully, which it absolutely deserves, by a politically correct label of root or first chakra. Chakras are focal points of psychic energy which revealed themselves to me spontaneously as my mind became progressively quiet. I didn't go looking for them. Initially the root chakra, terribly contracted and squeezed, came into clear focus while I was waiting in a line. I was shocked at the sheer ferocity of tension and tightness extending from the anal area to the base of spine, perineum (area between anus and scrotum or vulva), and my vagina, into my belly button area. My ex-guru Osho said that the body has two poles. Head as the upper pole has to do with the intake of food, air, impressions and thoughts. The lower pole, below the navel is for release and relaxation. Most of us are focused on and treat the upper part of the body with full attention, respect and maybe even pride, and the lower part, which is considered smelly, as dirty and even evil. The lower part has not only a lower location but also lower and negative value and meaning in most cultures. This, even though without the lower part humanity is virtually up shit creek. In my case, whenever my attention visited the lower pole of my body, it was invariably met with chronic tension and tightness, although I had no medical issues, not even constipation at the time. What's going on down yonder? Over time I developed a tender relationship with my root center. I would remember to wash and dry it with awareness which means bringing my attention down below.

For me, experientially, the three energy centers below the navel, and the crown center on top of the head, have been the most important. Root and crown chakra seem to be connected via a tube of energy which so far, I have only vaguely felt. Consciously contracting and releasing the root chakra relaxes it, enhances awareness of perineum which links the front with the back of the body and also strengthens pelvic floor muscles. Working with the root center is a big win for existential activities of sex, pooping and peeing.

Suzy's holistic spiritual vision for her "Poo-Pourri" business is urging people to "letting shit go" along with the dead and toxic past. Another of Suzy's crazy maxim, "Do epic shit," requires a relaxed and healthy root chakra (uncommon in modern speed and stress-ridden cultures), a healthy diet of fiber, and some degree of relaxation around and below the belly button area. Most of us, me for certain, hold a lot of tension in the stomach area and below, of which we may become aware only if some problem develops down there. First time I became aware of merciless tightness and unconscious holding in my stomach area was when I tried to quit smoking cigarettes following Osho's instructions. His advice to wanna-be quitters was, pay your full attention to the smoke pattern from start to finish. Why and when you reach for the cigarette and how it's affecting your body according to your experience not according to Surgeon General's warning on the package. I immediately noticed tightness of my diaphragm (a major breathing muscle) as a result of chronic, unconscious holding of my breath. The act of sucking on the cigarette and breathing in seemed to relax the diaphragm. The act of smoking, which let me take the deep breath that had been prevented by spastic diaphragm muscles was perhaps the lesser of the two evils at the time. Pretty soon I realized that not only the diaphragm muscle but also the root chakra and my sex center were being chronically pinched and constricted by my unconscious and repressive thought patterns. Seeking truth, my primary search rather than struggling with addictions, helped dissolve a lot of dysfunctional thought patterns. My nicotine addiction dissolved as my awareness of breathing increased and my relaxation deepened.

Simple act of resting my attention in my stomach area was the magic which liberated my attention from the head, relaxed the constricting patterns of energy, resulting in "epic shits" and epic orgasms. Since Suzy has tripped on "Ayahuasca," I'm wondering whether her idea of "Do epic shit" is a by-product of that. First time I did an epic shit which had a deep orgasmic feel to it was on LSD. At the time I wondered about my first independent shit as a baby. Although I had no clear memory of it, it felt like it must have been an epic event. Then I tried to imagine my last shit before death which was so difficult that it messed up my mind. My first two Ayahuasca trips delivered epic shits of orgasmic proportions, the internal delight of which lasted for more than a week. However, it's not something I would put on my Ayahuasca trip agenda. It's a by-product of it.

I was happy to note in the article that as a result of her spiritual practices and Ayahuasca trips, Suzy lives more in her body than her head. According to me it's a huge step on the spiritual journey. The point I want to make is to let go of our archaic conditioning of guilt, shame and embarrassment associated with the lower half of the body. My suggestion is to bring your attention frequently down in your body. Play with your breath starting at the belly level, do some OMing, play with Kegel's exercises, relax and contract the root chakra while doing dishes or standing in line. In short, flood this dark and long neglected area with an increasing tsunami of life energy. The result is an uncreated abundance of well-being, which is our very essence. Another byproduct of visiting the root energy center whenever possible is the refreshing mini break provided from the relentless chatter in the head. Hopefully, this distancing of attention from the head will give precious insight that you're not your thoughts but awareness of your thoughts. Awareness is prior to thoughts and also prior to the energy body, which is extremely subtle. But pure awareness, or Presence, is even subtler than that, and it is our essence. To rest in essence free of attributes is the delight of my life.

My thanks to Suzy Batiz, the writer of the article *Carina Cocano* and *The New Yorker* magazine, my muse in Mexican solitude, for helping me push the boundaries of my "good girl" conditioning. I felt encouraged to share my insights which are the byproduct of shining the light of my consciousness "down below." Typically not done in polite spiritual circles!

Chapter 58

Must I Meditate?

Do you know, even metals need rest, even metals get tired? So what to say about this subtle mechanism of the mind? It is the most subtle mechanism in the world. And you're continuously using it, uselessly, unnecessarily, you have forgotten how to put it off.

—Osho Radio, "The Path of the Mystic"

To understand the immeasurable, the mind must be extraordinarily quiet, still.

—Jiddu Krishnamurti

In Zazen, leave your front and backdoor open. Let thoughts come and go. Just don't serve them tea.

—Shunryu Suzuki

Meditation is not a way of making your mind quiet. It's a way of entering into the quiet that's already there, buried under the 50,000 thoughts the average person thinks every day.

—Deepak Chopra, *The Human Condition: Lost in Thought*

The stream of thinking has enormous momentum that can easily drag you along with it. Every thought pretends that it matters so much. It wants to draw your attention in completely. Here's a new spiritual practice for you: don't take your thoughts too seriously.

Eckhart Tolle, *Stillness Speaks*

"Meditation is the ultimate mobile device; you can use it anywhere, anytime, unobtrusively."

Sharon Salzburg, *Real happiness: The Power of Meditation*

I'M LUCKY TO HAVE ONE family member who meditates. I was explaining to her on the phone my version of meditation. She requested that I email her my instructions. I hadn't written anything of that nature for a long while. Miraculously writing about meditation primed my creative pump, which has materialized into this book. Here is the highly edited format of my original email.

Meditation basically means no thoughts and silence, while mind means thoughts and noise. Meditation begins where the mind ends. Why is meditation gaining popularity on the planet? Other day I heard Hollywood heavy Bradley Cooper, one of my favorites, say on Oprah that he meditates daily. Then I saw Lupita Nyong'o, starring in her latest movie release "Us," saying she had just returned from a meditation retreat. Oprah is a pro at it. Anderson Cooper of CNN is interested in it. It seems to me that everyone is talking about meditation because of our addiction to smartphones and social media, which results in hyper stimulated, hyper connected minds. Consequently the modern brain is exhausted, earning itself the moniker of 'The sleepless generation.' Paradoxically, to point to the meditative silence, which is wordless and thoughtless, I must use words. There's no other way.

In my case, one fine lucky day after a couple of years of meditation, what is commonly known as personal consciousness or attention had freed itself from its habitual perch in the head. It was floating in front of my closed eyes. I couldn't see it or grasp it but I could sense and feel it — a dimensionless point. I wondered whether the ancient label of soul equals my modern label of attention. Pharrell Williams, singer, rapper and songwriter, on Oprah, called it the unit of consciousness which is very accurate. The itty bitty point of consciousness loves its dark cave-like residence in the head and is more addicted to thoughts than any humans addicted to substances, even heroin and opium.

The personal consciousness, or the 'I am', is identified with thoughts and the body: I'm pretty, I'm short, I'm a loser or a winner, create sensations in the body which are recognized as good or bad feelings. It is this identification with body-mind that walls off the universal consciousness, which is essentially indivisible and whole. Thus is created the illusion of a separate self. As a meditator your heroic goal is to turn your outbound attention inward. Liberate it from its all-consuming addiction to thoughts and beliefs in which it is virtually drowning.

I have further noticed that the brain can't think without the attention being in the head. Attention, clearly, is the switch which turns on/off the unstoppable chatterer in the head. Now the instructions for Vipassana meditation, sit straight and keep your attention on your breathing, make perfect sense. Also keep in mind that attention can focus only on one thing at a time, either thoughts or breath. So, if you find yourself thinking, silently redirect the attention to breathing. Your mind isn't going to like this, not even a tiny bit. The definition of the mind is movement, movement of thought. The mind is deeply habituated to movement and now it's being asked to stop. Expect extreme resistance and momentum of habit from the mind.

Early on I was instructed at the Osho ashram to watch or witness my thoughts with disinterest as if they belonged to someone else, like a chilled watcher on the hill observing the world. But my attention was too identified with thoughts, too interested in them. Then I tried focusing on my breath, in the nose or my belly but my attention would run away to my head again and again. I found it most effective to sink my attention in my belly button, maybe because of its distance from the head. Instant peace of mind! Instant meditativeness! Focusing on the heart or the center of the chest, works well too. Added benefit of focusing on the navel is that it's the source of life energy. Watch a baby breathe with constant up and down motion of the diaphragm. A baby has a small chest but a big and relaxed belly. As a result of focusing in the belly area I have noticed that my breathing has become very deep and subtle. So artistic and filled with unnamable ecstasies! An outcome of much meditation.

I want to make it clear here that there's nothing wrong with thinking — it's absolutely necessary for survival. But the mind is usually out of control and doesn't know how to stop. Osho compares it with walking, which requires your legs to move. But now you're sitting down and yet your legs continue to move all by themselves, unable to stop. That would look funny, huh! But such is the situation with our mind. It thinks ceaselessly and relentlessly, mostly unnecessarily. It stops in deep sleep and in some cases not even then.

Once you get the hang of meditation and are able to hold your attention at your favorite spot in your body or able to focus on breathing, notice the deep and all-pervasive peace surrounding you. It is already here, has always been here, without any effort on your part. This all-inclusive and uncreated peace gets covered up by thoughts, like clouds covering the limitless sky. Even a brief dip in this ocean of peace, which is our essence, is experienced as deeply nourishing and hydrating by the body and soul.

A playful attitude toward meditation is recommended by the masters. No effort is required to close your eyes and move your consciousness from head to heart or navel. But to ask your attention to abide in any of those areas, it'll resist fiercely. No wonder the ancients called it the monkey mind. The modern mind drowning in its epic content is portrayed accurately for our current times by Gail Tredwell, "fidgety as a monkey tied up in a patch of biting ants." Being addicted to content, it'll want to go back again and again to its cozy and familiar dark cave in the head. Some days sticky worldly issues will demand your full attention. On those days you may want to contemplate the thoughts which are troubling you. But still, don't forget to sink your attention into the infinite silence of pure consciousness. Even a few moments of resting attention anywhere in the body below your head will suffice. Even hands and feet work well. In this inner journey of meditation there's no success and no failure. You're already the meditativeness and the peace and joy you're seeking. But you can't see it because of the spiritual sleep caused by your attachment to words and thoughts. If you're already the meditativeness, then meditation cannot be a doing. It's a state of being and resting in your own presence. The rest enjoyed by your tired brain is akin to deep sleep but more precious because you're awake and alert. This state is called Samadhi in yogi language. As a novice, you'll get to taste the nectar of Samadhi in dribs and bits. As your skill level increases, you'll find yourself soaking effortlessly in the fathomless ocean of peace, your very essence. You have at last come home!

Chapter 59

For You, Bill Maher

"The gods sent hemp to the human race so they might
attain delight, lose fear and have sexual desires."

Hindu scriptures, written around 2000-1400 BCE.

WHY YOU, BILL MAHER? FIRSTLY because of your fearlessly
unbending commitment to marijuana. Me too! A committed
stoner! Total dedication to the sacred plant. In India a medicinal plant
called Tulsi is worshipped. As far as I'm concerned, the only plant, as a
matter of fact only form, I could bow to and worship is the marijuana
plant. Ancient Hindus called it a sacred plant, "which releases us from
anxiety." They also praised cannabis as "joy giver" and "liberator." It has
been my guru, guide and a reliable buddy on my fabulous inner journey
of self-discovery. Before I proceed further, Bill, I wish to share how
much I love your sharp, witty, informative, brilliantly intelligent and
yes, crazy creative HBO show "Real Time with Bill Maher." If I had
to describe in one word your TV persona, it would be "Wild." But wild
in a responsible and mature manner. I recall with a thrill the time you
pulled out a joint from the breast pocket of your sharp and chic business
suit during your live show on TV. Another word comes to mind for you
is "openminded."

On your TV show you're uninhibitedly passionate about cannabis,
sex, the Democratic Party, and your atheist worldview. Your catchy
sound bite, "No, to god. Yes, to drugs," initially impressed me as so
hip and right. My life has been a thumping yes to high times in all

their available forms. The process of writing this book has brought into sharp focus how god has managed to sneak into my life via LSD and cannabis. On acid I became aware that god is not a being or an entity or a miracle worker with moral commandments for the erring humans. God is not an object that can be taken apart, scrutinized or even talked about. God is the subject, the life force or Spirit which animates us all. One conscious breath on marijuana gave me such an intense taste of life, of high times that I became its instant devotee. I observed that there is a natural meditative space accompanying cannabis which is the very source of high times. I realized that I could deepen it by meditating. So was born a mad meditator out of greed to prolong the chemical high times! Meditation is a shift of attention from the left hemisphere of the brain, which houses the ceaselessly chattering restless ego, to the right hemisphere, which is ever cool, peaceful and naturally high. Anxiety, fear, low libido, which the ancients in my quotes above claimed are relieved by cannabis, are ego's nasty family members residing in the left brain. Drugs and meditation, both bypass the ego to reveal peace and wholeness of existence.

Another of your brilliant sound bites, Bill, which appeals to my quest for high times forever, is "masturbate, don't procreate." My meditative mind seized on it as the third cozy cousin of my high times trinity of 3Ms: marijuana, meditation and masturbation. They release a blitz of dopamine and anandamides (bliss chemicals found in cannabis and meditators), etc., in the brain. The cool cocktail of feel-good chemicals helps to free up the attention from the head and zoom it to the genitals during sex. If for some reason attention stays stuck in the head, then a tepid or no orgasm is the result. Sex with a partner? Same process, although richer and more potent.

Did the word meditation make you nervous because of religious overtones, mainly Eastern? Meditation has nothing to do with atheism or god or religion. It simply dials down the hyper-dominant and hyperactive left hemisphere of the brain, so that the right brain, which is naturally high, is able to come online. Marijuana does exactly the same. It's the gateway to tasting Existence, the flavor of which most of us have forgotten due to our lethal preoccupation with thoughts. Most of us eat like robots without tasting food and screw, too, like robots, without being present. Meditation and marijuana get us out of the rigid and narrow box of our safe self-narrative into relatively expanded narrative and open vistas. Two together help free up the personal consciousness, so it can move to the genital area, an absolute requirement for spectacular orgasms. All three together open up fountains and waterfalls of aliveness and wellbeing which is our essence. Originally this realization rattled me to the core. My essence, our essence, as the inexhaustible source of high times! Who knew! The cocktail of high time chemicals one day totally quieted the ceaseless chatter in my head. I had landed in the invisible lap of pure life energy/ god energy beyond chemicals and molecules. What went wrong? Or, rather, what went right for me! Combination of meditation, marijuana and an ancient Indian sex technique which unsurprisingly I came across in America, known appropriately as OM, or orgasmic meditation, were my liberators.

In order to make sex meditative, all you have to do is bring your attention below the head, preferably in the genital area. Easier said than done. Attention is totally enslaved and under the spell of the voice in the head which loves to point out our flaws and foibles. I have found the technique of OM or orgasmic meditation mentioned in the preceding chapters very valuable for freeing the attention from the head. It consists of having a partner lightly, very very lightly, and very slowly stroke a woman's clitoris. It virtually nails the attention of the woman on her clitoris and her partner's on the tip of the index finger doing the stroking. The technique helps to bring both partners into the here and now, the only place and time where orgasm happens. Attention fully engaged and present in the body rather than lost in dark and dreary corners of the mind, as usual. You can't get any more meditative and orgasmic than that. Nicole Daedone in her seminal book "*Slow Sex*" — a must read if you wish to elevate sex to an art form, emphasizes again and again that the clitoral strokes should be very slow and soft. Hard and fast strokes may mean the attention has drifted back to the head and is focused on thoughts of outcome, performance etc. OM brings sex from head to the body where it belongs.

The life sucking chatterer in our head loves feeling sorry, guilty, ashamed, worthless, angry, embarrassed and may even enjoy porn fantasies. I recently read that approximately 40% of females in America can't reach an orgasm because they are caught up in the head criticizing their body, their performance or concerned about their partner's pleasure. Possibly the unquestioned belief that they are less than or undeserving is blocking them from an orgasm. Cannabis, masturbation/sex, and meditation all serve to liberate us from time bound finite mind. They give us longed for experience of timelessness, connection with the self, with the other and most certainly with existence. Perhaps this is an important reason for humanity's obsession with sex and drugs and its willingness to sometimes risk all for this transcendent experience of timelessness and loss of control of the ego.

Nicole, however, doesn't recommend using OM for self-masturbation. Her point is that with self stimulation, mind remains in control, and orgasm is about joyous loss of control. She likens self OMing to tickling yourself. No fun I agree! I have personally found self OMing very beneficial in freeing my attention and directing it in my body away from mind. During regular masturbation and sex, I wasn't aware where my attention was, so, bringing attention to a precise location, the clitoris, from start to finish is very liberating, especially from performance anxiety and addiction to outcome of orgasm. Attention freed from the head is life's secret sauce of enjoyment. Self OMing has helped me immensely with peace of mind, increased relaxation and increased awareness in my body below the belly button area, which most people are reluctant to visit or talk about. My ex-guru Osho said that he had asked hundreds of women in India whether they have had an orgasm during sex. He said all of them looked at him with innocent curiosity and asked, "what's that?"

For men, Nicole recommends OMing an inch long area below the head of the penis as being sensitive and rich in nerve endings. Most important ingredient of all is attention. Success here would mean that the attention of both the partners is locked at the point of contact between her hand and his penis. Should your attention wander, which it will, bring it back to the point of contact. Anyone wanting to take sex to another level of fulfillment, or taste the juiciness of life, start with moving attention from head into body, such as chest, navel or feet. Attention stuck in the head is often stuck in the negative pole of duality, which will not permit enjoyment of sex or life. Masturbation, especially, and sex generally, are condemned by most religions of the world which are life negative, in that sense. I see masturbation, which in its current iteration I shall call self OMing, as holy and healthy. Holy because it helps to free the attention from the mind trance in a relatively easy and pleasurable manner. By healthy I mean intense feelings of well-being and bliss which accompany 3Ms. The highs keep getting higher because their source is infinite existence itself.

Laughter, especially deep belly laughter, which I frequently experience on your show, also helps to temporarily stop the internal dialog in the mind. If meditation is a pause for the mind, then so is the laughter. It's of the family of merry 3Ms. Deeper the laughter, wider the gap between two thoughts and deeper the silence in the mind. Also, deeper the feeling of relaxation. That's what humanity is seeking consciously or unconsciously. Well being generated by such a lifestyle creates natural care and respect for the human body — another of your pet projects.

P.S.

Please don't proceed with OMing, self or with a partner, before seeing Nicole Daedone's YouTube video or reading her book, *"Slow Sex: The Art And Craft of Female Orgasm."* It has many valuable details regarding body position, stroking and grounding, etc. In reality it is a manual for living a truly juicy, blissful, and fulfilling life.

Chapter 60

Magic of "The Work" of Byron Katie

He said "How long will you journey on?"
I said, "Until you stop me."
He said "How long will you boil in the fire?"
I said, "Until I am pure."

Rumi, *In the Arms of the Beloved*
Translation by Jonathan Star.

I HEARD OF BYRON KATIE AND met her for the first time at least a couple of decades ago in Maui. I used to go to Satsangs in an opulent up-country house with gorgeous views of the Pacific Ocean. At the end of Satsang, the host announced Katie's arrival next weekend. Since she's vegetarian, they needed a volunteer to cook a veggie dinner for her and approximately twenty more people. Since no hands went up, they repeated the request and still no takers. So, I volunteered, seemingly reluctantly, and I was given a helper. I'm kitchen averse. Don't own recipes or cookbooks or have ever even opened a cookbook. This is much before the internet and google era. I had willingly offered to lay my head on the chopping block. What a fool!

At home I smoked a joint to figure out what I should do and above all why an unskilled person like me, who can barely wield a knife safely, volunteered to cook for twenty people. After the joint, I sat down to ponder and naturally my eyes closed. Pretty soon I was in my mom's kitchen. She was one of the finest vegetarian cooks in the world. She was cooking Aloo Gobi or cauliflower and potatoes curry. I was watching her cook, which I never did when I was growing up despite her urges, advice and even commands. At the end of my meditation I had a fairly good idea of what I was going to do. I figured I must have indirectly and sideways observed my mom and aunties over a period of many years. My mind under duress had put together and condensed all its observations and analyses of the veggie curries consumed by me. I made curry early in the morning with my helper as we both wanted to attend the daylong session with Byron Katie. My spiritual circle of friends had heard about her but didn't wish to attend the meeting because they found her too mental. Luckily, I had no such luxury, since I was in charge of the food. At the meeting I fell in love with her boundless compassion, sense of humor, laser like focus and her technique for investigating stressful thoughts, which bears the super honest title of 'The Work'

My answer and reward — why the moron and spaz in the kitchen had offered to cook for the illustrious gathering — came when I served her dinner. It was an extremely simple meal of veggie curry and brown rice, which most Indians would rather die of shame than serve at a gathering. No chapatis, no samosas, no papadams or even pickles or chutneys. The voices of my dead aunts and cousins were disrupting me at every step but I clung to my defense that I was in America and cooking for the Americans, some of whom, perhaps, may be testing curry for the first time. When I presented the meal to Katie she gave me the most tender and loving look and said softly, "love on the plate. Thank you." I nearly dissolved into tears of joy but pulled myself together as I had to serve other guests.

Later, at home, over a joint, I started to bawl remembering Katie's gracious comment of "love on the plate." I had been served "love on the plate," three times a day for more than twenty years by my mom and later my husband. I had willfully rejected my mom's love on the plate while growing up because it had resulted in me packing on pounds. I had lost the weight with great discipline and difficulty. In my marriage, love on the plate was making us both obese, which was ok by my husband, but I wasn't willing to accept the love handles and a sagging tummy. I demanded different kinds of love unfamiliar not only to them but also to me. Later I would receive glimpses of a new kind of love from within. An unconditional love of my being, which would eventually turn me from a beggar for love in the outer world into a royal. In that moment I also saw my expertise at creating misery out of absolutely nothing while growing up and in my marriage. Hitherto I had seen them as the perpetrators of my misery but a casual yet authentic comment had revealed my responsibility in the bitter drama of my past. That night I lost a lot of ancient and entitled anger and resentment, my reward for being a fool. By the way, Katie and the rest of the guests enjoyed the curry.

I have not only read most of Katie's books but grokked them i.e., eaten and digested them with fervor. If ever I still suspected some attachment to my mind and could only have one book, it would be Katie's book, *"Loving What Is: Four Questions That Can Change Your Life."* I have noticed again and yet again that the only cause of my suffering has always been attachment to an untrue thought. There isn't anything else, if there is I haven't found it. Neither has Katie nor had Buddha. Or Jed. I have done 'The Work' on myself several times by following the instructions on her website "the work.com," with palpable psychological benefits. I came to Ajijic, Mexico with one purpose: to die of flesh, to die of my separate personhood and be reborn in the spirit. For a couple of years, I kept Katie's book *"Who would you be without your story?"* in a very visible spot on my bookshelf. It was my nano-bomb for destroying all kinds of stories, positive or negative, sweet dreams or nightmares. I was heading for storyless and conceptless silence of pure existence.

From my current perch of storyless life, my inner journey replete with terrifying monsters and emotional slippery slopes, seems more a comedy fest than a tale of tears and sorrow. All my trials by fire were made of concepts and thoughts onto which I was hanging relentlessly until I couldn't. I'm reminded of Katie's grandson Race's story, from the book, *"Loving What Is."* Katie had gifted him a plastic Darth Vader toy from the movie Star Wars, which he hadn't seen. The toy operated by a coin played Star Wars music and had Dart Vader's heavy breathing. She writes, "his (Darth Vader's) voice says, 'Impressive, but you're not a Jedi yet,' and he lifts his sword as if to emphasize the point." Three-year-old Race took it to his tender little heart that he wasn't a Jedi, although he didn't know what a Jedi was. Katie tried to humor the little guy saying that he can be her little Jedi but he wouldn't have it. Whenever asked, he would reply "in a sad little voice, " Grandma, I not a Jedi." She took Race for a plane ride over the desert and asked her friend the pilot to announce at the end of the trip "Racey you're a Jedi now." She writes "Racey rolled his little eyes in disbelief." Upon arriving home, he rushed to his toy Darth Vader for confirmation, which wasn't forthcoming. Katie asked him one more time if he was a Jedi yet and he sadly replied, "Grandma I not."

Katie summarizes the human condition, "Many of us judge ourselves as relentlessly as that plastic toy played its recording, telling ourselves over and over again what we are and what we're not." I, too, had many deeply buried menacingly insistent recordings in my brain, many of which dissolved spontaneously with meditation and spiritual autolysis mentioned earlier. Some I dismantled with "The Work" and some by deeply understanding where Katie was coming from. For example, during nearly a decade of solitude in Mexico, every now and then I would become painfully aware of the passage of time which would cause unbearable feelings of impending doom. It was perhaps on YouTube I heard a question put to Katie asking if she were in solitary confinement, how would she handle that. Her peaceful reply was that whether she is in a heartwarming company or in solitary confinement, it's the same to her. I know exactly where she is coming from because I live there too. But in that moment my attention was flirting with and attaching to an untrue thought: my friendless and loveless life is unbearable. Just hearing Katie's response vaporized my anxiety and angst over my endless loneliness which is an untrue concept. That's how flimsy is the dream state reality. Katie frequently says that when she enters a room filled with people, she knows everyone loves her, only they don't know it yet. Everyone usually chuckles. Only when I was established in the ground of being, which is the being of all, did I understand what she meant and then I howled with laughter.

Katie in her book, *"A Mind at Home with itself,"* says "in that place there's no death and you live alone forever. There's no light, no up or down, no possibility of movement, no anything. There's nothing, forever, with no way out. I felt such terror." With inquiry she became as comfortable in immovable nothingness as she is in the world of ever changing somethingness, of "a Katie, a window, trees, mountain, sky." A little further she writes, "After that trip, everything was play, the freedom, the dance and the bodylessness of it all." I have been consciously living in this place of forever alone but lonely no more. This place in reality is not a place as we normally think of it, being all pervasive. It is uncreated and deathless, free from all distinctions. The Eastern sages are very comfortable living here. For them somethingness is an illusion, like a rainbow, and dreams which seem to exist but don't. Somethingness is ephemeral in relation to its source of no-thingness, which alone exists yet seems not to exist. The concept of "seem" common to both is going to cause me problems moving fluidly from silence and peace of the infinite into noise and pain of the finite.

Chapter 61

Super Soul Sunday:
Oprah's Popular Qs-and-As

Nothin but the truth now
Everything is sweeter
CLOSER TO THE BONE

Kris Kristofferson, *Closer To The Bone,* Lyrics

ONCE UPON A TIME IN Mexico, when my TV was hooked up, I used to watch Oprah's "Super Soul Sunday." I wasn't yet fully awake spiritually. I wrote down the questions she would frequently ask her guests on the show. I intended to answer her questions for myself, if and when I became fully awake and Self realized. Blessed me, I'm ready for the super challenge, even very excited to see how I fare.

The first question: how do you define religion and spirituality? Or the difference between religion and spirituality?

Spirituality begins where religion ends. Spirituality is my direct experience of formless and invisible pure energy, stripped naked of all content, distinctions and attributes. Accurately speaking it's beyond experiences, which come and go. This pure energy or spirit is our essence and the ground of being of the entire universe. It, alone, doesn't come and go. It, alone, doesn't move or change, yet it's always fresh and new.

Religion is based on the direct experience and understanding of spirit or pure formless energy by its founder. And also the relationship of the founder to the relationless energy. For example Jesus called the formless universal energy Abba or father. Buddha chose not to choose a name and remained silent. He described it as Nirvana, or the end of suffering, to keep it free from grubby paws of the ego. And for Sufis it is the Beloved. Most religions also contain the insights of the founder, after his finite identity was annihilated and boundless pure consciousness was revealed to be the true identity. For example, Jesus urges his followers with, "But I say to you, love your enemies and pray for those who persecute you," Matthew 5:44. These words of Jesus are coming from and are pointing to the vast ocean of pure energy beyond the duality of the mind. The concepts of friend and enemy, victim and the perpetrator exist only in the mind. Oneness of essence is Jesus's living reality from the highest peak of consciousness. We have all seen photos of the earth taken from deep space showing earth as one whole and undivided planet. While at the earthly level, it's divided into countries, nations, and religions and we are willing to die for these imaginary, though utilitarian lines and boundaries. That there are no enemies and perpetrators was Jesus's direct experience, not a practice. But the followers have to practice on faith because it's not their living reality. Merely practicing the insights of the founder may make you a better person, may even give you glimpses of whole and undivided Christ consciousness. But is not going to transform you into Christ, free of duality, which is the ultimate goal of life. Spirituality then is the ever fresh and direct taste of the divine. While religions talk and preach about the taste of the divine, often neither the preacher nor the congregation has tasted the spirit, but they are taking it on faith. This means that no one is going to directly taste the divine because of the erroneous belief that god is already known and has been tasted.

Second question: definition of prayer.

Talking to the higher power to express gratitude or to ask for a favor or to fulfill a need. Most of the time prayer is a form of asking, which strengthens the belief in duality, in a separate self which is lacking something. Too often it is a beseeching of the higher power, which is seen as the universal wish-fulfillment center. Prayer focused on lack is perhaps natural in the early stages of human development. My favorite mystic and sage, Byron Katie, says, "I don't have a prayer because I don't want anything but what I have." Super cool way to be. Elsewhere she says, "I see life and death as equal. I'm a lover of what is. I love sickness and I love health." When both poles of duality are embraced, the only prayer left for Katie, like Meister Eckhart, is that of gratitude, of "thank you." Gratitude becomes truly authentic when you are able to see, in Katie's words, your "worse loss as the greatest gift." She lights a match to human desires and dreams and our praying for this and that. When you can do that, you're done. You're a spiritual royal! Your war with reality has ended, along with your prayers. You have now joined the ranks of unconditionally unperturbed sages, tremendously satisfied with whatever life brings them.

Third question: what's the purpose of human experience?

To awaken the human from spiritual slumber, which, as I see it, is the only game being played by existence on the planet. By taking on form, we become players in the existential game of hide and seek or asleep and awake whether, we're aware or not. We are all in different stages of sleeping and waking states, whether we realize it or not. We are immersed in our experiences, either rejecting or embracing them, always yearning and manipulating life for desirable outcomes. This, then, is the hiding or sleeping part of the game. Who is hiding and from whom? Personal consciousness or separate self, by becoming lost in experiences, by identifying with them, is doing the hiding or sleeping. It is pretending to hide from the ocean of universal consciousness of which it's an extension. It's the destiny of personal consciousness to return home to the universal consciousness. That's what it is seeking and silently screams inside "I wanna go home" to my true identity. The personal consciousness wants this merger and yet resists it fiercely because its complete dissolution is required. It's either personal consciousness or universal consciousness, my will or thy will. You're either asleep or awake. But ego, in order to protect itself, wants to remain asleep and dream that it is awake, rather than to be awake.

Fourth question: how do you stay awake?

Sleep is the identification of consciousness with the content of mind, which is thoughts, feelings, images, fantasies and sensations. Waking up is disidentification with content and realizing your identity with pure contentless consciousness. Simple in theory but a real bitch in practice. Contentless consciousness is the harrowing nightmare of the ego because ego is the content, or object of the subject, which is pure consciousness. I use a version of Vipassana meditation in which I bring my attention to breathing and anchor it either in my nose or navel or solar plexus at the very bottom of the rib cage. Instant peace. Exactly what ego despises, and it tries to run back to the head, its control tower, its power center and refuge. The attention can attend to only one thing at a time. Think in the head or focus on the breath or rest in the belly button area. I redirected my attention again and again and again to the breath. In my case, ego eventually started to enjoy time away from the head and now finds it more delightful than its most alluring fantasies and irresistible thoughts. Besides bringing my attention to breathing, I also slowly and consciously relax my lower jaw, the main hangout of the big mouth ego, to derail unnecessary trains of thoughts. At other times I open my mouth wide several times as in a yawn. Another powerful yoga technique is to gently close your mouth and bring your tongue to the roof of your mouth. Instant silence or significant slowing of thoughts.

Fifth question: what happens when you die?

Absolutely nothing happens to our uncreated essence which animates us. Only the person, the story, which is a cluster of accidental attributes such as an Indian-American, dope head, a woman, single, loves reading New Yorker, etc., dies. Personal consciousness becomes almost inextricably mixed up and deeply identified with the story and therefore believes itself to be finite. From the perspective of pure consciousness, my essence, this changeable and shifting self has never even existed. One who dies then is a figment of our imagination although necessary for survival.

Now I'm going to go Hindu on you because you're Oprah and can handle it. No race has explored consciousness as deeply and as thoroughly as Hindus and Tibetans, who single-mindedly journeyed inward at the cost of inevitable chaos and squalor in the outer world. Personal consciousness or attention, being an extension of deathless awareness, survives the death of the body. Consciousness, stripped of the personhood at death, is transformed into the immortal soul, which rests in the timeless ocean of energy and is reborn according to how far it moved in the existential game of spiritual sleep/awakening. In the case of Buddha, his soul was completely freed from his story and totally dissolved into universal consciousness while he was alive. No rebirth for him. Buddha declared there's no soul because it has no independent existence apart from pure consciousness just as a wave has no independent existence apart from the ocean. Buddha had no desire left in him that could pull the personal consciousness out of universal consciousness and start the game of hide and seek all over again. Hindus call this "moksha" or liberation from the wheel of birth and death. This is not my belief because I was raised a Hindu. It is my experiential knowing, revealed to me in meditation when my attention became freed from the mind.

Sixth question: what's soul?

It's the evolution of personal consciousness. Soul is the personal consciousness stripped naked of the personhood and its manifold entanglements either while alive or after death. The consciousness directed outward is attention/ personal consciousness. The soul is the personal consciousness turned inwards where is found the kingdom of god. Personal consciousness is immortal regardless of its in or out going orientation because it's an extension of undying and uncreated universal consciousness.

Seventh question: what's your definition of god?

Absolutely undefinable! Who can name the nameless, define the limitless which precedes the finite mind filled with limited concepts and words? I arrived at the wordless pure energy by the process of subtraction or neti, neti — neither this nor that. Whatever can be experienced with the five senses, talked about, or internally observed or witnessed is not god. Peeling the layers of an onion with weepy and teary eyes is an extremely apt analogy. What is left is the indescribable and uncontainable emptiness, or That. God is a lover's name for That, or pure consciousness, or truth, or reality, or non-dual awareness — all such clunker names for it. Thank you, existence, or thank you, non-dual awareness, are so unpoetic, although more accurate. As pure awareness, god is not only bodiless, genderless, nameless and formless but also fatherless, motherless, friendless, alone, forever alone. It has no religion, no nationality and no favorites. Silence is its language and stillness its being. Its unconditional love and peace are beyond duality.

Eighth question: if you can ask one question of god, what will it be?

Questions, answers, dialogues and discussions are in the domain of the mind. As my mind became quiet and clear, all the questions were directly and spontaneously answered and understood by the personal consciousness. Existence is prior to the mind, therefore, beyond the duality of Q. and A.

Ninth question: what's the lesson that has taken you longest to learn?

It's friggin moronic to fight with life/reality by believing untrue thoughts about what should or shouldn't be happening. Million, no, a zillion times have I butted heads with life and lost. Finally, with my skull shattered, brain badly bruised and body old and wobbly, I have come to my senses. At last, I am in sync with life and know that whatever is happening should be happening, from pandemics to infanticide. My personal will is toast. Reality, what is, or "is-ness," rules supreme.

Tenth question: what do you know for sure?

I am or I exist. The rest are opinions and therefore can be peeled off, leaving behind pure emptiness or "am-ness," which can't be discarded.

Eleventh question: what's the best piece of advice you were given?

No thought is true thought on the journey of enlightenment, by Jed McKenna. The advice is a vacuum cleaner sucking up all thoughts, even of god, enlightenment, pure consciousness, etc.

Twelfth question: who have been your greatest spiritual teachers?

I have mentioned them in preceding chapters, but most impactful have been three contemporary teachers; Osho, Jed McKenna, and Byron Katie. They have helped with dismantling and unraveling of my personhood — the main obstacle to enlightenment. They have saved me from the brink of insanity, by which I mean belief in untrue thoughts, several times during my perfect solitude phase in Mexico. There's one very very dead master from antiquity, Adi Yogi Shiva, whose invisible hand has seemingly steered and continues to guide me through my adventures with chemical mysticism, stillness and pure energy. Why me, the irreverent un-devotee? No idea! I have never prayed to him, bowed or worshipped or consciously asked for his protection or guidance. However, I have done a lot of psychotropic drugs, which I continue to explore. Shiva is also known to be an avid stoner and consumer of psychedelics. He showed up twice on acid trips: once in his popular Hindu form and the second time as inner sensations. In Mexico during deep meditation I have felt his formidable presence as a barely perceptible vibration of extreme stillness bordering on death. An unforgettable experience — eerily unpleasant at the time. To hang out with Shiva at his depth of stillness initially was an acquired taste for me. But now, a blessed addiction, and matchless supreme joy.

Below are fill in the blanks from Super Soul Sunday.

The world needs … us to wake up.

I believe ……in no-thingness which is not a belief but reality.

I am most grateful for …… having completed the cosmic game of hide and seek, supremely thrilling, sooo fulfilling and totally liberating!

Chapter 62

The Cosmic Game

"This consciousness which is functioning in you, in the garden slug and earthworm outside, is the same"

UG Krishnamurti

N O ONE, NOT EVEN A diehard atheist or even a theist, would disagree that there's only one life animating the entire humanity, as a matter of fact, all sentient beings. Furthermore, the one life is conscious. All you pet lovers would agree. In humans, life is conscious that it's conscious. If I were to ask a human, are you alive, do you exist? the answer would be a thumping yes. You have to be alive even to say no, I'm not alive, which means you're alive. So far we all agree that there's one life and it's conscious. There's no separate Hindu life or a separate Christian life or an atheist life. No such thing as a separate life force for dog, spider or a garden slug. It's much like one invisible electricity powering various visible appliances and toys, etc. There's one invisible life expressing itself through myriads of visible forms. That life loves diversity is evident all around. Something humble like leaves on the trees and bushes — so many different sizes, shapes and colors! Nonetheless gazillion forms and more are all powered by one life force. All our modern appliances and toys are dead without electricity or some form of energy. Similarly, all forms are dependent on one life force which, when departs, the form is declared dead and useless. Unlike appliances powered by electricity, a human form is intricately entwined with formless life energy. Just how deeply fused and entangled the two are becomes clear only when their unraveling is initiated!

A baby born anywhere is pure life, pure being, not knowing its name, gender, color, religion or nationality. She doesn't even know she's human. Her being will slowly be conditioned and molded into a human by the milieu of her birth. A baby born in India inherits a network of Hindu concepts which will create a Hindu mind set. Buddhist, Christian and communist mind sets have similar origins. Thus, pure life, absolutely free, is conditioned and constrained and will behave robot-like according to its conditioning. The fact of its infinite beingness is forgotten and replaced by identification with the finite human form. The visible human form, although brilliant and beguiling, is the surface covering over invisible life. The finite form is totally dependent on the invisible and infinite life energy, much like the light of the moon depends on the sun. Existence being infinite can never get lost. It simply pretends to get lost in the transient world of forms so it can play the game of finding itself. The mystics in the East, after awakening from the illusion of the mind, have howled with laughter at their turbulent and sweaty search for that which is always here and present. These lines from T. S. Elliot blow life's cover and reveal its play with no rules,

> "We shall not cease from exploration,
> And the end of all our exploring
> Will be to arrive where we started
> And know the place for the first time."

The ancient longing of existence is to explore the form identity and then return home to the formless. Or "where we started," which is pure being free from words and thoughts while still in the form. The journey of exploration — getting lost, existential angst, then being found — all that movement happens in the conditioned mind, which only seems to exist. The concept of "seem" or "apparent" is the open secret of life's play with itself. For this play to be amusing and entertaining the limitless being must forget itself completely. Now it will see itself as a human, separate, sovereign and independent of the life which animates it. The plot of getting lost is thickened by the outward focus required for survival of the form. Life thus becomes alienated from itself. It sees itself as Sogyal's "unnerving stranger" which it must shun at all costs. The more a being gets lost in its human identity, the more is its enjoyment because deep down it knows it's too vast and infinite to pull such a caper. It can only play at being lost.

Pure existence is god itself. But life identified with complex human form becomes so utterly confused and blind that it's unable to acknowledge its own godliness. Through the agency of the mind, life creates god as a being or a thing to be worshipped, scrutinized, feared, blamed or praised. Life identified with human form chooses to philosophize and debate about god, wage holy wars, rather than wake up from its identification with form. It's all in the spirit of play, of hiding from itself. Itself being the source of all forms both gross, such as physical, and subtle, like thoughts and feelings, sensations and images. It even allows humans to declare that god is dead because it knows that only the god created by the fake finite mind is perishable. Life in the human form, as a perfect player, will learn to abhor and kill those with different mindsets. It'll learn to loathe itself, its faceless face of pure invisible energy without any attributes.

Life has not only forgotten it's naked "am-ness" but finds its natural state and its radical simplicity as horrifyingly unpalatable. Spiritual sleep, then, is about devotion to the mind directed outwards and preoccupied with piling on accidental attributes. Awakening is looking inwards and discarding all the non-essentials, until indescribable void that contains everything and is the same for all humanity, is reached.

Looks simple but not easy. It's a huge effort to turn deeply entrenched human consciousness away from the magical mind and direct it inwards toward the emptiness of Being. The simplification process of throwing out the attributes of a woman, angry, worthless etc. is not like throwing out furniture or old clothes. For the formless to awaken to its godly identity, the conceptual veils covering it, much like an onion, must be peeled off. Extremely painful process which Jed, in *Enlightenment Trilogy*, likens to acid baths and skin being peeled off with a scalpel. Endless ouches! The most excruciating ouch is the dire loneliness of the seeker. She is going inwards and discarding everything accidental. The collective humanity going in the absolutely opposite outward direction is dedicated to adding on attributes, the more the better! The inner journey therefore tends to be a big deterrent to most people who are content to read scriptures, visit temples, churches, do good deeds, take self-help courses to improve their ego, and argue about theism vs atheism. It's through a small number of humans, life ventures out to find itself.

Personal consciousness, having painstakingly freed itself from the clutter of thoughts, realizes that it's an extension of pure formless life or universal consciousness. Consciousness thus awakened in the human form no longer sees itself as separate from life and other humans or as having its own will and being captain of its own ship. The main attribute of an awakened human is connectedness with all, along with fearlessness, playfulness, creativity, joyful wonder, awe and overwhelming gratitude. The personal consciousness loves the inner journey to its transformation into soul. Soul can still remain separate knowing it's oneness with the source. A perfect win-win scenario for the soul, which loathes to disappear and dissolve into the source. Now the human, awake to its identity as pure consciousness, can grow and mature into an adult human.

Jed, in his *Enlightenment Trilogy*, according to my understanding, advises personal consciousness to go no further, if possible. He mentions all the perks and privileges available to the consciousness that is awake "in" the dream. He is 100% right. Enlightenment, according to me, means dissolution of personal consciousness in universal consciousness, or soul into the spirit, into not "twoness." The mystic, Mooji Baba, calls the first half of the journey tasting the honey of existence. There's still duality here; the taster of honey and the honey. The last leg of the journey is about complete erasure of duality. According to Mooji and other teachers, most people are satisfied with tasting the honey but aren't willing to "be" the honey. Fear of total annihilation, dying into no-self, grips the personal consciousness. It doesn't wish to lose its seeming sovereignty consciously and willingly.

Merger of the personal consciousness into universal is aptly named, by sage UG Krishnamurti as "the natural state." The endgame. The one who was lost and was seeking is seen to be a figment of a fake mind.

The personal consciousness is fully awake — awake not only "in" the dream state but also awake "from" the dream state. Jed, in *Article Zero: Readme 1ˢᵗ*, says "Right now you're asleep in the dreamstate; a child. Other options include being awake in the dreamstate — an adult and awake from the dreamstate — enlightened. The latter includes the former, but it's really the former you want, the latter being an over-hyped booby-prize."

Unconsciously compelled by life to awaken "from" the dream state, I parted from my beloved guide Jed and turned my gaze toward the mystic East. Since enlightenment includes both tasting the honey and being the honey, it truly signifies the endgame of life. Life cares naught for anyone's opinions, not mine, nor even those of my wise gurus and guides. Its mission accomplished, life lives in simple silence accepting and embracing all. Its nourishment, clarity, joy and laughter come from within itself. There's only unknowable truth or pure existence living through me freed from the familiar morality, rules and regulations, purposes and plans of the mind. It visits the mind, uses it but lives beyond mind, alone forever. Such is my experience.

Since my dissolution in no-thingness, my ancient longing for a romantic relationship and desire for like-minded friends have also dissolved. They were the earthly veils covering my one and only longing for eternal love affair with the divine, or no-thingness. Divine romance is experienced as a continuous celebration of never ending festivities. Says Byron Katie, "the only true love affair is one with yourself. I'm married to me." She adds, "I'm married to god, to reality. Until you marry truth, there's no real marriage." It's the only love story on the planet — the prototype of earthly marriage and earthly love stories. The cosmic game of soul's seeming separation, getting lost in the world and then reuniting with itself has been the only game played on earth since time immemorial. Universal consciousness is the ultimate good and personal consciousness disguised as ego resisting and opposing it is the ultimate evil. Good vs evil is the prototype of game from which are derived all the other games, dramas, movies, even Star Wars, all the epics and stories of the past and future.

Chapter 63

Dark Night of the Soul

"I'm off the planet, call back later."

Message on the answering machine of American
astronaut Marsha Irvin, when on a space flight.

Tough love romance is what I can say I'm having with existence. Sweet and tender moments, I have noticed require my full presence while killer punches render me totally unconscious. Well, life sent a knockout punch to one who had died from her life, one who had committed willing and voluntary suicide. It shouldn't even have registered, had she been really dead. Instead, she was resurrected! Disoriented and wobbly, I managed to stand up but repeated jabs knocked me out for days and weeks with searing pains and fatal psychic confusion.

Here is how gut-wrenching conflict unfolded and played itself out. Results have been an extreme cleansing of my psyche and transformation of my inner bitch. My manuscript is nearing completion and I need to connect with the world to gather data for publishing it. All the forces are pointing toward self-publishing, but I'm told I need an editor. Before any of that, I felt I needed someone to read the entire manuscript and give me their opinion if I have overstepped the cultural red lines of both East and West. Will there be blood because I'm spotlighting violence and sexual abuse in some spiritual circles, de-iconizing totems of Hinduism, seemingly exalting metaphysical sex, masturbation and drugs. Also exulting in extreme meditation Shiva style. My feared future seemed to be being burned at the stake. Am I willing? Or is a course correction needed?

Prior to completion of the manuscript, a couple of friends, not spiritual seekers, showed interest in reading it. One read a couple of chapters and some didn't read at all. All gave lack of time as an excuse. Does the manuscript simply suck? Are they just being polite? I needed someone to talk to, someone in academia or a book lover or a writer. I found out that a retired friend with academic and administrative background, an ancient spiritual seeker, an old devotee of sex, drugs, rock 'n' roll was already in Ajijic on a vacation. What are the chances of such a miracle! Giddy with joy I virtually floated off the earth plane. I was feeling insanely grateful to life for sending me such handy high caliber help the moment I needed it. Ha, ha, ha! I'm being cynical. As Jed puts it in his *Enlightenment Trilogy*, the disciple asks life or guru for a fish and she gets worms. Such has been the rule on this long pilgrimage which I would forget for now. My expectations of creamy luscious fish would be the blinders which would make me heartless and compassionless toward my friend. My expectations working underground had already started my seemingly dangerous disconnect from the pure energy.

I emailed him my manuscript and he said he was enjoying it. In the early part of our meeting, for the sake of his safety and my desire to see him as much as possible before he left, I offered him my more than two decades old car. I live up on a hill and the roads are cobblestones with potholes. Within a few days we collided with each other creating searing sparks. From hindsight I see two entrenched mind patterns crashing into each other head on: mine time centric and his opposite and lax. Half an hour late is acceptable to me because of "mucho trafico" during the winter months. But two hours and plus is crossing my red line. My lifetime of experiences with the tardy bunch from India, North America and Mexico had led me to the conclusion that tardy bunch is unkind, confused and spacey. Under the influence of my righteous judgements, I was shooting death rays at him and not even feeling guilty.

Post my hissy fit he said he was reading my manuscript. But his overall response felt rather lusterless to me. I started to take his perceived lack of enthusiasm personally. After all, the overall interest of the few with whom I had shared parts of my manuscript had been tepid to nil. My self-doubts were proliferating like a deadly unstoppable virus. Another challenge was getting permission from the authors of the books I had quoted in my manuscript. What a daunting task! I had no clue. The process of writing, for the most part, had been delightful, effortless and seemingly divinely inspired. Why was everything swiftly sliding south? I tried to steady the ship of doom by consoling myself that the discipline of writing had not been without its rewards. Dazzling clarity, silent confidence, and thorough cleansing of my soul had certainly been accomplished. The manuscript may not morph into a book, but it hadn't been in vain.

Around this time, I started to feel concerned that my friend was driving my old car rather excessively from running his errands to familiarizing himself with the lakeside lifestyle. He started to cancel our meetings, which chafed my ego.

I sent him an email which, in hindsight I would see as inflammatory, asking him to limit his use of my car. Things went very dark, very quickly. I verbally abused him on the phone for stubbornly insisting on returning the car immediately even though it was late at night. He sent me a couple of nasty emails saying my peace and bliss were fake adding that the goddess on the hill (me!) will not tolerate tardiness or overuse of her car on bumpy roads because it undermines her peace. Very true! I shared with him that I was myself feeling like a fake and a fraud. I'm even wondering who wrote the manuscript. Whatever happened to my new universal identity? What about my new divine romance, which had barely bloomed? The publication of the manuscript now seemed unnecessary and irrelevant.

Had I thought my freedom was unassailable? Absolutely! The challenge of completing and recording my journey seemed a proof and validation that I had been permanently liberated from meta twists and tangles of my mind. But life was revealing otherwise. Maybe there's no permanent freedom from the mind as long as I'm alive. Not true. I knew one person, Byron Katie, who is fully free and so cozy with her mind! Many freshly baked humble pies were sitting on my counter with more on the way.

On his last day in Ajijica he came to return my car. He seemed to be thoroughly frustrated by the traffic and other typical Mexican annoyances. I too was feeling very frustrated with myself and my reactivity. My ego was writhing in pain of worthlessness which hadn't visited me for years. The thoughts and feelings whirling in my head were: he doesn't really care for me, he is avoiding me, otherwise why would he cancel our meetings. I'm happy to see him leave. He only wants to use me and my car. Had I traded my car for his attention? An immutable habit of my mind. Was I pissed because the trade hadn't been to my advantage?

As I was walking down the stairs to let him in, I kept silently chanting "be kind, be kind, you don't know what he's going through." A sign that my heart had turned to ice. Indeed, he was going through a lot of mental anguish and frustration along with physical pain in his body. But my self-absorbed eyes were blinded by my own emotional pain which I was projecting on him. Too late! Our thought monsters were fully awake, at least mine were, ready to smash through walls, guns blazing. He looked deflated and despaired. In retrospect I saw that his own thoughts and beliefs were eating him alive, and the moment required endless compassion. Instead, I dumped my cruel thoughts onto him. It looked like a re-enactment of my marriage scene from more than thirty-five years ago, just before it finally disintegrated. Now, just as then, trust had vanished and we were struggling desperately to protect our raw psyches from further trauma. Only with my ex it had taken us several decades to sink to this level. The current crisis had taken less than three weeks to reach this shocking depth of toxicity. Could this be called progress? Maybe! Between us we had several decades of spiritual strivings of all sorts. I had spent an entire decade in solitude, meditating and writing my brains out. Now I was drowning in a smelly swamp unable to see a way out, my eyes tearing from toxic fog.

Through it all, I could see my old tendency of wanting to blame him for my misery. After all, hadn't my world been a Zen temple of silence and simplicity for at least two years before his arrival? But I knew it wasn't his fault. At least I had matured some! He wasn't the cause of my misery. My mind was. Life hadn't turned against me. It was teaching me how to re-enter the earth atmosphere smoothly and safely. It had sent me Jed early on who, like an astronaut, had taught me what it takes to leave the warm and weighty earth plane. Meditation taught me to float and dance weightlessly in deep space which I had embraced as my home with no boundaries. My re-entry into the world had been embarrassingly rough and jagged. Life was enrolling me in Byron Katie's earth school. All the while, as I was chronicling my gurus earthly misdemeanors, I was ever aware of Katie whispering in my ear that if I think they need "The Work," it's me who needs it the most. So true, groaned my humbled and battered psyche, optimistic that her wounds bleeding life energy, no matter how grave, would heal quickly and completely.

Chapter 64

Here Comes the Sun!

"There's a style, a way to prostrate and bow. Bow in such a way that when you stand up you're headless. Bow in such a way, that you are totally destroyed. No one should be able to raise you or put you together again."

My translation of the Hindi song of Sufi Fareed as sung by Guru Ma.

AFTER HE LEFT I STARTED journaling like a mad woman to unearth my complexly layered psychological struggles. From the massive emotional debris I sussed out simple judgements required for Byron Katie's "The Work." I downloaded the judge-your-neighbor worksheet from her website for free. I noticed whatever I was projecting on him outward was true and truer of my relationship with myself. I was very impressed with the awesome consistency with which every outward projection turned out to be a reflection of my own inner state in that moment. It never failed.

"The Work" on judgement: he is exploiting me, when turned around, hits me straight in my third eye as I am exploiting him. Embarrassingly true! My ego was shredded by shock and shame on seeing my hidden exploitation scams with him and others. Another turn around was that I am exploiting myself. True again! My freshly freed attention was obsessively focused on him, his lacks and my silent weeping over the perceived death of my manuscript. Was I finding rest in the egoless and storyless ocean of silence and stillness too vanilla, too boring? Was I looking for my old identity addicted to misery and pain? Was I feeling drama deprived? I croaked an anguished and embarrassed yes! When I sat down and closed my eyes, the ocean of unfathomable peace and silence was here as always, undisturbed and undisturbable. It, being impersonal, had nothing to do with being bored or deprived. My hard-won superpower of resting in the depths of the ocean of peace was intact. Roaring restlessness and confusion were merely on the surface. For the first time my soul had access to both and was genuinely interested in understanding the disturbed and whirling mind.

I continued "The Work" of asking the four questions and the turnarounds on other wrenching beliefs: he doesn't care for me, he shouldn't have driven my car so much, he should have apologized for being late, he should have read my manuscript with interest, and so forth. All like mirrors reflecting my own inner states. I turned another belief around: I need his opinion became, I need my opinion on my manuscript. Very impressive! So I impressed myself by writing my opinion of the manuscript, which I used with an interested publisher, but it didn't work out. Next layers were of shame and guilt; Judas effect, for betraying my beloved truth. I had devalued it! Just to protect a prosaic old car so I wouldn't be inconvenienced! And my ancient need for feedback and praise for my manuscript!

What about my inner bitch who had unexpectedly emerged after a long rest? All charged up as a man-eating monster, a headstrong believer in her thoughts! What are the beliefs which are stoking her never ending rage, violence and vitriol? The same ole, same ole screaming and thumping belief tormenting her and humanity — "this shouldn't be happening" (injustices, inequities, exploitation, mass violence, gang rapes, police brutalities, Coronavirus pandemic etc.). They are wrong, very very wrong. Other unholy beliefs which were wrenching me: "I shouldn't be suffering. Certainly not after my holy pilgrimage seemed to have reached its finish line. I have ruined everything. I have wasted my entire life chasing stupid nothingness! So maddeningly obvious! So unsexy! Hardly a human wants to attain it. It's good that my dull and limp manuscript is dying of despair. It needs to die. OMG! WTF is wrong with me? Why am I not enlightened yet?" Explosive laughter! I was reminded of Katie's little grandson, whom I have mentioned earlier.

In my mind I looked at Katie with the saddest baby face crying out to her, "Granma, I not Jedi. I the same. I not enlightened." More laughter. The old lens of wrongness had smoothly slipped over my eyes. For once I was not in a crazy rush to remove it. The lens was getting foggier with my habitual language of extremes; all or none, always, never, no one, everyone etc. Virtually unshakable belief in all-knowingness and wrongness had revived the heartbeat of my nearly dead ego.

The gift darkly wrapped in layers of complex psychological half-truths and delusions was starting to reveal the radiance of the jewel within it. The remaining tentacles and hidden roots of my personhood were being destroyed, which absolutely needed to be destroyed. There's no other way. Life had indeed sent me a "spiritual friend of the year." A destabilizing muse to help me tear down my remaining psychological defenses and already cracked and wobbly walls. Thank you, friend. Thank you, life, my guru, for mercilessly crushing my personhood. Thank you, Katie, for showing me that everything in my life is happening to awaken me and to keep me awake.

For in-depth cleaning of my mind I decided to hire a professional "The Work" facilitator. We worked on the belief that my friend shouldn't have driven my car excessively. The turnaround, which was a click for me, was truly comic. It was, I shouldn't have driven my thinking excessively. Well yeah! He is driving my car excessively and I'm driving my mind excessively. An increase of at least 90% in both forms of driving. The excessive and obsessive driving of my mind after prolonged meditative rest was the source of my mental exhaustion and aggression. The crystallizing moment of my session was when he said, according to Katie there are two ways of dealing with inconveniences of life, absolutely all inconveniences from Corona virus to cancer. Resist or surrender. Peace or panic. Sanity and efficiency or exhaustion and high drama. I knew that but this time it sunk in deeper. Reality however, continued my facilitator, will not budge with either choice. I had met with the inconvenience of a long wait from my friend with a habitual hissy fit, which had scalded both of us. The reality was that he was late and no amount of rage and sadness was going to change that. So why not stay connected to peace and silence of truth? I clearly saw that these deeply baked thoughts of resistance, like vampires, sucked inordinate amounts of life energy to no good purpose. Armed with the new energy efficient behavior, I re-enacted all my wrathful behaviors recorded in this manuscript. With new behavior I got what I needed from the world with minimum expenditure of energy devoid of heavy burdens of guilt and shame. Even if I don't get what I need, coming undone is seen to be inefficient and immature. I also started to watch Katie's YouTube videos. A garden variety domestic scene caught my attention: Katie's husband had promised to take out the garbage, but he didn't. In my mind, upon seeing the garbage, my brain reflexively spazzed out. He gets not only a death ray from my stink eye but also a few smelly aggressions which I would regret later and apologize for profusely. Katie, pre-awakening, more or less had similar wrathful channels operating her mind. Awakened, Katie simply notices the garbage without any judgements. When her husband comes into the kitchen she says "sweetheart (her favorite term of endearment) I noticed the garbage is still here and you promised to take it out. I thought I'll remind you." If he still forgets to take it out, she said, then she would do it herself because she is the one wanting it out in the first place. I love that. Peace is truly energy efficient. Her peaceful way of having her needs met is not a learned or practiced behavior. It's a direct outcome of questioning her stressful thoughts, which we have all imbibed unconsciously from our family, religion, culture, educational institutions and society, etc.

Keeping in mind my chronic addiction to suffering and pain, I have been repeating to myself the final wisdom of "The Work," deeply grounded in reality. "I'm ready and willing, looking forward to all sorts of inconveniences from my friends, family and life. I'm willing to be molested by my mind, anytime, anywhere. Bring it on baby!" There could be more mind attacks. Why not!

Epilogue

It's peak COVID period across the planet. The unfamiliar sensation of confinement at home has become a fact of life for most humans. I remembered with compassion my own stubborn resistance to self-imposed solitude. What to say of isolation imposed by circumstances! Friends and fiestas are bygone experiences for most of us, for the time being. My teeny-tiny social life has further shriveled with collective shrinking of human contact and connection. I'm more alone than before. My unwavering love for the being has transformed my loneliness into aloneness — the basic human condition. Soul at home in the spirit gets limitless joy, peace and laughter directly from the spirit. The splendorous fulfillment that doesn't need the other for love and connection, that doesn't need anything, not even god or enlightenment, is my finest accomplishment.

The last holy humdinger highlighted the necessity of maintaining a clean and empty mind. No-mind or clean-mind offer no resistance, as if there's nothing there. If thoughts linger, they are met with two questions of "The Work": is it true and who would I be without this thought? The last question makes my soul sing! Songs such as; without the thought I'm limitless and inexhaustible peace, always here and now, Ms. know-nothing, silence sublime, pure life energy empty of words and thoughts, filled with wonder and richness of possibilities. Free, gloriously free! Free even from the concept of freedom. Free from fabrications of the mind, sweet and wicked both! Mind dethroned and willingly and joyously resting in the spirit. The same spirit which mind had earlier vehemently denied because it can't be described, named or felt. Now the same mind, the indisputable ruler of the dream world, is its impeccable servant.

I see meditation and writing as ways to examine false beliefs, which put me on a fast track to enlightenment. Somehow for me, writing alone, wasn't creating enough enjoyment of pure consciousness needed to naturally abide in it. My love affair with the silence of spirit happened in the relaxation of meditation or simply when sitting silently with my eyes closed. Over a period, residing in the radical simplicity of truth has become a beautiful benediction.

From my new clarity I no longer see the gurus as "Failed Gods" because of the impossibility of ever disconnecting from existential essence or truth. I see them with compassion as failed humans just like myself who occasionally believe their thoughts, resulting in bad judgements, causing chaos and commotion. I have decided to leave the original chapter headings of "Failed Gods" because they so clearly show the evolution of my personal consciousness. In any case it never really was about the gurus. It was about my lack of ease with my own mind and my unwillingness to take full responsibility for it.

I lay garlands of lotus flowers at the invisible feet of life for allowing me to indulge in the belief that I was its only neglected and abandoned stepchild. Until I no longer could! My surrender to life was forged in the hot hell fires of my fierce resistance to its Will. One with existence, its Will is my will. No obedience is required, they are one and the same. No mind or mind free from thoughts, mirrors the indivisible unity and all-embracing oneness of life. Only a belief in thought can create the black magic of hell and separation from existence from god. I'm grateful to Jed for inspiring me to take the inner journey of tasting existence with my own tongue rather than relying on the reports of others. There's truly no other way.

Bibliography

Jill Bolte Taylor, Ph.D. My Stroke of Insight.
USA: Viking Penguin, 2008.

Louis Bradley. Goner: The Final Travels Of UG Krishnamurti.
UK: Non-Duality Press, 2011, 2013.

Byron Katie with Steven Mitchell. Loving What Is:
Four Questions That Can Change Your Life.
USA: Harmony Books, 2002.

Byron Katie with Steven Mitchell. A Thousand Names for Joy.
USA: Harmony Books, 2007.

Byron Katie with Steven Mitchell. A Mind At Home With Itself.
USA: HarperCollins Publishers, 2017.

Christine A. Chandler, M.A., C.A. G.S. Enthralled: The Guru Cult
of Tibetan Buddhism.
Christine A. Chandler 2017.

Nicole Daedone. Slow Sex: The Art And Craft Of The Female Orgasm.
New York: Hachette Book Group, 2012.

Ma Anand Sheela. Don't Kill Him! The Story Of My Life With
Bhagwan Rajneesh.
New Delhi, India: Prakash Books, 2012.

Bill Maher. The New Rules: A Funny Look At How Everybody
But Me Has Their Head Up Their Ass.
USA. Penguin Group, 2011.

Jed McKenna. The Spiritual Enlightenment: The Damnedest Thing.
USA. Wisefool Press, 2002.

Jed McKenna. Spiritually Incorrect Enlightenment.
USA. Wisefool Press, 2004.

Jed McKenna. Spiritual Warfare.
USA. Wisefool Press, 2007.

OSHO. The Book Of Secrets.
OSHO International Foundation, 2012.

Nina Paley. Director. Sita Sings the Blues.
2008 American animated musical romantic
comedy- drama film.

Michael Singer. The Surrender Experiment: My Journey Into Life's
Perfection.
USA, Harmony Books, 2015.

Jane Stork. Breaking The Spell: My Life As A Rajneeshee,
And The Long Journey Back To Freedom.
Copyright Jane Stork, 2009.

Gail Tredwell. Holy Hell: A Memoir Of Faith, Devotion, And Pure
Madness.
Hawaii, Wattle Tree Press, 2013.

Printed in the United States
by Baker & Taylor Publisher Services